SURVIVING WITH UNCLE

SURVIVING WITH UNCLE

Janka Goldberger

JANUS PUBLISHING COMPANY
London, England

First published in Great Britain 1995
by Janus Publishing Company
Edinburgh House
19 Nassau Street
London W1N 7RE

British Library Cataloguing-in-Publication Data.
A catalogue record for this book is available
from the British Library.

ISBN 1 85756 112 0

Cover design Harold King

Printed and bound in England by
Antony Rowe Ltd., Chippenham, Wiltshire.

To my children Nina, Stephen
and Robbie

Contents

Introduction

My husband, Egon, whose adolescence is described in "Surviving With Uncle", died of cancer at the age of forty-three. I sold the comfortable house in Kent where we had lived and moved to London with our three children because it was easier for me to work in town. Eventually the children grew up, I remarried and found that I had time for myself. It was then that I started writing.

I decided to write "Surviving With Uncle" for my children, because I wanted them to know something of their father's incredible life during the second World War. He had not told them very much because they were too young. When I first heard his reminiscences in 1946 I suspected that he was indulging in a spot of storyteller's licence in order to impress me. Later I met his uncle who independently confirmed every detail.

Egon had kept the various identification documents he was given, but the paper was of such poor quality and the words so faded with time, that the printers said they would not be able to reproduce them. It is a pity because he took great pride in them.

However, his badge of the Home Army is still in my possession. So is the little amulet of Holy Mary and Child, which he would certainly not have bought for himself. His drawings are included in the book. I think that the tragic face of a woman may have belonged to the lady who kept repeating her story in the Warsaw cellar.

Before writing the book I confirmed the essential accuracy of the events I have described against contemporary documents as well as compilations published after the war. Both sources verified his reminiscences and gave me the atmosphere of the period.

I have changed all the names, because people see themselves from different angles and I did not want to give offence. Some of the place names remained in my memory, but others I looked up on the map as being most likely.

Finally I wrote everything down, as simply and unsentimentally as I could, in the form of a novel, both in order to make it readable and to give me the freedom of including background details which would make people's actions understandable to those who have no knowledge of what happened at the time I describe.

In contrast, my own story of the same period, "Stalin's Little Guest", which was my first book was written as an autobiography, because I was actually there and could describe the events as I saw them. I am at present writing a third book describing what we, and others like us, made of our lives after such unpromising beginnings. This book will attempt to present the unusual view of the world and the purpose of living we developed as a result of being catapulted into disaster while still young enough not to lose the ability to laugh while, at the same time, being able to view events and people against the background of our experience.

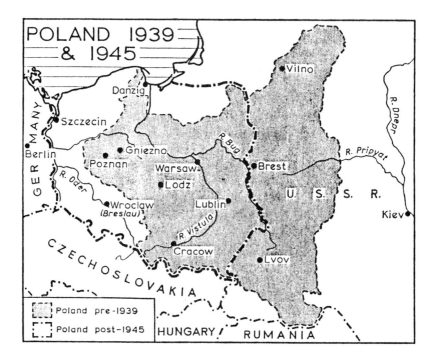

CHAPTER 1

GROWING UP

Die urdeutsche Stadt Krakau muss judenfrei werden. Jeder Jude der sich versteckt wird sofort erschossen.
(The ancient German city of Cracow must be free of Jews. Every Jew who hides will be shot at once.)
General notice.

*

Any Pole helping to lodge, feed or hide a Jew, or not reporting the presence of Jews, will be punished by death, together with his family.
General Notice 1941.

*

"There are only two ways of dealing with the Jews in the Ghettos: let them die of starvation or shoot them."
Dr. Jost Walbaum in Krynica, Poland, soon after the occupation, during a conference of German doctors. The audience cheered and clapped.

*

Egon lay absolutely motionless under the blazing rays of the sun, as close to the earth as possible. His parents and his brother lay near him, hidden in the tall corn. They all fervently hoped that once more they would escape discovery. All that Egon could see without moving his head was the clear blue sky above him. It seemed preposterous that it should look just the same as it did that other summer four years ago in Soniec near Krolewska Huta. He willed his mind to dwell on the memory to keep himself still.

*

They were spending their holidays with Great Uncle Ernst Weiner. The old house had been newly whitewashed before the summer holidays began. Egon watched uncle Ernst dozing in his favourite armchair, resting before the numerous members of the Weiner family arrived later in the afternoon. For the moment all was quiet in Soniec. It was such a happy place. Ernst and his wife Ruth had bought the manor house with all its outbuildings for their family of twelve children.

There had been Weiners in various parts of Poland for hundreds of years, but they lived mostly in the towns of Upper Silesia and Uncle Ernst's country estate was an exception in the family.

All Ernst's and Ruth's children were grown up. They had completed their studies and achieved independence, but they still loved to return to the farm in the summer. There was enough room and help to look after not only the children and grandchildren, but any of the more distant family who wanted to come. And they came from as far as Prague and Berlin; from Warsaw and Katowice, not to mention Krolewska Huta (still sometimes known by its German name Königshütte) where most of them still lived. There was no great luxury to be had at Soniec, but there was a warm welcome and plenty of space. There were hills and woods for the children to explore, riding for the energetic, and music and cards in the evenings. Most of the Weiners played at least one musical instrument and the piano in the main room was the centre of attention as soon as supper was cleared away. Egon remembered the flower garden, which spilled into the tidy vegetable beds and the orchard, merging into the fields beyond.

He once saw smoke coming out of the kitchen window and furiously pedalled on his tricycle to the local fire station where he explained that he did not want to waste time talking about it to people who could not really help.

But during that last summer of 1938 he was older, nearly nine, and he and his brother Kurt, who was eleven, were going to play a new violin duet, which Kurt had composed. Kurt was very clever and very kind, but he was shy and did not have many friends. It was through Egon that he communicated with the rest of the world, because Egon was always doing something, or talking to somebody. Kurt's red head was for ever bent over a book.

When Uncle Ernst woke up from his afternoon doze, the house was full of people. Groups of children delirious with their newly found freedom were playing in the orchard, surrounded by all the farm and hunting dogs, which yapped with delight and excitement.

Egon in particular was happy. His family had to leave Krolewska Huta and go to live in Prague. He could not understand why, but mother said it was no longer safe at home.

It seemed to have something to do with his father's getting the Iron Cross for bravery from the Kaiser during the last war, which was not considered a good thing by the Polish authorities. At the same time many of the local Germans made threats towards the Jews. Good friends from both communities came to warn his father.

Of course, Prague was very beautiful, and their flat comfortable enough, but Soniec was freedom. Egon decided to pretend that he was a train. He charged puffing between his cousins until he came to a standstill when he saw a parked van, which had just delivered some extra supplies. He immediately changed from being a train into being a van driver and climbed into the van. He remembered that when his father drove his car he first released the break. That was easy. Egon did it using both hands. Father then used keys to start the car. He resolved that a safety pin he had in his pocket might serve as a substitute, and fiddled with it in the lock while crouching on the floor and pressing the side pedal. The van obligingly cleared its throat and started. Egon knew what to do. He pressed the other pedal with his foot and moved the gear lever into place; now he stepped on the gas and the van moved off. The road was straight.

There was no traffic. Egon thought he had gone a long way before the pin fell out and the van stopped, but it had not been far. He left the van where it was and walked the short distance back to the house. On his return he saw a crowd of aunts and uncles surrounding the driver, and his mother looking for him. His father was not there. It had not been safe for him to come. Egon was very proud of his achievement, but the driver was furious and Egon knew he would be punished, though he could see that the grown-ups were trying to hide their amusement. He was the first to hear the sound of an approaching car.

"Look!" He shouted glad of being able to turn their attention away from himself.

They all turned to look and saw the large, open topped Mercedes Benz ponderously making its way along the dirt track which served them as a road. It stopped, and they could all see that it was Uncle Otto and Filomena – both dressed in leather travelling coats. Some of the ladies gasped. Filomena and Otto were not married. Furthermore, she was not even Jewish. It was a shocking thing to bring her here. But Otto was oblivious to the general opinion. He stepped out of the car, smoking his large cigar, and put his arm round Egon.

Most of the family were tall, but Otto was also broad, and Egon had the sensation of standing next to a mountain. He felt safe and happy, breathing in the mixed smell of cigar, eau de cologne and leather. A faint whiff of perfume came to him when Otto opened the other car door for Filomena.

*

For a moment he thought the baying came from the friendly dogs of Soniec. But then total awareness flooded over him, and with it the overwhelming feeling of utter terror, which stiffened his whole body and made him want to scream.

It was summer of 1942 and they were far from Soniec, in Brzesko, near Cracow. The blades of corn stood high in the fields around Brzesko. High enough even to hide an adult if he crouched a bit, and stayed still. The family had hidden like this before and the Germans had not found them. Now, all four of them, Siegfried, Frieda, Kurt and Egon were stiller than the shimmering golden corn around them. Even the birds, the only free creatures in Poland, seemed not to see them crouching close to the earth. They circled and went about their business above them, as if there was no human presence in the field. The sun casually picked out the brilliance of the scarlet poppies and sapphire blue cornflowers dotted in the pale yellow, softly rolling hills.

The dogs were looking for them, and Egon knew that this time there would be no escape. Frieda Weiner realised this too, and the awareness of this made her feel freezing cold in the heat of the summer day, cooling her brain to an icy clarity. Her nose was aquiline, her eyes dark, her hair black and curly. She knew that any Pole would know that she was Jewish, and many would be found who would give her away to the Germans.

Her husband Siegfried was tall and fair. Nobody knew him in this part of Poland and he could have made an attempt to survive on false papers. On many previous occasions she had tried in vain to persuade him to part with her in order to give himself a better chance.

"Life without you," he had said, "would be a kind of death." She could understand that easily because she felt the same about him.

Kurt had red hair, and it was mostly Jews who were red-headed in Poland. Frieda had tried to dye it blonde for him, but the hair had grown, and she had no more peroxide. It now looked odd, and made him even more conspicuous. But little Egon with his shock of silky fair hair rakishly covering his jet black eyes looked like a Polish or a German boy.

Frieda came to a sudden decision: "Run," she said to Egon, pushing half of their money in his pocket. "You're the only one who has a chance. If at least one of us survives we'll have a small victory over Hitler. Try to live by any means but remember that you are a Jew. Use your wits! Run!"

Egon obeyed, because nobody argued with his mother.

He ran as fast as he could along the path leading to the stream, which gurgled through the cornfields, sparkling in the sunshine. Then he heard the dogs coming nearer. He stopped, wiped the tears which flowed down his face, and began to think; the terror concentrating his thoughts like it did his mother's. He knew how dogs behaved, having played with them in Soniec. They would find him if he kept running or tried to hide. He could not swim so he could not get across the water and throw them off the scent.

His eyes now focused, because thinking stopped the tears, and he saw the nice, slim, long stick. He picked it up, as an idea came to him. In his pocket amongst the many things he collected, was a piece of string, and a bent nail. He ran again to sit down on a rock he noticed by the stream. Quickly he tied the nail to one end of the string and the stick to the other.

Then he took off his shoes and socks and threw them into the bushes; rolled up his trousers and shirt sleeves, and dropped the nail into the water. His fair hair fell over his forehead, and he presented a perfect picture of a boy happily fishing.

A few moments later he clearly heard the dogs find the rest of the family. Although it seemed he had run a long way, the excited barking of the dogs and the German command "Juden raus!" reached him with terrible clarity. His whole body tense he waited for the shots, but they did not shoot them then like the Himmerlfahrtskommandos of the SS shot all the Jews who had obediently gathered in the market place some weeks previously. It was the ordinary German soldiers of the Wehrmacht who led his family down the path a few steps away. He heard one of the soldiers say in German.

"Look at the lad. You'd think there wasn't a war on. He's fishing!"

Even then he did not look up, fearful of the tears, which pressed so hard on his eyeballs. For all the world he looked as if he was entirely concentrating on his fishing.

There was a terrible dryness in his mouth, the tears seemed to burn holes inside his eyes, which saw nothing except flickering black and red fragments.

It was only when they had passed that he had dared look up to see his family disappearing into the distance, pushed along by the German soldiers with guns. He followed them with his eyes as long as he could; until they disappeared behind a clump of trees. Then he was alone in the bright sunshine, by the rippling stream. All alone in the world which had been so friendly, and had now turned so hostile.

Egon no longer saw the blue of the sky, the gold of the corn or the scarlet of the poppies. The colour went out of everything, turning all his surroundings into a meaningless, colourless limbo. He had been through bad times before, but these were bearable while they were all together.

Two years ago the news had reached his parents that all the Soniec family had been taken away to the ghetto. Every Jew in Poland had been either killed, or put in concentration camps or ghettos. Egon knew what a ghetto was like. He had been with his parents in the Cracow ghetto, but they had escaped when his father heard that the Germans were going to lock them in. They had been in hiding since then, and he had seen so much horror, that he thought he was no longer a child. Now, for the first time, there was no one to look after him. The awareness of this brought a convulsive flood of tears, which shook his whole body. When this last act of childhood left him, he realised that the final responsibility for his life rested with him, and he became an adult, though he was not yet thirteen.

He dried his eyes. There was still pressure behind his eyeballs, but it was no longer due to childish self-pity. It was now caused purely by blind hatred and a desire for revenge. Yet even that subsided after a while, when the hopelessness obliterated all else, until a flood of memories submerged it.

They had been running away since he was five. First from Upper Silesia to Czechoslovakia. He had to cross the border pretending to be a strange woman's son, his mother's jewellery strapped inside his briefs, so that they would have something to sell when they needed money. All their household goods had been left in Silesia to be later sent to London by the family.

People in uniform asked Egon to tell them where his parents were, and gave him sweets, but he did not tell them, because his mother had told him not to. He had denied all knowledge of his parents though he knew that they were hiding in a house near the border waiting for him. Siegfried and Frieda praised him when they met.

Then they came to Warsaw, because their British visas were waiting for them at the embassy, but the officials did not want to issue them, because of diplomatic difficulties. Too many Jews were trying to escape. They escaped to Cracow, because the German army was advancing, and they had heard from their family what was happening to the Jews in Germany. Now there was nowhere and nobody left. Except . . . possibly . . . Uncle Otto. His father had taken him to Otto's new office in Warsaw, when they were hoping to go to England.

Even the thought of Uncle Otto made him feel better. Perhaps his family would escape. Surely Uncle Otto will be able to help. They could never catch him. He was too big and too cunning.

Calmer now Egon retrieved his shoes and socks, tidied himself up, and started walking towards Brzesko railway station. He knew that the station was normally watched by the Germans, and the sale of tickets controlled. It would not be possible to just go to the booking office and buy a ticket, but the daily train was not due to start for another three hours and would be standing empty at the platform. Perhaps somehow he would be able to get into it. Every step along the hot and dusty road demanded an effort. He was extremely tired, exhausted by his grief, by the heat, and by hunger, but he disciplined himself into an unfeeling automaton, which simply placed one foot in front of the other, and trudged on. He could now see the station, and the warehouse next to it. All was quiet in the hot sunshine. Whoever was guarding the station was inside.

Egon noticed a ladder leaning against the blind wall of the warehouse and, goaded by danger, quickly climbed to the roof to get a better view. He could now see the train. On the empty platform to the right of him a peasant woman was talking to the clerk at the booking office window. Egon heard them clearly in the stillness of the afternoon.

"I've come a long way, and I have my permit and money for my ticket. Couldn't I just sit in the train until it starts? I'm taking some food to my son in Warsaw, and the bundles are ever so heavy. Besides, when other people come one never knows what'll happen. I mightn't get a seat, or something might get stolen, or," she lowered her voice, "confiscated."

Egon could not quite see what was happening, but he heard the rustle of paper. Obviously some of the food was finding its way to the clerk, because, after a pause, the woman walked up to the train, opened a carriage door, pushed in the bundles, and climbed in.

The platform was still empty. Egon slid from the roof, slipped across the platform and dived under a carriage to the other side of the train, so that he could not be seen from the station. Then he lay on the ground until he caught his breath.

He was now past fear. Any strength he had left served only his instinct of self-preservation. He picked himself up again, and walked along the narrow gap between the train and the fence between the railway track and the forest, until he came to the carriage where the peasant woman was arranging her bundles.

She was plump, and her voluminous skirt came right down to her scuffed shoes. Her head was covered by a large, flowered scarf neatly tied under her chin. Egon thought she was old, because her face was wrinkled, but her eyes were bright blue and sparkled in her sunburned face.

She was startled when she saw him walk in, but was re-assured when he bowed politely and said,

"Madam, I have lost my parents and have to get to my uncle in Warsaw. Please help me."

The act of having to beg for help released all his accumulated tears, which flowed silently down his face. The woman looked at him unblinkingly. "What a nice boy," she thought. "And so sad."

Egon stopped crying and continued, "If I climb up into the luggage rack, and you put your bundles in front of me, no one will know I'm there. You can always say you don't know how I got there."

She nodded and helped him to conceal himself behind her bags. They were both so afraid that they waited in silence, even though there was nobody around.

The woman put an apple and a piece of bread in his hand and he ate them greedily, chewing as quietly as he could. Slowly the carriage filled with people, but Egon did not see them, because his view was obscured by the bundles, and he dozed.

He was wide awake when the control officers came through the train. He heard voices, both Polish and German, and the fear came back.

But they did not find him, probably because they were not looking for young boys, and, after an eternity, the train arrived in Warsaw.

It was easy to slip out after the woman deliberately slowly unloaded her bags. Their eyes met, and she whispered,

"Go with God."

"May God reward you," Egon answered, as he had heard the beggars say when his father gave them money.

The few remaining Poles, who saw him climb down from the rack did not say anything. They did not want to associate themselves with any trouble.

The familiar streets of Warsaw were shabby, people moved furtively and Egon's unkempt appearance blended well with the surroundings. He was not sure where to go and he knew that it was quite impossible for any Jewish business to exist in Warsaw in 1942, but the medical supplies shop was the only place which had any association with Uncle Otto. So he trudged towards Koszykowa Street where it had been.

CHAPTER 2

OTTO WEINER

Otto Weiner was a very tall man. Sufficiently tall to allow his frame to carry the considerable weight of his body without too much difficulty, and without interfering with the lightness of his step, which seemed belied by the heavy walking stick he always carried. He had the typical black Weiner eyes, which gleamed darkly with intensity, directness and intelligence, though, in his case, they were somewhat lost in the vastness of his face. Similarly, the toothbrush moustache seemed incongruous – too small to be wedged between the large cheeks. Otto's hair was dark and sleek, but in spite of his dark colouring, he did not look Jewish. He looked more like a bigger and better edition of Hitler, and, having been born in Silesia and educated in Berlin, spoke better German than the great leader of the Teutonic race.

When he and Filomena, dressed in their leather coats, travelled through Poland and Czechoslovakia in their large Mercedes Benz, they were frequently taken for German spies, questioned and then released. It became an almost routine inconvenience, but they liked the car, and the coats were the only comfortable thing to wear if you wanted the roof down.

Filomena's blonde hair was always fashionably waved, the blue eyes and lovely smile could have belonged to any Northern country, but her tall, rather full figure, balanced on shapely legs looked a bit German, and the leather coat emphasised the impression.

On a sunny day in August 1939 they were both seated in Otto's small new office in Warsaw. He – behind the modern desk, and she – in the armchair opposite. In spite of the modernity of the desk, the floor was old-fashioned parquet with a Persian rug covering most of it. At the other end of the room white-lacquered glass-topped cabinets displayed the medical supplies in which Otto dealt. These were largely imported from Germany and sold to the main hospitals in Poland and Czechoslovakia. The evening sun came through the large window bringing out the colours of the rug, and touching the painting on the wall behind Filomena, who sat motionless, listening to Otto.

"It's too late now," he was saying. "It's a great pity, but it's too late. You couldn't leave your mother, and I didn't want to leave you, but now we're stuck. It will not be so bad for you, but it could be death for me, though I'm going to do my best to avoid it. Now that the Germans have attacked there is no chance for a Jewish business to survive. I think the time has come for you to go back to your family. We've seen what is happening in Germany. Any association with a Jew will be dangerous for you, and I don't want you harmed because of me. If we both survive we'll meet again."

Filomena stood up and looked out of the window. They were quiet for a time, and then she turned to him. There were tears in her eyes, but there was a great determination in her voice.

"We've had a marvellous time together, and we would have been married by now, if it had not been for our different religions. Most Catholics and Jews in our country hate each other, but perhaps after the war things will change. I'm willing to take the chance. I want to stay with you, and help you all I can, but I would be stronger and happier if I knew, that if we both survive we will be married."

Otto walked across the room and put his arms round her. He also did not want a parting, but he knew the danger of letting her stay. He acknowledged to himself that if he did let her, he would have to give her the promise of marriage. He never broke a promise, but such a marriage would be extremely difficult. Not in every respect, of course. Their two bodies seemed to be made for each other. Even at this moment the touch of her breasts against his chest aroused him. But the differences in their background could easily lead to strife. He had heard so much of this before.

"What will you do when she calls you a bloody Jew?" his brother had asked.

During all the time they had been together she had never shown any inclination to do so. She had been loyal and loving at home; intelligent and efficient in business, and was too precious for him to allow her to be killed for his sake. He stepped back, and looked at her, trying to fix her picture in his mind.

"You must go home, my love. I'm not going to let you be taken to a concentration camp because of me."

"Nothing is going to happen to me. You and I have managed to wriggle out of many difficult situations before, and we'll do it again. I am staying with you. You know that once I've made up my mind, there's no budging me."

"There's no budging me either."

They were both very stubborn.

"But you know," she continued, "that your chances will be better with me here, and if I'm prepared to take the risk why can't you?"

This was a challenge. She meant, if she was willing to risk her life for him, he should be willing to promise marriage.

"I don't want to see you hurt," he said, gently drawing her to him again.

"I'm a grown woman, and it's my choice. I'll not go away."

"We'll be married if we survive," he said with his face buried in her neck, and they stood clinging to each other for a long time. Eventually Otto stood back.

"If we're supposed to survive together," he said, "I'd better tell you of the arrangements I've made, because if you want to stick around, you'll have to be a part of them. You know that I have not been to Germany and to Silesia in the last two years."

"I know, but I thought you didn't go simply because Jews were not in favour with the Nazis."

He smiled at the understatement in spite of the seriousness of the situation.

"That too, but there was also another reason. I didn't want you to know too much, in case there was trouble. The Germans gave me VIP travel documents, because of the value of the business I brought," he continued. "But I didn't want to take you with me on my last trip, because the actions against the Jews were becoming worse. I've been helping people during all my travels and have got away with it. Eventually someone was caught, and my name came up. They arrested me and confiscated the car, but, according to the law, which at that time my German friends still managed to enforce, they had to present me and my passport, to the Polish Authorities on the border before committing me to trial. You know that no matter what, the Germans obey orders and laws. Two guards took me to the border. I insisted on being allowed to keep my walking stick, having convinced them that I can't walk any distance without it. They had one look at my size and didn't fancy carrying me. When we reached no-man's land I used the stick to hit them both over the head, and ran across into Poland. The German guards started shooting, but by that time I was over the border, and they didn't want to provoke an incident. The Polish border guards enjoyed the whole thing and welcomed me when I produced my Polish passport, which I was supposed to show them anyway in order to be identified. To add insult to injury, the Germans had to return the car, because without getting an admission of guilt from me, they couldn't prove the charges. Of course I wouldn't have got away with it these days, but at that time my influential friends could still see to it that the formalities were observed."

"I wish you had told me," Filomena giggled. "I'd have dined out on the story for weeks."

"That's precisely why I didn't. My popularity with the German authorities was not improved by this incident, and when they come into Poland they will be looking for me not only as a Jew, but also as an enemy, so I have set about creating alternatives. I'm hoping that this is not going to be a long war, and I think my plan will enable me to last through it, otherwise I wouldn't have let you stay with me. My greatest worry is the rest of the family. I've been warning everybody to get out, but everyone thinks it will blow over. Nobody believes me when I tell them that what is going on in Germany will be considerably worse in Poland. Even the tales of the refugees don't seem to convince them. They have all grown up in Silesia mixing with the Germans and cannot accept that their highly cultured friends will put up with Hitler for much longer. But culture is only skin deep and anti-semitism has always been a popular policy. The only thing that motivates most people is self-interest."

He stopped, and lit a large Havana cigar, which was as much in keeping with his personality as the heavy walking stick.

No wonder they let him keep his stick, Filomena thought. It seemed a part of him.

"Tell me about your plan," she said aloud, thinking of the various members of the enormous Weiner family, whom she had visited with Otto.

He had advised them all to leave Poland, but everyone had good reasons to stay. Many of them were reluctant to leave their comfortable homes and possessions. Some were too old to go, while others had business committments or important work they did not want to abandon. All believed that somehow it would be alright. After all, many of them could remember the First World War, and, apart from those who were killed in action, everybody had survived.

"Well, first of all I've decided to have papers in a different name. I cannot be an ordinary Pole, because I speak Polish with a German accent. I have therefore acquired papers in the name of Herman Schmidt, a citizen of Bohemia. I'm a travelling salesman with an address in Warsaw. In fact, I am, on paper, a boarder at Professor Wolkowicz's flat. As you know, he has been my friend for years and thought it a capital idea after I told him about the border incident. We had a bottle of vodka and a good laugh." Again they were silent remembering the parties they used to give for their clients. Professor Wolkowicz of the City Hospital had been one of their most important customers. Many of the prominent doctors, politicians and dignitaries of the Catholic church were on their invitation list, because they were all involved in looking after the sick. Most became friends, because of the integrity and the spirit of fun which Otto and Filomena shared.

"I'm sure you've done something about the business as well," Filomena prodded.

"Yes. You know me well. You've also met Franz Mitke. Although he is Silesian, he was one of the directors of the Polish State Bank, but they recently retired him because of the general anti-German feeling in Poland at the moment. He was at a loose end and came to see me. He's another man I feel I can trust. I therefore had papers made up showing that the entire business, both here and in Silesia has been sold to him for a small sum, much under its real value. He paid for it in cash which is not a bad thing, because I have bought gold coins with it. One never knows what will happen to the currency. Our arrangement is that I shall run the business in the background, because he doesn't know much about it, and, after the war, he will become *de facto* a fifty-fifty partner. Now that there is a possibility of your participation, you can become his assistant and be paid an official salary. This will be on a generous scale, so that we can live on it if necessary. Furthermore, he has now closed the Silesian business, and will concentrate on the shop downstairs here in Warsaw. We can keep this office as a flat, where we can live."

"You've thought of everything."

"I've tried. I'm a realist, and don't like pretending to myself that things work out on their own. It's a great relief to be able to talk to you openly. I was just trying to think of an excuse to send you back to Silesia for a few days, so that you wouldn't see the builder who's coming to make an inconspicuous staircase from here to the back of the building, so that it will be possible to get in and out without going through the shop."

Filomena thought how very matter of fact Otto was in spite of the imminent danger. He always planned ahead and his mental processes were faster than anyone's she knew. Of course, he lost his temper frequently, but she sometimes wondered if even at those times he was only pandering to the current fashion of people shouting at each other. She did not quite understand him, but she loved him for the sheer excitement he brought to her life and for taking her away from the respectable boredom of her home outside the small Silesian town of Krolewska Huta.

Her father had been a petty government official, and her mother a pious, prim woman. There was never quite enough money. Constant squabbles with her brother and two sisters provided the only diversion. When she had qualified as a secretary, her first job had been with Otto. She had to work hard, but he paid well, because both her German and her Polish were excellent. She enjoyed the work and the easy comradeship of the office, so different to the stilted formality of her home and school.

Often she had to stay late to finish outstanding letters, and heard him talking on the telephone to his various friends and family. There was a glamour and a variety to his life, which she envied and in which she wanted to participate.

Filomena was not unaware of her beauty. Many a young man took her to dances, and many a kiss had been exchanged under the lime trees in the local park. In fact, once or twice, she had to go to confession and say hundreds of Ave Marias for allowing more than a kiss, but none of this mattered too much.

After working for Otto for about a year, she was delighted when he started bringing her presents from his frequent business trips. There were bottles of expensive French perfume, scarves, pretty beads and handbags. Finally came the dress.

Otto came back late from Berlin that day, and she was still in the office typing. Almost shyly he handed her the large box he carried.

"I thought you would look lovely in this when I saw it, and couldn't resist buying it for you," he said, and she, in turn, couldn't resist trying on the shimmering blue silk dress, which matched her eyes, and kissing him instead of just saying "thank you". She had to take the dress off again in order to change into her normal clothes, and that was when they first became lovers four years ago.

Yes, Otto Weiner was an unusual man. He travelled a lot, read local papers wherever he was, saw a lot and understood people. Although his upbringing had been German, he thought, that when Hitler came to power, the Polish leader Piłsudski was right when he proposed a preventive war to his French ally, who, alas, rejected the proposal. Poland was wedged between the two great dictatorships, the Soviet Union and the Third Reich. On his deathbed Piłsudski is supposed to have said, "Do a balancing act while you can, and then set the world on fire."

Otto could see what was coming, and knew that it was imperative for him and his family to leave. He was not sure exactly who was responsible for the death of the Berlin Weiners. The large restaurant they had, had been one of the capital's best known. It was burned down during the winter of 1938, probably by the SA thugs whom Herman Goring had made into an auxiliary police force. The whole family had died in the fire, which, he was sure, was not accidental. By that time it was no use asking too many questions. The neighbours assured him that they saw the charred bodies of the parents and three sons. The auxiliary police force was dealing with the case. Otto knew better than to look for justice. He had read Goring's election speech concerning his duties as Prussian Minister of the Interior, in which he had said,

"The measures I take will not be inhibited by any legal considerations . . . my job is not to administer justice but only to destroy and exterminate, nothing more!"

Otto's parents remained in Soniec with Grandfather Eric. His father, told him that he also read newspapers.

"You're not yet thirty, and you want to tell me what to do. First of all I am too old to move, secondly Poland has a good army. Of course, it's only half the size of the German army and not so well equipped, or trained, but our French allies alone have the biggest army the world has ever known, and the British have the world's largest navy. Together they also have tanks and planes, which are more than equal to the Germans. The Polish army is bound to last out for the couple of weeks it will take the Allies to get going. Furthermore, the Germans have now put up with Hitler for a long time. It is quite impossible that this nation of intelligent, and well educated people will allow him to stay in power much longer. He'll be removed, and things will return to normal."

In vain Otto told him about the German secret police, the Gestapo, against whose activities there was no appeal, so that anyone who even breathed a word against Hitler was put in a concentration camp or killed.

His father looked at him quizzically and asked if he was sure this was not just Polish propaganda.

So they all stayed, because Otto and Siegfried's father was much respected in the family, and his opinions were generally accepted. In this particular case they also represented the most convenient alternative.

The only one who had tried to go had been Siegfried, but he had to return to Poland when Czechoslovakia was attacked, and was now waiting for a British visa.

Otto hoped that they would get away. He had all their household goods packed by the famous German removal firm Schindler in Silesia, and shipped to London. Siegfried had also tried to send some of his money out of Poland. It could not be done legally, so he had entrusted it to an acquaintance who was going to United States through Switzerland, but he proved to be a rogue. It was impossible for Siegfried to leave Poland, but his wife Frieda somehow managed to get to Switzerland and recover a small part of it. She was back in Poland because she did not want to leave her family. Otto did not know all the details, but it must have been quite an adventure. There was no doubt that Frieda was a clever and an energetic woman. Better at business than his brother, Otto had not seen them since. All he knew was that she had found the swindler, who convinced her that he had already spent most of the money. Somehow she persuaded him to put the comparatively small sum he still had into the Swiss bank account, so that they would at least have something when they came out.

Desperate times, desperate measures, thought Otto.

There had been truth in everybody's thinking. The Germans and the Russians divided Poland between them, so Psudski had known what he was talking about.

Otto's father had been right, because the Polish Army held out for a month and five days, and Hitler was right, because he knew that the Allies would quarrel, dither and miss the opportunity of attacking while his army was engaged in Poland.

The worst tragedy of all, Otto himself had been right, because from the very beginning the occupation was totally barbaric.

As was his habit, Otto read all available papers and saw that the Soviet German friendship blossomed in every respect. It was very useful to the Germans, who explained to all left-wing parties of the world, that the Third Reich was fighting against imperialism and therefore everybody should stay out of the war. The Gestapo and NKVD (later known as KGB) held mutually satisfying conferences regarding exchange of experience and mutual co-operation in future.

The Soviet NKVD, as a friendly gesture, returned German communists who had escaped to "the Fatherland of the World Proletariat".

In February 1940 the Soviet Union and the Third Reich signed a trade agreement, which arranged for "Hitler's best ally" to supply oil, cotton, metal, phosphates, platinum and animal fodder. In exchange, Berlin was supposed to send shipbuilding materials, plans of tanks and aeroplanes, precision tools as well as radio, and telephone and telegraph equipment.

The Germans were deliberately very slow with their deliveries, but the Russians delivered regularly until the 22nd June 1941, the day of the invasion.

CHAPTER 3

WARSAW

Egon noticed little, as he almost mechanically followed the people leaving the station. The streets of Warsaw, which, he remembered as bustling with life and cheerful noise, were now silent and shabby. Many buildings had been damaged by bombing and not repaired. People moved furtively, and Egon shuffled along like everybody else. He was tired, hungry and overflowing with a grief, which he could not even formulate in his mind. His brain did not function normally, and it was only his instinct of self-preservation which made him go on.

He had almost reached the shop of the medical supplies firm "Esculap", when he heard a commotion behind him. The Germans had sealed off the street at two points, and were checking the documents of the people trapped in between. Groups of men were being forcibly dragged off. Without thinking, Egon walked into the shop. He did not know what to expect.

His relief was almost total when he saw Filomena behind the counter. She was speaking to a tall German in a Wehrmacht uniform, and became aware of Egon before the German noticed him.

With great presence of mind she exclaimed:

"Holy Mary, if it isn't little Wojtek come at last from Silesia! Will you excuse me a moment, Herr Doktor, while I show him where to go to clean himself up from the journey. He's an orphaned boy, my sister asked me to look after."

She was so charming in her explanation, and smiled so prettily that Dr. Fritz Meyer politely clicked his heels, and assured her that he could come back another day, when she had more time. And when I have more time too, he thought. Most of the pretty Polish girls would not look at anyone in a German uniform, but of course there were ways to make them comply. He had to make sure that this one was not a Volksdeutcher a Pole of German origin – because a Volksdeutcher, in contrast to a Polish citizen, had legal rights. Her German was as good as his, so she could be one.

All he saw of Egon, as he walked out of the shop into the street, was the back of his fair head.

Filomena hugged Egon. She still smelled of perfume, and the comfort of her warmth made him cry.

"Don't cry, little son," she said, "Run upstairs. I must stay here in case someone comes. There's some food in the cupboard. Eat. Otto should be here soon."

So Egon went upstairs and found some bread and cheese; drank a glass of water with it, and felt better. He had had nothing to eat for two days except for the small piece of bread and the apple the peasant woman had so silently put in his hand when he was climbing into the luggage rack. Then he fell asleep.

*

Otto was indeed on his way back, and he was deeply troubled. Professor Boleslaw Wolkowicz, from whom he had so farsightedly rented a room, had been one of the first to be collected by the Germans and sent to a concentration camp, from which he was never to return. The Germans had a list of prominent people, who were engaged in education, which, they felt, was a commodity not needed in Poland. Otto had gone to the flat and found the maid crying bitterly. She told him that when her master had protested against being taken away, they beat him with rifle butts. That had been two years ago, right at the very beginning of the occupation. Otto continued using the flat, until one particular day during the previous month. He had gone in as usual. All had been quiet, but when he walked into the study, he saw the dark shape of a man sitting at the desk.

It was too late to run away, so he stopped where he was. There was no one else around, and the man did not seem to be holding a gun.

"Don't put the light on," the man said. "I don't want you to see me. We've been watching you, and have questioned the maid, who told us that you are a friend of Boleslaw's. That's why I've come to warn you. One of the residents has seen you and suspects that you are a Jew. He told the cleaner that next time he sees you he'll report you to the Germans. It will be dangerous for you to come here again."

Both men were silent for a while, listening for any noises outside, but all was still.

"Thank you." Otto said at last. "Boleslaw is an old and trusted friend. If I'm ever in a position to do anything for you, you've only to ask."

"We are asking. We need bandages, disinfectants, pain killers and poison capsules for our people to carry. In fact any medical supplies at all." The man spoke urgently but quietly.

Otto considered the matter for a few minutes. "It will be best if you come to the shop openly," he said at last. "It would also help if somebody could look as if he was doing deliveries for the Germans, and if he could carry some official looking document with a few stamps on it. You know how the Germans love rubber stamps. He is to say that he has to collect two parcels. They'll be ready for him. You can keep phoning 'orders' through, saying when you can collect, and you'll be told if the goods are available. Say that you want them for Herr Wolf – it's the nearest I know to Wolkowicz. I'll do my best."

"Thank you." The man stood up and offered his hand. "We must all help each other. I'd have the traitor who wanted to give you away removed, but we're not allowed to shoot Polish citizens without a trial, at which, of course they're not always present."

"I understand. Nobody wants lynchings, either now, or when the war's over."

Otto saw the precarious safety he had so carefully built up being eroded. He had not lived in Warsaw before the war, and most of the people he had known there had left Poland, but still he was afraid of being recognised. Franz Mitke was mostly away on buying trips in Germany. Otto did not know if any of his German business associates could be trusted.

Fortunately so far none of them had visited Warsaw, or was likely to do so. On the whole Franz was better at managing a bank than a medical supply business, but he was learning.

It was a touch and go existence, but so far it had worked. Otto spent most of his days reading papers in cafes, because he had nowhere to go. Today he had been sitting as usual in a cafe, reading a newspaper, holding it up so that it obscured him from general view, when a man walked past his table, turned around and sat down on the vacant chair opposite. Otto looked up and froze.

He had known the man in Silesia. What was he going to do? Give him away to the Germans, or demand money for his silence. It was bound to be one of the two. Otto looked up enquiringly.

"I must speak to you," the man said quietly, bending forward so that no one but Otto could hear him. "I must tell somebody, and you can't give me away because you're a Jew. Don't worry, I'll not give you away. You see, I became a Volksdeutcher – most people from Silesia can manage this, because we speak good German – and was then made to join one of their special units. The pay was good, and I've always been a bit wild, but after what I've seen, I'm legging it. They made us "work" in the Cracow ghetto. We had to kill all the old, the sick and the children. Thin little children, and helpless, starved wrecks. It didn't matter how we did it. Those who could still move they took to the camp in Belzec. We only needed to "work" till five o'clock. Bloody German office hours. You've never seen so many corpses. We just left them lying there. The bloody Germans organised it, and did most of it, but the ones who really seemed to enjoy themselves were the Ukrainians, the Lithuanians and especially the Latvians." He shuddered.

"A man has to live with himself," he continued. "With God's help we will meet again after the war. I'm off to the forest to find the partisans. Perhaps one of us will survive to tell the tale. I'm now also on the run, like you."

The man, whose name Otto could not remember, got up and left as abruptly as he had come, and Otto stayed, unable to move. Every nerve in his body seemed to jangle and then freeze.

It was a great effort eventually to stand up and go. He made himself walk fast in order to regain his composure, but he was lost in thought otherwise he would have been more careful.

Too late he realised that the street in front and behind him had been closed off by the Gestapo. They were loading everybody into closed vans. This was happening all the time. It was called by the Poles "lapanka" and had become a commonplace procedure, used for getting slave labour to be sent to Germany, or taking hostages to be shot in reprisal for any action taken by the underground army.

On occasions it was possible to get out with valid papers, which he had, but they often made all the men lower their trousers if they suspected them of being Jewish and circumcised, and he could not take the risk. There was only one thing to do. It was better to be shot at once than being killed slowly, and Otto preferred to take a chance. Very purposefully he strode to the group of Germans at the end of the street.

"Let me through, my man," he said imperiously in German to the Gestapo officer who was busy using the butt of his rifle to help in the loading of the vans.

"Of course, Sir," the other one saluted, "but may I first see your papers."

Instantly Otto slapped the man's cheek, and said furiously: "D'you know to whom you're speaking?"

"I'm sorry, Sir. I didn't know. Please go through," the man blurted out. This was the language he understood.

"Alright," Otto said, "but next time you'll be reported."

"Thank you, Sir." The officer was obviously relieved, clicked his heels, Heil Hitlered and hit the next man twice as hard with his rifle butt.

Otto walked away slowly swinging his stick, and exercising every bit of the will power he possessed not to break into a run. As soon as he turned the corner he stopped and hid in a number of doorways, looking back to make sure he was not followed. Then, very cautiously, he made his way towards the back stairs which led to his little flat. The special handle he had fitted showed that no one had come in that way, but even so he stopped on the landing and listened.

He could hear Filomena moving about the shop, but did not dare to go in or give her a sign in case anyone was with her, because he had no official reason to be here. He slipped up the stairs, as quietly as possible, opened the door and saw Egon asleep on the floor.

Egon was not relaxed even in his sleep and his closed eyelids registered Otto's shadow above him. He opened his eyes, and saw the large face, which looked naked without its small moustache, shaved away in an attempt to change his appearance, and threw himself into Otto's arms.

"Don't knock me over," Otto tried to joke, but Egon clung to him for a long while and cried silently. After a short while he composed himself and told Otto about the last hours in Brzesko. It was then Otto's turn to put his arms round the thin body of the boy and weep. Siegfried had been his favourite brother, and he knew there was little hope for him, his wife, or his brilliant son Kurt. This is how Filomena found them after she had locked the shop for the night. They took control of themselves at once when she came in. Their masculinity would have been affronted if they were seen crying by a woman. But it was allright for her to cry when they told her.

They comforted her, and by doing it comforted themselves. After all, both Siegfried and Frieda were very able people. If there was a way out Egon's parents would surely find it.

But in their hearts all three of them knew there was no way out, and they had to think very urgently about their own survival.

"He'll need good false papers," Otto said eventually. "Genuine ones of someone of his age who died. If you called him Wojtek in front of Dr. Fritz Meyer, who by the way is the new German supplies buyer, the name will have to appear on his papers. I know people who will get them for us, but it'll take time if we have to find some with the name Wojtek on them. Odds are that the Herr Doktor who was in the shop when Egon came in will not remember the name you used, but we can't take the chance."

He turned to Egon. "You'll have to stay here until we have the papers and not go out at all. Not even go up to the window. If you hear anyone coming upstairs you have to go in there and stay until they have gone."

"There" was a coat cupboard in which coats were hanging in the normal manner. Otto slid a panel behind the coats, which revealed a space under the new staircase he had built. The panel could be closed and opened from inside the cupboard, and could not easily be discovered unless someone knew of its existence.

"Remember," Otto said sternly. "As soon as you hear anyone on the stairs you are to go behind the panel and close it. You'll not be able to see or hear anything, but you'll be safe. We will tell you when the coast is clear."

So day after day Egon stayed alone with his thoughts, and lived again through the first days of German occupation, when they all had to put on the armbands with the star of David. He saw the Germans amusing themselves by pulling out the beards and sidelocks of the religious Jews. They would also make them do gymnastics, until they dropped from exhaustion, and Egon had seen one man have a heart attack and die.

And then, one day, a group of Polish boys started chasing his family, because his mother and Kurt looked Jewish. They screamed abuse at them, and the grown-up Poles smiled at their children benignly. Nobody did anything to stop them. A woman even shouted.

"That's right! We don't need the likes of you!" It was happening more and more often, and Egon was learning to hate. It was December then and they had to sweep the snow off the streets.

They had not yet become accustomed to manual work, and it seemed hard at the beginning, but they still tried to joke about it, because they could return to the privacy of their own rooms.

Then they had to go to a walled place in a part of Cracow unknown to Egon, which they called the ghetto. His father had counted the bungalows

and one-storey houses. There were three hundred and twenty of them altogether. Egon heard him telling his mother that the Jewish authorities estimated that around fifteen thousand people had to be re-housed there, and they were lucky to get one tiny room for the four of them. Everyone was told that, although uncomfortable, they would be safe in the ghetto, provided they worked.

Those who were being taken away, were only going where there was more suitable work for them.

But Siegfried became suspicious when he heard that the Germans were going to lock all the gates to the ghetto, and took his family away into hiding, moving from place to place, until they had reached Brzesko. Egon tried not to think about Brzesko and what had happened there. He buried it all in the furthest corners of his mind and could not even bring himself to tell Uncle Otto. But every time he closed his eyes he saw it again:

"Go to the village and get a loaf of bread," his mother said and Egon obediently went out from the cellar where he and his family were hiding. It was safer for him to go than for anyone else. The local policeman always smiled at him when he crossed the road near the prison, and sometimes he chatted to him. That day he waved to him conspiratorially and showed him his fist, the knuckles of which looked cut and bruised.

"D'you know how my hand got that way?" he asked.

Egon looked into the stupid, cruel face, illuminated by a cunning grin.

"No," he said politely, "but I am sorry you're hurt."

"Don't worry y'r little head about me," the policeman said bravely. "It was all in the line of duty, but it didn't go unrewarded. We were knocking the gold teeth out of some Jews this morning, and got quite a few. Better for us to have them than the Germans, what? But I know where other Jews are hiding in a cellar. I'm now waiting for some Germans and we'll flush them out. Be off with you now, and mind the road."

And Egon ran back, forgetting the bread, because he thought that they were coming for them. He had barely got back and was telling his parents what he had heard, when a Gestapo car pulled into the courtyard.

The Weiners stood motionless behind the wooden walls of the basement and watched the courtyard through the cracks between the planks.

There was another Jewish family in the cellar across the courtyard. The Germans were going to have a good haul. For a moment all was quiet. The Polish policeman was just about to say something, when the cellar door opposite burst open. Oblivious to danger in her fantasy world of childhood the little Jewish girl escaped from her hiding place, carrying her doll. Egon had seen her many times doing just that, and heard her mother calling her Rachel.

Rachel's golden curls fell to her shoulders, and her enormous dark eyes always sparkled with laughter. She was totally irrepressible and could not keep still, darting here and there like a ray of sunshine reflecting into the cellar. Even in these terrible times she made everyone smile when they listened to the stories she told her doll.

When the shot killed her, she lay with the smile still on her pretty face, like a larger version of the doll she held in her arms. Her mother ran out of the comparative safety of the cellar and threw herself towards the child, still holding the baby of the family in her arms.

One of the Gestapo troopers grabbed the baby by its feet, swung round with it and smashed its little head on the wall. So much blood out of such a small head, and the screams of the mother still rang in Egon's ears. He did not see any more because he must have blacked out. That time the Germans did not find the Weiners, but every time Egon closed his eyes he saw the blood. Sometimes he dreamed of it. Like now.

All of a sudden he heard the sound of footsteps coming up the stairs. He had not yet had the time to pull across the partition behind the coat cupboard, when he heard the door to the flat being unlocked.

"I see that you were telling the truth and there's nobody here," a voice said in German. "Where has the boy gone to?"

"I've sent him back to get his papers," Filomena's voice did not seem to be very steady.

"So he had come without papers, and gone back without papers. That, as you know, is punishable. Often by death, usually by deportation. Blonde Polish girls are in great demand by German brothels to produce heroes for the Fatherland. However, we can make ourselves comfortable here from time to time and nobody will be the wiser. What d'you think?"

"You know that I mustn't leave the shop unattended, Herr Doktor," Filomena sounded out of breath.

"I've taken the precaution of locking it, and if there's trouble I'll deal with it."

"Can you promise me that nobody will know about it?" Filomena's voice sounded desperate. "If anybody at all finds out I'll be killed by the underground. There would be no way of protecting me."

"This I'll promise. I'd much rather have you willing."

Filomena was a practical girl. There was not much point in being heroic.

They would probably all be killed eventually if she refused. She loved Otto but he was not much interested in lovemaking these days, and there was no glamour in their present existence. Fritz Meyer was a large man with healthy pink complection, short blond hair and fair eyelashes. Filomena thought he was quite good-looking. Furthermore, she had been fitted with a birth control device before the war. One of Otto's gynecologist friends had checked it recently, so she knew she was safe. All that Egon could hear after that was some very heavy breathing. When eventually he heard the door close behind them, he went to the back of the cupboard and pulled the panel behind him.

Filomena came back to let him out and looked at him carefully searching for any sign that he had seen or heard anything, but Egon's face was totally blank and innocent.

"It was Dr. Fritz Meyer," Filomena said finally. "He came to check some accounts. He's a very suspicious man. Anyway, you must always be absolutely sure that the panel is properly shut if anyone comes."

Egon's curiosity was so great, that in spite of her warning he took the risk of watching through the tiny space between the cupboard and its door every time Fritz Meyer came. He did not hide behind the panel, and had nearly been discovered when the German decided to hang his coat in the cupboard. Fortunately he was very slim and Filomena's coat had hidden him. He took great care, however, to retain the pretence of going behind the panel immediately Filomena let Dr. Meyer out, so that every time she arrived to tell him to come out she found him hidden out of sight and out of sound.

It was in this manner that Egon received his sex education.

He felt that what they were doing was somehow wrong, and that there was a betrayal involved, but he was both fascinated and excited by their bodies moving in the total abandonment of lust, by Filomena's large round breasts, and the urgency of their desire. At first he thought that they moaned in pain, but then he realised that the moaning was an expression of extreme pleasure.

He became aware of a stimulation in himself, which resulted in erection. Imitating the action he saw, he learned to relieve the tension and found that the resulting climax relaxed his nerves.

In the long hours of his solitude he wondered if he should tell Uncle Otto, but he knew himself to be the cause of the situation, and another betrayal would serve no useful purpose.

He had a lot of time to think, and his active mind went beyond the immediate events. His parents had inculcated in him very clearly their ideas of what was right and wrong, and he tried desperately to find a way to be good and to live up to their expectations, but it was difficult. He knew lying was bad, but he had to become a consummate liar if he was going to pretend to be somebody he was not. This did not worry him too much.

They had told him that it was all right to lie to save life – his or anyone else's. What about concealing the truth? Yes. That too could be alright. When he had wanted to tell his mother's friend, Mrs. Katz, that he thought her new hat was hideous, his mother had said that one did not need to tell the truth if it was going to hurt others. Apparently Mrs. Katz had cared about her hat, and Uncle Otto definitely cared about Filomena. Furthermore, Dr. Meyer had promised that no one would know.

Egon grew up and matured much beyond his years in the weeks he was alone. He played a game during which he asked himself difficult questions and tried to answer them truthfully. Some he registered in his mind and promised himself to ask if he found anyone who could answer them.

CHAPTER 4

FRANZ MITKE

The pretty office in which Otto and Filomena had discussed their future had been transformed into a store-room which was kept full of large cardboard boxes, leaving only a small space for the desk and two chairs. All other furniture and the carpets had been removed. There was no longer a framed painting facing the tall window, which looked drab, deprived of its curtains and covered in grime. Still, it was lucky that the glass panes were still intact, though cracked in places, following the early bombing of Warsaw.

Every day, except when somebody came to the office, Egon was left alone. Even at the time when his thoughts had been cheerful, he had disliked inactivity. Now, when only blackness filled his mind, he desperately tried to find something to do.

The first thing to come to his attention was the unfortunate fly, which kept buzzing and which made him nervous. He caught it, taking the risk of going to the window, and took it apart, trying to see how the wings were attached. Then he looked around for something else. He knew that no electricity was supplied to Warsaw during the day, so he decided to dismantle and put together first one and then all the other electric switches in the room. The only tool he had was a penknife, his father's last present to him.

He experienced considerable difficulty assembling the first switch, and was very concerned that it might not function, but all was well. Nobody noticed, and in the evening the light went on as usual. This seemingly futile activity taught him how electric switches worked, and kept his mind occupied. He was more careful with the telephone, and only opened the bakelite lid to look inside. He had plenty of time and exceptional eyesight, so he could follow the wire pathways with his eyes, but did not touch them.

Egon indulged in these activities only in the mornings, because it was then less likely that anybody would come in. In the evening, as soon as darkness fell and the curfew hour came, Uncle Otto would creep in to spend the night. Filomena went back to her mother, whose address was shown on her documents. The upstairs office was registered as belonging to the shop and was supposed to be unoccupied, so they could not switch the light on at night. As electricity in Warsaw was only sporadically available, it did not really make all that much difference. They kept their food behind the panel. Otto slept on his desk and Egon on a shelf.

It was now November and darkness came early.

In the afternoon of the third day Egon heard voices on the stairs and quickly dived into the cupboard.

"It's alright. You can come out of there, Egon," Otto's voice sounded more relaxed than usual, as he slid open the panel and turned on the light. Egon came out and saw that his uncle was accompanied by another man, smaller and slighter and dressed in a well-cut business suit, something Egon had not seen for some time. The man patted him on the head and, like all grown-ups, commented on the fact that he had grown.

"Do you remember Mr. Mitke?" Otto asked. "He now owns this shop. Furthermore he has received papers which recognise him as a real German and not just a Volksdeutcher."

"Oh, come on." Mr. Mitke was obviously embarrassed. "Both are just for the duration of the war, and only because there is no other way. Incidentally, I have been reading the official German newspapers, and they say that the Russians have sustained enormous losses in tanks and heavy guns. This means that they had them in the first place, and surely must have used them. Reading between the lines, these papers give more information than they are intended to. Perhaps the war will not last much longer."

Egon remembered Franz Mitke, though he now looked thinner than before the war. Also his hair had turned completely grey. He still looked just as distinguished, and his pale blue eyes remained kindly. "Sometimes I can be here quite officially to discuss business with Herr Mitke in my capacity as the Bohemian representative of the respectable German firm Esculap." Otto now turned to his partner.

"So you tell me that the authorities have confiscated the main stores in spite of the fact that you now own them."

"I had to give them up for 'purely patriotic reasons', as they had belonged to a Jewish firm and had not been specifically shown on the document of my purchase."

"That's alright. The important thing is whether they gave you the receipts for all the goods. I have explained to you how important this is. If we survive, and that will mean that the Germans had lost the war, we will be able to claim it all back."

"Of course. They were delighted to give me receipts, all properly stamped and signed. Everything has to be done correctly. In the meantime some of the usual manufacturers still deliver goods, and the German hospitals in Poland have the right to purchase, so that we have a modest income. Incidentally, I have been discreetly approached by the suppliers and asked whether I would like to distribute some goods to the black market. I have equally discreetly replied that in my precarious position as an honorary German I don't want to do anything risky. They understood. As you have told me, I make only a minimal mark up on the sales price, and say most patriotically that this is not a good time to make big profits. All I do is purely in the service of the Fuhrer and the Fatherland. Incidentally, it is becoming more and more difficult to get cyanide. It's obviously much in demand, and anything that is in demand is stolen by our good German soldiers and officials and sold on the black market."

"Yes. I see all this in the cafes, where I have to spend the days. Although there are many German cafes and restaurants, the Wehrmacht seems to prefer the Polish ones. The food is better in spite of the shortages. Also you can buy pretty well anything if you have money and it is in the cafes that the soldiers make contact with the Polish 'businessmen' to make the money. It is interesting to see how it is being earned."

"The stories I hear from my German friends," contributed Franz, "are quite incredible. Nearly all the petrol used by the Polish population is bought from the German soldiers, the German director of the Gas Works has been arrested for selling coal at a thousand zlotys per ton. They say he has sold one thousand tons. Not bad."

"No. Not at all bad," agreed Otto. "And in the cafés, where I hear all the gossip, they say that the recent lowering of sugar prices is due to the Polish workers stealing large quantities of sugar from the chocolate factories working for the Germans. But the best trade is in documents. You can buy any kind of identification. German officials sell them at regulated prices, and the Polish forgers can produce anything. The current joke is that the chief of police has been offered his own ID card for ten thousand zlotys." Otto paused for breath.

"It is purely a matter of economics," Franz Mitke was now in his element. This was something he understood. "The official prices fixed by the German government are below production costs; the Germans get allocations of pretty well everything and are well provided for, but they feel that here is an opportunity of getting rich, and they don't want to miss it, so they get whatever can be sold, wherever they can. The Poles can't survive on what they get. Somebody made a calculation and worked out that an average worker could officially purchase a pound of butter a month and nothing else after he'd paid his rent. They have no option but to trade on the black market, which they do with great daring, and enormous loss of life, but, as I said, they have no choice."

"Thank God for human greed," Otto said piously. "Otherwise we would all die of starvation even before the Nazis killed us."

"It's being said that Warsaw has become the black market centre of Europe" Franz Mitke wanted to impart all his news. "If the Germans need something special and they can't get it, they locate it through the ghetto. They needed milk churns, which they couldn't get anywhere, and the milk situation was becoming serious. A Jew in the ghetto arranged for supplies at a suitable price, and they didn't kill him for a while, because they wanted the supply to continue. The same thing happened with, of all things, clover seed and many other things. The Jews try to manage but mostly they're dying out, both from starvation and from typhoid. As they have officially 184 calories a day, which they don't always get, and even if they did, it's almost no food at all, the only way some of them survive is through children managing to smuggle black market goods into the ghetto. It's being done with the co-operation of the Poles. I heard someone say that after the war they'll put up a memorial to the unknown smuggler."

"This is primarily why I arranged for us to meet," Otto's voice previously animated by the opportunity of exchanging news now returned to the heavy monotone with which he covered his constant distress.

"We haven't spoken on our own for some time. Have you heard of the "action" in the ghetto. D'you know that nearly everybody has been killed or taken to Tremblinka concentration camp, and that only a fraction of the population is left?"

"Of course I've heard something, but these things are not much discussed by those amongst whom I live."

"Of course not. But by now only about one out of six Jews in the ghetto is left. I've been getting false documents for those who had a chance to survive outside, so I have information. They want to defend themselves, and I need an excuse to go in and find out with whom to deal. I've been talking to the Germans with whom I do business, and playing on their paranoic fear of typhus infection from the ghetto. I said that I may be able to get some supplies of vaccine and take it in myself. Now that Egon is here, he can come with me. He can talk to the young. Between us we should be able to make some contact. By the way, he's going to be registered as a delivery boy here. His official residence will be with Dr. Koronski, but I don't want him to be there too much. The Koronskis are marvellous people, and have offered help, but I don't want to endanger them more than necessary. In the meantime, can you get me supplies of the vaccine?"

"I'll certainly try." Before he could say anything else a loud knocking on the door interrupted them.

Without saying a word, Otto indicated the cupboard to Egon, who dived in silently closing the door behind him.

Otto picked up his heavy stick and limped towards the door, opening it with a flourish. A small man in the dark navy uniform of the Polish police rushed in accompanied by two Gestapo troopers.

"You see," he said in broken German, "there are two men here, and this is an office, which should be empty at night. A good friend of mine in this house heard them. She thought they may well be some of the Jews that ran away from the ghetto."

"Please take this officious Pole away," Franz Mitke totally ignored the Polish policeman and imperiously addressed the Gestapo officers in German. "I am the owner of this business and Herr Schmidt is my Bohemian representative. We came here this afternoon, and have not yet finished discussing our business, which concerns medical supplies for our soldiers who are fighting the Russians. I find it quite intolerable to be interrupted in this manner."

"May we see your documents just the same, Sir," the Gestapo man was not going to be put off.

"Certainly." Franz took out his expensive leather wallet and produced his impeccable credentials.

"Sorry, Sir. And what about the other gentleman". The trooper was now more polite.

Otto showed his papers, and the Gestapo man looked up distrustfully.

"This man is not allowed out after the curfew. How is he going to get home?"

"He has my permission to stay here overnight. In any case, we still have a lot to discuss, and I'll be glad if you take your informer with you and allow us to get on with our work. We still have all these documents to go through." There was indeed a pile of printed papers on the desk. "Many thanks for the polite way in which you have conducted your investigation." Saying that, Franz opened his briefcase and took out two packets of cigarettes, which he handed to the two Germans. They took them, Heil Hitlered, and walked out, followed by the Polish policeman, who mumbled under his breath in Polish.

"You told us to look out for Jews, and that's what I was doing. The German I'd have left alone, but I'd have had the trousers off the Bohemian, just in case, to see if he is circumcised."

Otto stood by the window until he made sure that all three had left.

"We've survived once more," he said. "That was a good performance. Thanks."

"Sons of whores," Mitke said in Polish, which he obviously found more suited to express his feelings at the moment. He knew that if they had been found out he would also have finished up in a concentration camp, but there was no other way for him to act. He felt betrayed on behalf of both his Polish and his German ancestors. Thank God he had no close family, and he was no longer young. He had had the best years of his life. His father had been a German mechanical engineer in charge of development of coal mining machinery in Silesia. Both his mother and his wife had been Polish. Whenever his father had a drink with him, after he had married Maria, he always proposed a toast:

"To Polish women! The most beautiful in the world." There was a lot of truth in this. Even now in the greyness and dirt they managed to look beautiful.

Egon sat in his dark hole and fought the fear and the approach of panic.

The dryness in the mouth and the cold, clammy sweat, which covered his whole body had become familiar to him. He had experienced them many times before. The worst of it was the inactivity. If he could only be doing something instead of sitting motionless and just being afraid.

He thought that one day he would simply walk out and be killed. It would be easy if they would just shoot him, but one never knew if they would take him in for "interrogation" to find out where other Jews were hiding, and who had helped him. He had heard about those interrogations, which had become routine. Death was a friend in comparison.

As Filomena opened the shop in the morning, Mrs. Piasecka, who lived on the second floor followed her in. She had obviously been waiting for her.

"You should've warned me that there would have been somebody in the office last night. I've reported that I heard people there, and the Polish policeman was furious with me for having raised an alarm for nothing."

"Did you need to raise an alarm at all? There's surely no harm in people talking in an office." Filomena tried not to sound too worried.

"How can you say a thing like that, Miss Filomena? Don't you know the sort of times we live in? They could've been Jews escaping from the ghetto, and if the Germans found out they'd shoot most of us, or take us to concentration camps."

"Not necessarily, if you didn't know anything about it, though I admit that often they shoot first and ask questions afterwards. Mr. Mitke must have come in after I left. I also didn't know. Will you excuse me now. I've a lot of sorting out to do."

But Mrs. Piasecka was not in the mood to go. She stood there implacably, her greyish hair carefully combed back, her small brown eyes in the high cheekboned face glimmering darkly, and said menacingly:

"I can't make you out, Miss Filomena. Surely it's better to raise an unnecessary alarm than to be accused of hiding Jews. If you ask me, it's good riddance, and it's no good you looking all holy. I've seen you flirting both with the big German who comes here, and with the Bohemian salesman. If the right people come to hear about this they'll not like it. I'll go now and let you get on with your important work." And she strode out of the shop, the whole of her square shaped body quivering with righteous indignation.

As soon as she was sure that Mrs. Piasecka had gone back to her flat, Filomena dashed upstairs, and threw herself at Otto and Egon, who were occupied with their morning ablutions.

"Thank God you're O.K. That dreadful Mrs. Piasecka has just left. In addition to everything, she implied that I could be reported to the Polish Underground."

"Don't worry about them. Their leaders know where their medical supplies come from, but what did she want to report?"

"She said I flirted with you and with Dr. Meyer."

Filomena clung to Otto and shivered, because the Polish Underground was particularly vindictive towards Polish girls who "fraternised" with the Germans. All the unspoken words hung about them, and Otto began to suspect that the friendly banter between Filomena and Fritz Meyer was not entirely innocent, but he held her close just the same.

Early next morning Egon had to dive into the cupboard again, this time on hearing a strange woman's voice, but he left the panel open and listened to the conversation.

"It's getting more and more difficult, Miss Filomena," the woman was saying. "You know I'm not asking for extra because I'm after making a fortune, but they're bringing more and more laws against selling food, though they'll never stop it. The peasants are being legally paid three hundred zlotys for a pig by the Germans, and they get a thousand from our people. Apart from anything, they don't want to help the Germans, who have been confiscating their stores, and taking their young people for work in Germany. Except, of course, that up to now the penalty for most things was death, and now they've started taking people to camps, and that's worse."

Filomena's voice sounded friendly, when she answered.

"I know you're not trying to take advantage of me, and I'm afraid to go to the market, where people are caught every day. Besides which, I earn my money by being here, and have no time to go round looking for food. You and I have known each other for some time. I know you get food, and you know I pay, and we both know that neither of us will give anything away, but the prices seem to go up every week."

"Not all of them, but the more laws come in, the more the Germans have to be bribed to let anything through, and that costs money. That's why the prices go up. Also the risks have gone up, and people charge for taking them. You didn't know big Maria Augustyn, who brought meat from Karczew? Well, she had bags stitched to the inside of her coat, and put sides of pork fat and sausages in them.

The Germans regularly stop the trains outside stations and do spot checks, but our railwaymen are paid to warn us, and the drivers pause for a moment before reaching the place where they had been instructed to stop, so that the traders can jump off. Well, Maria jumped off, but the stuff she carried was heavy, and she fell and broke her leg.

The Germans were furious that they found nobody carrying food on the train, and made the driver back up. Maria couldn't run because of her broken leg. The other traders would've helped her, but when they saw the train coming back, they had to run away. Even her son, who was with her, only watched from the tree he had climbed. They searched her, found the meat without any difficulty and shot her there and then. Young Jasiek, the son, saw it all, and watched them searching the area, but they didn't find him. He does the trade now, but he's only young and can't carry as much. She was a good woman. God rest her soul" There was a pause then, probably the woman stopped to cross herself, Egon thought. "There's no way that family can survive without the trade. The rations are allocated to them, but you can't survive on them and down in the country people don't always get the little that's due to them.

There are six children, the father, if he's still alive, is working somewhere in Germany, and they've no land of their own. That's why poor Jasiek has to carry on, but he doesn't want to sell his life too cheaply, and who can blame him."

"That's terrible," Filomena's voice was quiet, and for a moment there was silence.

"I've brought you meat, milk and bread as well as some eggs. I'll try to get some potatoes tomorrow. I can only carry so much at a time."

"Thank you. I can see why it was so much money," Filomena's voice sounded tired. "Would you like some coffee? There's gas on today, and we've a ring here. I'm afraid it's only acorn coffee, but at least it will be hot."

Egon would have loved some coffee too. He was freezing. It was a very cold winter, and there was little fuel in Warsaw. Anyway, it would have been risky to heat the office, because it was supposed to be primarily used as a store. He had piled all the spare clothes on top of himself, and he continuously flexed his muscles as his uncle had shown him, both to keep warm and to keep fit. He didn't make the effort to creep up and look. It did not seem worth it, but he continued to listen.

"You're lucky to have this job, Miss Filomena. What with the good pay, and being fairly safe. Though nobody really is. Everywhere I go there's somebody missing."

"My brother has also been taken to Germany, but he's working in a factory, and is not in a camp," said Filomena. "It was still hard on my mother. He has always been her favourite. My sisters stayed in Silesia."

"Nobody's safe. Two other families I go to have had relatives in the Pawiak prison. One managed to get out, but he's died of his injuries since. He knew he was dying, but said that it didn't matter because what he had seen was so awful that he couldn't have lived normally any more anyway. They don't seem to care whom they kill and how. Even small children and their own people. He said that a famous German chessplayer, his wife and little son, were brought to the Pawiak while he was there, and they hanged them all."

Once again the two women were silent, and then the unfamiliar voice resumed.

"And those who can't buy on the free market get ill mostly with tb. And if you think our prices are high, they're still higher in the ghetto.

They've killed most of the Jews already, and any food that gets through seems to be carried by the little children. Many of the policemen can be bribed, but the Gestapo just shoot.

You can always see little bodies outside the ghetto walls. Poor bloody Jews. I don't much like them, but to shoot children! And they try to take all our young people for work in Germany. I worry about my son. He has a job in a factory. That is he goes there in the morning, does as little as possible and comes back. They all put in as much work as they're paid for, and that's nothing. You can only earn something if you do some trade, but it's dangerous, and somebody in the family has to have documents showing he has a job."

"I was told a story about that," Filomena's voice sounded less serious.

"A man met an acquaintance in the street, and asked him what he was doing.

'Working,' answered the other.

'And your wife?'

'Both she and my daughter sit in an office.'

'So how can you survive?'

'Thank God my son is unemployed.' "

"It's always nice to come to you Miss Filomena. We need to laugh. If it wasn't for the fact that the bloody Germans are so ridiculous I think we would all have kicked the bucket.

My lodger always reads the lies in the Polish papers allowed by the Germans. We call it the reptile press, and when we don't get too angry, we can have a bit of a giggle, but still I don't know how we'll last till the end of the war. I hope it will come soon. It's a pleasure to see all those frost-bitten Germans coming through Warsaw. I was chatting to my friend, waiting at the station, and next to me was a woman watching a transport of wounded.

'Be quiet,' she said to me.

'Are you sorry for them then?' I asked her.

'Don't be so silly,' she said. 'I enjoy hearing them groan.'

But I must go now. Thank you for the coffee."

Egon was nearly caught eavesdropping by Filomena because she came to let him out almost before he managed to close the panel behind him, and only then followed her guest who had gone down the stairs by herself. He dashed out of the cupboard as quickly as he could, because his sharp ears caught a sound of singing in the courtyard below.

Very carefully, so that he could not be seen from the outside, he edged to the window and peeped outside.

A boy, probably younger than he was, was standing in the centre and singing an old folk song with new words,

"An axe, a hoe, what's in store?
The stupid painter'll loose the war.
An axe, a hoe, a glass of beer,
Soon they'll go away from here."

There were many couplets to the song and an unusual cheerfulness emanated from the cheeky lad in the courtyard, but he finished up with a plaintive little tune, showing his need.

"Give me, oh give me, my dearest people,
Only fifty groshes for my song,
I can then buy some bread and milk,
And keep my spirit strong."

And windows opened all round. Little pieces of paper were wrapped round coins, so that they wouldn't roll away when thrown down. The boy picked them up, waved his arm and disappeared into a doorway.

And Egon, who never used to cry much, sat down on the floor to fight his tears. It was the sound of music, however rudimentary, and the fact that people were still capable of kindness, which touched him in spite of himself.

At last his papers arrived. His name was to be Wojtek Romanski, son of Helena and Witold Romanski, who had died during the occupation of Upper Silesia.

He was now formally introduced to Dr. Fritz Meyer, whom he had for so long been observing through the crack in the cupboard door.

"So you're an orphan," Dr. Meyer said. "Mind you obey your Aunt Filomena. Where exactly did you say you lived?" But Egon had been very thoroughly briefed and could even describe the house where he was supposed to have spent his childhood.

When the German had left and Otto appeared, Filomena said:

"Meyer has been asking Egon questions. Fortunately the good doctor is not a Pole, otherwise he would've asked him about religion, which is what every Pole does when he suspects anything. Egon had better be taught the catechism. I can't do it, because I haven't got all the books, and I've forgotten a lot of it."

"You're right," Otto said thoughtfully. "Now that he has papers, I'll arrange for him to go and see Bishop Podolski. He'll find somebody to teach him. I wouldn't trust every priest. Many of them are quite glad to be getting rid of the heathen, but he's not like that."

CHAPTER 5

JANUSZ

A t first the beautiful weather intensified Egon's feeling of desolation, as he trudged in the brightness of the morning towards the church near the Square of Three Crosses, where Uncle Otto told him to go. But then his young body began to enjoy the crispness of the air and the freshly fallen snow under his feet. He had been confined to one room for nearly three months. Otto and Filomena managed to get some food, so he had filled out a little, and they made him do exercises to occupy the time and to keep fit. His legs moved easily, his lungs filled with fresh air. It was very cold, but the sun glistened on the snow, and he could not help smiling to himself.

His father had been a Latin scholar. During their enforced inactivity he taught them Latin out of an old copy of *Juvenal*, whom he particularly admired. The last text on which they had worked came to Egon's mind:

"Orandum est ut sit mens sana in corpore sano.
Fortem posce animum mortis terrore carentem,
Qui spatium vitae extremum inter munera ponat Naturae."

A part of the first line was in common use in Poland, but Siegfried knew the whole verse and explained it to them:

"Your prayer must be that you may have a sound mind in a sound body. Pray for a bold spirit, free from all dread of death; that reckons the closing scene of life among Nature's kindly gifts."

The old Roman knew what he was talking about, but it was not easy to achieve. He could only try.

Suddenly a conversation between his parents came back to him. Kurt and he were translating another quotation from *Juvenal*:

"*Summum crede nefas animam praeferre pudori*

Et propter vitam vivendi perdere causas."

"Deem it to be the summit of impiety to prefer existence to honour, and for the sake of life to sacrifice life's only end." Kurt had translated this one. He enjoyed Latin. Their mother, who was listening, suddenly said:

"Would it therefore not be more honourable to just allow ourselves to be killed with everybody else?"

"Only if our death would help anyone. Remember our culture is older than the Roman, and we believe in life, though never survival at the cost of others. It's our duty to try and survive." Siegfried had been quite adamant.

The rays of sun splintered into a multitude of lights as they poured through the tall stained glass windows of the church, but the church itself was dark and smelled of candles and incense.

Egon barely had time to adjust his eyes to the change of light, when a priest silently approached him and asked him to follow. He was shown into a small, hidden waiting room, and asked to wait. There was a wooden bench beneath the winding stone staircase and he sat down on it. Very soon one of the heavy doors swung open and he saw the bishop's tall, dark figure outlined by the sunlight behind him. He followed him into the bright room.

"So you want to learn our prayers." The bishop's voice was melodious. "I'm not sure that prayers should be learned as a matter of expediency." He stopped, waiting for an answer.

"I could easily lie to you," Egon said, instinctively liking the man, "and say that I really want to believe your faith. It would be quite an easy way out. I am prepared to lie to save my life, but no more than that. Uncle Otto said that you are a 'Mensch'. Forgive me, but you know him, and you know that his German is better than his Polish. I think that I can tell you the truth."

"I'm honoured by Otto's high opinion of me." There was amusement in the bishop's voice. "And I also favour the truth. I must therefore tell you that I shall do my utmost to lead you towards the true path of Christianity. It is my duty, as a Catholic priest to try to save your soul."

"That's fair enough." Egon relaxed. "One thing we can both be sure of. In the hour of need, whichever prayers I recite will be sincere."

They both laughed then, but the priest could not know, Frieda Weiner's last words to her son. He was to remain a Jew as long as he lived.

"I shall start teaching you myself," the old priest continued, "and will do so for a while, but later on it will be safer for you to go to the Church of St. Mary, where Father Michal can continue your instruction. I am not sure how long I'll be allowed to stay at liberty."

A few months later the bishop was indeed arrested and taken to a camp. After the Jews, the Germans concentrated on the inteligiencja and the priests.

Egon visited the church at irregular intervals, and the colourless young priest, called Father Michal, who was to continue teaching him at St. Mary's, always collected him from the little waiting room.

By now the whole of Warsaw was one big conspiracy. There was hardly a family who had not lost a member in the constant executions, arrests and deportations, and the common tragedy of the city produced a comradeship of misfortune, surmounting the class divisions, which had previously divided its society.

On a cold day during February 1943, when Egon was as usual shown into the small waiting room, he saw that there were two other men already sitting there. One of the men was tall and blond. He reminded Egon of someone he had met before. The other, shorter and darker, looked stern and worried. They had to wait for a very long time and Egon curled up on the bench, closing his eyes. As soon as the dark man thought him to he asleep he started talking urgently:

"We must have more information about the trains. That consignment must not get through. What shall we do if no one can be found who can get it?"

"Yes, what we need is somebody inconspicous, who can speak perfect German. I'm afraid somebody would suspect both Tadek and me, if we were to start asking questions." The tall man spoke beautifully, and his voice also seemed familiar.

"I can speak German," Egon said opening his eyes and sitting up.

The two men eyed each other questioningly. Eventually, the taller one said.

"He wouldn't be here if he couldn't be trusted." He then looked at Egon intently and asked in easily flowing German.

"What is your name?"

"My name is Egon Weiner," Egon replied also in German, realising that this was a test, and in the excitement forgetting to use his new name. He was now quite sure that he had seen this man at home before the war.

"You have grown. I wouldn't have recognised you. If you remember me," the man said very quickly in German, obviously making sure that his companion did not understand, "do not under any circumstances mention my name. Now describe this gentleman to me in German."

"He is of less than medium height," Egon said, carefully accentuating his words, as his German governess had told him. "His hair is thick, dark and straight. Wrinkled forehead. Sunburned. Eyes light brown. Rather shaggy eyebrows. Upturned nose with a wart on the left nostril. Shabbily dressed as we all are, but neat. Appears middle aged to me, but I am not good at judging people's age."

"He observes well and he does speak perfect German." Martin Gold said. He had changed considerably but Egon now remembered the name of the Jewish professor of history, who had been a close family friend and had often come to see them, when they still lived in Silesia. "If you dress him up in a Hitlerjugend uniform, and let him speak a lot about his father, the general, he can ask questions, and get through anywhere." He turned to Egon:

"You seem to have volunteered for a job. If you really want to help, follow me, and we'll have a talk. Bolek, whom you have so well described, will stay behind and make some explanation to the Father on our behalf."

Egon ran after Martin Gold over the old cobblestones of Warsaw, not sure where he was, until they walked through an ornate doorway into a dilapidated courtyard, down a broken staircase and into a deserted cellar which showed signs of habitation. There was a desk, two chairs and a bundle of bedding in one corner.

"Sit down," Martin gestured towards one of the chairs, while seating himself behind the desk. Egon thought that his face looked terribly sad. It was the sadness which had made him difficult to recognise, because he had always laughed a lot when he came to visit the Weiners in Krolewska Huta. Also a new tension and purposefulness appeared in him which frightened and encouraged Egon at the same time.

"I was glad to see that, although you recognised me, you knew how to keep your mouth shut," he continued. "Now I am known as Janusz and am the commander of a group of resistance fighters, within the Home Army, the AK, but if they knew that I am a Jew I wouldn't be safe. There's always somebody who doesn't like Jews. Are your parents in Warsaw? Where's Otto?"

He listened carefully to Egon's story, and said:

"I brought you here primarily to give you this capsule of cyanide. If ever you're caught you must take it at once. It acts quickly, and you'll be dead before they start on you." He gave Egon the small capsule, and Egon looked at it doubtfully.

Martin glanced up at him, shook his head and turned around to fumble with a brick in the wall. It came out, leaving a gap from which he extricated two photographs. He gave one to Egon.

"You knew my wife Hanka, " Martin said.

The picture showed a beautiful girl with wavy hair falling down to her shoulders and a heart-shaped medalion round her neck. Her warm smile displayed even, white teeth, and the eyes above the pretty, slightly aquiline nose, laughed more obviously than her well-formed mouth.

"And this is the photograph of her," Martin continued, "after they finished questioning her at the Pawiak jail. It was taken in the mortuary at the Oczki Street. It's no longer possible to take such photographs. I want you to remember it in case it gets lost."

Egon looked with horror at the second picture. The limbs were spread out at odd angles, showing that the bones had been broken.

The head was a wound, where the hair had been torn out: the open swollen mouth showed no teeth, there was no nose, only a dark patch, and the eyes . . seemed to be missing. Only the heart-shaped medalion was unchanged.

"I am not showing you this to make you hate more, nor to have your sympathy, but to ensure that you do not forget the importance of taking the cyanide quickly." Martin spoke in an expressionless monotone, which people seemed to assume when speaking of things which needed to be said, but which they found extremely hard to mention at all.

"I've been told that the SS take young boys and train them specially. As a part of their training they let them have puppies and kittens, and when they have grown to love them, they're made to strangle them with their own hands. I don't know how true this is, but I know that they are no longer human. Some people seem to acquire a taste for cruelty with practice, and it's certainly not only the Germans. They had no pity on my wife, and they'll certainly waste no pity if they catch you. The fewer people know about us, the better, so don't tell Otto. You'd only put him at unnecessary risk. Otto is a businessman – not a soldier.

Go back to him now, and say that your teacher has asked you to stay with him for a day or two to avoid difficulties with the curfew. Then come back here by five. I shall be ready for you. I'm not asking you to take the usual oath, because betraying me would not help you. Nothing can save a Jew from death except hiding, but I'll let you read the oath so that I·can truthfully say you know it."

So Egon read:

"In the presence of God Almighty and the Most Holy Virgin Mary, the Queen of Polish Crown, I put my hand on this Holy Cross, the sign of suffering and salvation – and swear that I will faithfully and unswervingly guard the honour of Poland, and that I will always and with all my strength fight for her liberation from slavery. For this I am ready to give my life. I shall obey all orders and will under all circumstances preserve secrecy, regardless of what will happen to me."

"We in this country seem to have a natural inclination towards the dramatic, " Janusz said when Egon had finished reading, "but I'm sure that you understand what is meant. I must add that we're not allowed to kill wantonly, or to inflict unnecessary pain. We are not going to succumb to the current 'German Morality'."

*

Egon returned promptly at five to find Janusz taking out a Hitlerjugend uniform out of an old shopping bag.

"Try it on," he said.

Egon would have liked to have seen himself. The belt and the straps of the short black trousers had to be tightened. They must have belonged to a much better nourished boy, but everything else fitted.

"One of our girls is working as a maid for a German family, and she has 'borrowed' it for you. With any luck we will be able to return it before anyone notices. It would be a pity if she was sacked for stealing. Now take it off. We must keep it clean. You'll have to start early in the morning. As in acting, you must try to think yourself into the part. If I remember your family correctly, it shouldn't be at all difficult for you to behave like a well brought-up young German. We all had to click our heels at proper times, say 'thank you' and 'please' more than necessary, and bow to our our elders and betters. The only additional thing is to remember to say 'Heil Hitler' whenever anybody else does and stretch out your arm. We'll practice this in a moment. Your job is to find out anything you can about train movements from the station. You will have papers proving that your name is Egon Blaskowitz – the youngest son of General Johannes Blaskowitz."

Am I right in thinking that Egon is your real name? I seem to remember, that this is how your governess used to call you. By the way, do you know what happened to her? I can't remember her name, but she was a nice girl."

So Egon told him about Fraulein Hedwige Hoffgarten, who had taught him his impeccable German, who had laughed and played games with him, and when told of the Nazi excesses went back home just to make sure it was all a lie. The first time Egon had seen his mother cry was when she received Hedwige's last note, brought from Germany by a mutual friend:

"Dear Mrs. Weiner," it said. "It is true and I can't do anything about it. I have been proud of being a German, and have tried to teach your children our beautiful language, our sense of honour, honesty and hard work. Everything in which I have believed has been befouled. I cannot go on living."

The friend said that Hedwige had shot herself with her father's hunting gun.

They were silent for a while, but then Janusz resumed his quiet instruction, and they practiced "Heil Hitlering". If anyone had seen them, or heard them they would have wondered what such devoted servants of the Third Reich were doing in the shabby cellar.

"May I ask you a question? Or are you in a hurry?"

Egon's anguished voice startled the older man.

He looked at the boy in front of him and thought that Ziggie was lucky to have his two fine boys.

He himself would never have a son. The chances of his survival were slim, and the years of his marriage had not brought him children. He felt a warmth towards the boy; the sort of warmth he thought he could never feel again.

"No. Of course I don't mind," he said. "It's most important to try to understand as much as possible, and without questions there can be no understanding. Don't forget I'm a teacher by profession and it's been my job to answer questions. Anyway, it's past curfew so we have to spend the night here and- it is too early to go to sleep."

"Why do they all hate us Jews so much? Some of the Poles seem to me even worse than the Germans, because many of them appear to do so of their own initiative, while the ordinary Germans do so because they're ordered." The words came out with such force that Janusz realised that the problem had been in Egon's mind for some time, and that he was the first adult whom he could ask. The boy was probably hesitant to ask Otto, because Filomena was not Jewish. What horrors had he seen? In any case the question was one on which he had spent a lot of his time. Furthermore, Martin Gold was not a professor of history for nothing.

He loved to teach, so, with a feeling of pleasure, which he had not felt for a very long time, he allowed himself the luxury of giving Egon a lecture, trying all the while to remember that he was talking to a child whose education had been picked up mostly through listening to adults. The necessity to keep it all as simple as possible, and to explain any words which Egon might not understand, made him hesitate occasionally, but he had given the subject so much thought, that he talked easily.

"Antisemitism is not new," he said slowly. "Jews have been killed simply for being Jews for very many centuries. Paradoxically, I think, if there had been no antisemitism, there would also have been no Jews. We would all have assimilated like the Jews of China. Within the animal kingdom, to which humans belong, any individual or group which is different is feared and therefore hated. That is the basic reason, if you can call it that, for the classical hatred of the stranger, which is present in all people who lack security of mind. It's called xenophobia. In addition, people always need a scapegoat – somebody to blame for their misfortunes and their own short-comings. In their wisdom the elders of Israel had, in fact, a real goat onto which people could load all their sins, and then send it out into the wilderness.

How easy it is to blame everything on someone you hate! Did you hear the old Jewish joke where an older Pole explains to a younger one that all the world's troubles are due to the Jews and cyclists.

'Why the cyclists?' asks the young man. The Jews he accepts as the cause of trouble without any hesitation."

"I heard my father telling this joke, but at that time I didn't understand why it was funny," Egon said.

"I see that now you do." Janusz nodded and continued: "Ours is an old culture. As, in most places, we were not allowed either to own land or to carry arms, we had to concentrate on developing our minds. Illiteracy among male Jews has been almost non-existent for about two thousand years. A Jewish boy was supposed to start learning his letters at the age of three. We also learned mathematics and thus could trade at a profit and calculate interest on lending, which was one of the few means of livelihood allowed to us. Our laws of hygiene and knowledge of medicine often saved us from contagious diseases, which raged outside our settlements.

"During the time that Christianity developed there were many prophets in the land of Israel. Basically they all wanted to ease the yoke of the Romans. The Jews are not allowed to proselytise."

Martin stopped for a moment sensing that the boy did not understand the word.

"Proselytise means, to try and persuade others to accept a belief, in this case our religion. But the Jewish sect which adopted the teaching deemed to have originated from Jesus wanted to change this law. In order to be able to spread their gospel among the Romans, and stop their own persecution, they had to dissociate themselves from the mainstream of Judaism. The Gospels, the New Testament stories of the life and death of Jesus, were written years after he is thought to have died, and the later the version the blacker their portrayal of the Jews, in order to prove that Christianity had nothing to do with Judaism. Given all this, it is not surprising that the ignorant masses regarded us with superstitious mistrust, accentuated sometimes by the differences in our dress and customs. This mistrust was quickly seized by those in power for their own ends. The princes, and others who owed money to the Jews, incited the priests to preach all kinds of fallacies to stimulate hatred amongst the populace, provoke pogroms and get rid of their debts in the process, at the same time distracting attention from any evil deeds of which they themselves were guilty." It was a long time since Martin had an opportunity to speak openly, so he took advantage of this one. "I am not saying that all Jews are good," he resumed. "In fact I have known a lot whom I intensely disliked, but that applies also to non-Jews.

"All mankind consists of good, bad and mostly mediocre people. Nobody is better or worse. Like others, we also have a percentage of those who are dishonest, though probably not as many murderers, thieves, wife or child beaters and drunkards as many other nations. I hear that there are some Jews in the ghetto who betray their own kind in order to save themselves, or their families. Some even to enrich themselves. There are a few, who co-operate with the Gestapo." Martin stopped because he did not want to allow himself to condemn out of hand. He always tried to be objective.

"Every nation," he continued eventually, "is cursed with some scum, and we're no exception. However, unless you yourself have been in a certain situation, you can never be sure how you'd behave yourself. You hope you'd do better, but you don't really know. It's wrong to believe in ones own moral superiority until you've tested it. You must always try to put yourself in the other person's shoes, in order to know how they feel. It weakens your arguments, but increases understanding.

It was always easy to ask the very poor of any country, and there have always been plenty of them, to compare their wretchedness with the relative affluence of some of the Jews, and life in the past was cheap.

Furthermore, Jews have always provided a spark in the societies in which they lived, supplying them with new ideas of every kind, and helping culture to flourish, but people fear and misinterpret innovation.

One of the excuses for killing Jews has been the so-called blood libel. It was used for the first time to incite the masses in twelfth century England."

"What is blood libel?" Egon did not like to interrupt, but wanted to understand.

"Well. The story goes that Jews kill a Christian boy at about Easter for ritual purposes. In later years this fiction was developed further. It was then darkly explained to the superstitious people of the time, that the boy's blood was used in making matzos the unleavened bread of Pesach, the festival which celebrates the Jewish exodus from Egypt," explained Martin, and continued his lecture.

"Instances of Jews being murdered by the mob, of Jewish villages being burned and women raped have been frequent in most countries. Eventually, even many of the educated but unthinking believed the stories invented for the benefit of the ignorant, although, it must be said that the blood libel charge against the Jews, had been condemned by most leading intellectuals and many of the Popes.

Poland gave us a refuge, when we were exiled from pretty well every other country of Europe, and that's why so many of us are Polish patriots, but, especially in the last years, antisemitism, which has always existed, has seriously increased. This, in addition to the usual causes, was mainly due to the fact that Poland had very little middle class.

We've had a lot of nobility and landed gentry, and a mass of peasants. The Jews became the middle class of Poland, prospered, and increased in number. Most of the doctors, lawyers, dentists, merchants, many teachers etc. were Jews. This created envy – a very human failure.

The Russian influence, – the Tzars sponsored anti-Jewish propaganda, and issued laws denying them most human rights, – resulted in pogroms in the east of our country. Within the western part antisemitism manifested itself in not allowing Jews to attend many university courses, as well as several other injustices.

Priests in country villages preached that we had killed Christ, and continued to spread the story that a Christian boy's blood had to be used in order to bake matzos. Some of the more ignorant ones assured their congregations that we have horns. Children were threatened that a Jew will come and take them away if they were naughty.

If you had told a peasant or an ignorant country priest that most of the Latin prayers are a simple translation from the original Hebrew, that Jesus and the Holy Mary were Jewish, not to mention all the Apostles and many of the saints, they would have lynched you for blasphemy.

And if, like me, you had studied history, and found out that the first Christmas was celebrated three hundred and fifty three years after the birth of Christ, when it conveniently replaced the feast of *Natale Solis Incvicti* – the birth of unconquered sun, you wouldn't dare to tell this to anybody, because they would say that you are a vicious liar.

Our code of ethics, as expressed in the Ten Commandments, seems to give many Jews an exaggerated sense of justice, which is deeply ingrained into our consciousness, making us subscribe to idealistic causes. This also doesn't make us popular.

The educated were jealous of our intellectual successes, and the simple taught to hate us instead of their oppressors. Unfortunately, there is only a very small step from hatred to murder if there is an opportunity. It's all precariously balanced between the strength of a person's moral scruples and the natural inclination.

The bible tells us, that, thousands of years ago, our people had also indulged in wars and stupid acts of vengeance.

I think now, in the main, we're not cruel – we've had a few thousand years to grow up.

You can hate people as much as you like, though, please always remember, that hatred destroys the person who hates, but one would have thought that even a slightly civilised person would stop at calculated cold blooded mass murder, a total extermination of innocent people.

What we are seeing now is how thin the veneer of civilisation is, if the piercing of it is cleverly combined with flattery and appeal to both self interest and the basic animal, which to some extent is present in most people. It's my belief that nations have to grow up, like children, and it takes time for the cover of civilisation to deepen sufficiently to gain control of the animal instincts which are buried inside us.

The Nazi propaganda machine is very clever. It tells people that they are threatened by the Jews, at the same time as making us appear inferior in every respect. You'd think that the contradiction would be obvious. How can you be afraid of someone who is cowardly, weak and stupid?

You will see from the posters and newspapers that we are guilty of causing all troubles which assail mankind; from starting the war, to causing shortages of everything, with the exception of lice and illness, which we spread around.

And people believe it, in spite of the fact that in all the Nazi occupied countries there are now no Jews left at large, except for people like us of which, we hope, no one is aware.

If you repeat a lie often enough, and print it, it will be accepted as the truth. Sadly, it will take a very long time to wipe this out, if it ever happens at all. That's why it is so important for some of us to survive and live in such a way that these lies can be disproved."

"My mother said so too," whispered Egon.

"Your mother has a great understanding of things that matter," said Martin. "I always liked talking with her." They were quiet for a time – thinking about the past, but Martin had the need to say more.

"The Germans and the Austrians," he went on, "are constantly being told that they are superior to everybody, and that the Jews are responsible for all their troubles and those of the rest of world, that the road to salvation lies in getting rid of the entire Jewish nation. The Germans are a people used to obedience. Moreover, they can see an immediate personal benefit, so most of them obey willingly. The orgy of killing has appealed to many of them; they began to enjoy it, and, in the process, lost all claim to being human. We're all to be killed, and all the Slavs are to become slaves to the master race, and are considered sub-human.

Polish and Russian prisoners of war are no longer considered to be within the Geneva convention, which is an agreement for humane treatment of prisoners of war.

The Poles betray us mostly because they have been told that they and their families will be killed for not reporting us, though some scum do it for money, or for fun. The betrayal comes quite easily to many of those, who are glad to be rid of us, but not to all.

I hope I have at least partially answered your question. Now we ought to try to make ourselves as comfortable as we can and go to sleep."

"But surely there must be some Germans who don't agree with this." Egon almost whispered as he tried to settle on the hard floor.

"Of course there are, but they're either dying in Dachau or keeping their mouths shut. Don't make the mistake most people do, that it's only the Germans. Judging by their accent, at least half of the SS and Gestapo appear to be Austrian, and remember that Hitler is an Austrian."

"But I thought the Austrians were not like this," interrupted Egon shyly.

"My father told us, when we were in Cracow, that German soldiers were quartered in his friends' house. We were then waiting for our British visa, and our friends had a possibility of buying a visa to America, but all their money had been taken away from them.

Their young daughter, she was a bit older than me, went to the only Austrian soldier, and told him that they'll be taken away within a fortnight unless they escape.

That young man had a heart and a lot of courage, because they would've shot him if they found out. He wrote to his mother in Salzburg to send him all his savings, which he gave to them. My father said that they escaped, although, of course, he didn't know how far they got."

"This is just what I'm trying to tell you. You must never condemn a whole nation for the evil done by even the majority of its people. That soldier is the only Austrian of whom you really know anything. A lot of people hate Jews without ever having met one.

You must not become like that. People have to be judged individually. There are good and bad everywhere.

Although I admit the temptation is great, if you say 'all Germans are bad', you'll reduce yourself to the level of the Nazis. Of course, it will be difficult at first to fight the revulsion against all things German, which we feel at the moment, but to condemn a whole nation out of hand is a crude, sweeping judgement, which we must never allow ourselves.

As I said before, I'm sure somewhere there is a large population of perfectly decent Germans, but they are either dead or in camps, or, mostly, so intimidated that they just sit still and do nothing. That's those who can think for themselves, which not many people are inclined to do.

For instance, there was a priest in Berlin before the war who ended his sermons with a prayer for the Jews, because he had seen what was happening. They took him away. He's probably dead now.

Naturally, you also have the worst elements of all countries doing the dirty work. The Ukrainians, Latvians and Lituanians we have here are particularly good at killing old men, women and children, but it would be wrong to assume that they're all like this.

The masses believe what they're told. Hitler wrote a book called '*Mein Kampf*'. He wrote in it that the receptive ability of the masses is very limited and their understanding small. They also have a great power of forgetting. As he had predicted, they forgot the truth, and believe the lies, especially as he has been phenomenally successful in all he has done.

On the other hand, I've been told that there is a prison in Berlin where

German political prisoners, which means those who have said anything at all against the Nazis, have to pay for their own keep and their own execution.

Under those circumstances most people, even those who are essentially decent, have learned to keep their mouths shut.

Although the majority of Poles do give us away, a very small minority almost makes up for it by helping us, because they do so with the full knowledge that the punishment for that is death to them and to those they love.

There is a true nobility of spirit among some of them. I even know of some pre-war antisemites, who still help the Jews because their conscience makes them do it.

If any of us survive outside the ghettos and camps it will be almost entirely because of the crazy courage these people have. There are probably a lot of Germans who would also help us, but very few of them have the blind courage of the Poles."

Martin Gold, known as Janusz, stopped talking, and they lay quietly, trying to go to sleep. They needed to husband their strength for the following day.

Their two fair heads contrasted sharply with the darkness around them. They were their good fortune. Anyone of even vaguely semitic appearance had no chance on the streets of Warsaw. The hunt for Jews had become a sport and it was the Poles who most easily recognised them. The small mannerisms of speech and behaviour, which would not be apparent to a German, were obvious to the Poles, and many of them would denounce the fugitives, whose death was then inevitable, though there were variations in its horror.

Both the man and the boy had an urgent need to be involved in some useful activity above and beyond the mere necessity to survive. There was a similarity in their unusual characters, which combined extreme sensitivity with great strength. They had been hurt beyond endurance, and instinctively knew that they needed to do something constructive in order to retain their sanity. The only thing they could do for the moment was to survive, and, if at all possible, to fight back.

They had both been born in Upper Silesia, and found it almost impossible to believe that the Germans, whom they had been taught to consider the most civilised people in Europe, could become mindless murderers and torturers of innocent people.

"Just one more thing before you go to sleep," Janusz felt he had to use

the opportunity of talking to this child of his friend, who was probably
dead, because the child might survive and bear witness.

"If you do live through this nightmare, try to re-construct a real life. A
life built on love and not on hate, on beauty and not on ugliness.

Humans were meant to be happy and good, and vengeance may be sweet,
but it begets only another, and usually a greater vengeance. I would happily
kill those who have tortured Hanka, or betrayed my Jewish friends, but if
I simply go out and kill German, Ukrainian, Polish or any other civilians, I
may be killing perfectly good people who have done no one any harm.
Then they in their turn may feel in duty bound to kill some other innocents
and so it goes on. Justice must be done, but random stupid vengeance is
an evil in itself."

He stopped for a while, and then whispered in the darkness:

"I have a feeling you might survive, and I know I will not. The odds are
against me because I have lost the will to live."

Egon had found a person on whom he could fashion himself. He admired
the knowledge, the detachment and the clarity of expression which Janusz
had shown.

He had spoken to him as to a grown-up. Egon did not understand it all
absolutely, but what he had heard had a ring of well thought out truth.
With the instinctive idealism of childhood he admired Martin's ability to
despise hatred and evil, but at the same time agree with the noble precept
of not blindly returning like for like.

There was also the beautiful wife, who had died in torture rather than
give him away. For the first time since Brzesko Egon slept well.

CHAPTER 6

THE RAILWAY STATION IN SIEDLCE

Early the following morning in the bitterly cold cellar, Janusz, formerly Martin Gold, and Wojtek, originally Egon, washed in the icy water from a tap outside, before the Hitlerjugend uniform was put on. Egon stopped shivering when he was completely dressed and his fair hair carefully combed. By sheer good fortune it had recently been trimmed by Filomena and, according to Janusz, he looked perfect for the part he was about to play. Egon wished he had a mirror to see himself, but Janusz could not provide one. Instead he vanished into the depths of the courtyard and reappeared with a thermos of hot acorn coffee and a pack of ham sandwiches, which he put on the desk.

"Just the right sort of food for a Jewish boy setting out on a mission," he said smiling wrily, "but our kind hostess wasn't to know that we shouldn't eat pork. Enjoy it. You'll need your strength."

Egon did not need any encouragement and he ate as he listened to Janusz, who continued speaking.

"You are the youngest son of General Johannes Blaskowitz, who really does exist. All I know about him is that he is a professional soldier, and comes from East Prussia, so that his son would have been brought up to click his heels excessively, and be as stiff and polite as possible.

"Also, it is highly unlikely that anyone at a comparatively small railway station would be personally acquainted with him, though they will know his name, which should carry a lot of weight.

"I want you to find out as much as you can about all trains travelling through Siedlce station. As I told you before, you must just think yourself into the part and then it'll be easy. Above all, you must act with confidence. Trains are your hobby, and your father would consider it a favour if you were shown around and told how timetables are made up. Have the cyanide at the ready, because if anything goes wrong they'll want to know who put you up to it, and they would never believe that you had told them all you know, even if you did.

"We are very fortunate, because we are amongst the very few Jews who can fight back. This is why I have no hesitation in risking your life. Anyway, according to the Jewish law, you'll soon be an adult. You would be doing your barmitzvah in a few months. As we are all supposed to be killed anyway, it is far better to die fighting the evil which besets Europe, though I am sure that you will fight and live." Having once allowed himself to give Egon a lecture, Janusz found it impossible to refrain from continuing to do so, while he had the chance, but then he became practical again.

"Tadek, with whom you are going, will be here soon. All your documents are perfect, though not genuine. We had our best forgers working on them during the night."

He was interrupted by three light knocks on the door, and peered through a crack, before letting in a young man, who slipped into the cellar in one swift movement and then waited for a moment, getting used to the semi-darkness of the cellar. He was broad shouldered and athletic looking in spite of being excessively thin. This thinness made the German army corporal's uniform he wore, look very elegant. His fine, elongated face was friendly in spite of its somewhat sardonic expression.

"Your car is waiting round the corner," he said with a grin. "We'd better go, before anyone starts making enquiries."

"Good luck. Go back to your uncle when you return. We can keep in touch through your lessons," Janusz said, choosing his words with care so as not to give away any names or the nature of the lessons. Although he had made a speech justifying sending Egon on this mission, his conscience was not satisfied with the explanation he had given it, and he did not feel happy, quite unlike the two youngsters, who walked away laughing. Janusz wondered if their laughter was genuine, or whether each tried to show the other that he was not afraid.

As they crossed the courtyard and went down the cobbled street, Tadek explained to Egon that a Mercedes Benz German army car had been "borrowed" for them from a garage, which employed Polish staff. They walked to the road, where it waited for them, parked inconspicuously behind a heap of rubble. Tadek sat down at the wheel and drove off, looking like any highly respectable German army driver.

Egon hoped that he looked equally convincing in his Hitlerjugend uniform. The knee length white socks seemed preposterous in war-time Poland, as did the black lederhosen, but it was nice to feel clean, which was a necessary part of his costume. It was not only pleasant, but it gave him the self-assurance necessary for playing the part. Although he was fully aware of the odds against them, he was no longer afraid but conscious of excitement, of anticipated adventure.

"I have to drive carefully, though I'd love to give this thing a proper go." Tadek said. "It could easily do up a hundred and fifty kilometers an hour! Can you imagine! One day I'll have a proper car myself. My father had a Tatra, but God knows where it is now. But I had better concentrate. All we need is to have an accident on the icy roads, and have to explain our way out of it!"

In his present mood Egon found it difficult not to show off about Otto's old Mercedes, which was a superior model to the one in which they sat, but said instead:

"Couldn't you just let her rip on a straight bit?"

Tadek grinned and put his foot down until the needle climbed up to a hundred and twenty. Then reluctantly he slowed down.

"That was super," said Egon. "And I'll also have a fast car when the war is over and I am grown up."

"I'm sure of that," Tadek said in a matter of fact way. "In the meantime it's all jolly exciting, though thoroughly uncomfortable. One day they'll put heaters into cars like these. They probably do in America. I'll have an American car after the war, I think, and perhaps a Rolls Royce for special occasions."

"I think I'll also have a Rolls Royce one day, but also a fast sports car," Egon said after considering the question for a while.

"I had a Jewish friend when I was at school," Tadek reminisced. "He told me a story about a poor man, who has bought a lottery ticket and hopes that he'll win a lot of money. He tells his children that, if he really does win, he will buy a horse and cart. 'I'll sit in the back,' says the mother, and the girls say they'll sit with her. 'And I'll drive,' says the father; 'I'll sit in the front next to you' says the elder son.

'No,' says the younger, 'I want to sit on the front seat'. 'You'll sit in the back with me like a good boy,' says the mother. 'No, I'm sitting on the front seat,' bellows young Moshe.

'Moshe, get off the front seat at once, or I'll smack your bottom,' says the father severely."

Egon laughed, although he had heard the story before. The old Jewish stories which made fun of poverty and trouble never failed to amuse everybody. He felt a warmth towards Tadek, who shook his head and said, "I hope somehow he's still alive, but I doubt it," then drove silently the rest of the way.

They were frozen when, after a few hours, they reached the small town of Siedlce and found their way along the railway line to the station. German soldiers were sitting outside it enjoying the sun, which had just broken through the clouds. It was evident that they felt completely at home, but continued to exercise caution, because a sentry stopped the two visitors before they came too close. Tadek stepped out of the car. After the correct exchange of "Heil Hitlers", he showed their papers and asked to see the commanding officer. His German was excellent. It sounded as if he came from Bavaria. They were instructed to leave the car and walk across to the little office, where a smiling, gentlemanly man in an army captain's uniform sat behind a desk, and welcomed them with another "Heil Hitler", eagerly returned by both of them.

While Tadek explained the reason for their visit, Egon had time to think about how odd it was that they were so completely and naturally accepted by the enemy, and to see how easily both he and Tadek could fit into German surroundings. As Janusz had told him, the behaviour expected at the Weiner's home in Silesia was also the norm for a German general's son, with the exception of the stupid Nazi greeting, which he had so well rehearsed. He relaxed into the part he had to play and looked at the man sitting in front of him.

He looks just like Uncle Herman Weiner, thought Egon. In spite of what Janusz had said to him, he found it impossible to reconcile the cheerful, human appearance of the Germans with their actions.

It was as if they wore perfectly made masks to hide their real faces, which, surely, should be marked with some signs of the terrible cruelty of their owners. Uncle Herman was either already dead or in the camps. At best he was in hiding. It was doubtful if any of his children with whom Egon had so often played were still alive. And yet here was this man, who looked just like him, smiling, as if he had done nothing wrong, but, of course, he was doing something evil by just being here. It was like a bad dream, during which a beloved face can change into a nightmarish monster. These thoughts slipped through Egon's brain mixing with the pictures of his parents going away, and the ever present scene in Brzesko. He always tried to avoid thinking about this, because it made him hate anything German as he now hated the German captain, although Janusz had told him not to hate unreasonably. In the meantime Tadek had finished his explanation and the man at the desk spoke. His voice, though that of an educated man, had the slight inflection of Silesia, just like Uncle Herman's.

"Stabsunteroffizier Bauman tells me that you're the son of General Blaskowitz, and that you are a train fan. It's nice to see the young taking interest in mechanical things.

Although Siedlce is a small station, it's a very busy one, and you can have fun watching the trains passing. I shall assign a man to take you round, and he will introduce you to the station master. You'll have no difficulty with the language. The man is a German. One couldn't trust the Poles to run a railway station, especially this one. Heil Hitler!".

Egon offered his profuse thanks, clicked his heels and Heil Hitlered, before leaving. Tadek, or rather "Stabsunteroffizier Bauman", was then taken off for a beer. Egon found himself following a young soldier to the stationmaster's office, suddenly feeling alone and afraid.

The stationmaster's name was Thomas Braun. He was fat, fair and obviously pleased to have a general's son so interested in his work. Egon complimented him on the orderliness and cleanliness of the station, and the man positively glowed with pride.

"It must be difficult," Egon said naively, "to make sure that all these trains don't collide. You must be very clever to be able to organise this. Are you supplied with a time-table, or do you have to do it all yourself?"

Otto smiled modestly, and told Egon that in fact he was responsible for organising the area timetables and that it wasn't all that difficult if you knew how.

"Oh! But it must take years to learn!" exclaimed Egon. "How do you set them out? It must be frightfully hard to put all this complicated information in a form simple enough to be followed by people who don't have your experience."

"Not at all." In all his life nobody had appreciated him as much as this charming lad. "Look! Here are my notes. I take a few carbon copies, and then keep altering them until I get a plan like this. Then I have some copies typed. They have to be changed once a month for security reasons."

"Naturally," Egon said sternly. "My father always says that security is always foremost in the Fuhrer's mind." He was now getting into the spirit of the thing and almost enjoying himself.

"D'you think I could have a copy of this plan and your notes to show my father what a clever system you have evolved?"

It was with great pride that Braun instructed his secretary to type out his notes, and make an especially neat copy of the time-table. Very casually he mentioned to her that the Herr General Blaskowitz was extremely interested in the work he was doing. The girl was most impressed, and, because she tried particularly hard, kept making mistakes, and starting from the beginning again.

It seemed to Egon that an eternity had passed since he had walked into the office. He cursed himself for overdoing his act, because he was now beginning to get worried about the duration of his visit. They should be getting back before someone discovered the loss of the car and the two uniforms. He tried to protest that he did not want to waste the valuable time of the stationmaster and his staff, but Thomas Braun insisted that it all had to be done properly for the Herr General. Egon could feel his heartbeat pulsating in his throat, which was dry with fear. But he smiled and chatted politely, as instructed by Janusz.

In spite of his constant hunger, he could barely eat the food offered him. Fortunately, Thomas Braun misinterpreted his abstinence.

"Of course, we cannot offer the sort of food you get at home, but you should try to eat. You're are a growing lad."

Egon said truthfully that his lack of appetite was due only to the fact that he was so absorbed in the train time-tables. Suddenly, the office telephone rung shrilly. Egon was sure that somebody, at the other end of the line, was telephoning to tell Thomas Braun that it was not the son of General Blaskowitz who was sitting in his office, but a Jewish boy, who was trying to find out how best to blow up a train carrying some special freight.

It took a great effort to remain in his chair instead of running away, while there was still some chance. How could he warn Tadek anyway. He stayed sitting quite motionless while Braun slowly picked up the receiver. Was it somebody telling him that General Blaskowitz had no son? Or that the son was in Germany? Egon thought clearly again, and knew that there was no chance of running away. He strenuously concentrated on producing a slight smile on his face, and waited.

"Sorry," Braun said when he replaced the receiver, "I have to go. They want me outside, but Fraulein Gruber will give you the timetable, when she has finally managed to finish it." He glowered at the unfortunate Fraulein Gruber, and got up.

"Thank you for giving me so much of your valuable time," Egon said with feeling, also getting up from the chair in which Thomas Braun had placed him.

Eventually he managed to pick up the finished time-table, for which he thanked the typist profusely. She was a plump girl, wearing round glasses through which her blue eyes looked up at Egon worriedly, and in a voice filled with doubt said:

"I've had to rub out once. Perhaps I should re-type the whole thing, otherwise Herr Braun will be cross with me."

But Egon kept a tight grip on the imperfect time-table, and assured her that his father was only interested in the principle of the thing. He thanked her again and walked out before she could say anything else.

They left with smiles and "Heil Hitlers" and Egon waved out of the open car window when the guards let them out.

Tadek drove the Mercedes back exercising great care.

It seemed to them that a very long time had passed since their departure from Warsaw. They were too cold and tired to be truly jubilant. Hunger bothered them too, but neither would admit that they had been too nervous to eat when food was offered to them. The grubby man, who took the car and the precious time-table from them, pushed them out into the street with a sigh of relief immediately they changed into their own clothes, which had been brought for them to the garage. He was sorry, he said, but he had to hurry to pass on the information.

Outside it was cold and getting dark.

"If I run," Egon said, "I may just make it home before curfew."

"I wouldn't even try," Tadek said. "If they see you running, they'll shoot first and ask questions afterwards. We'll go round the corner to my aunt. You can't sleep there, because she has no room, but she knows a lot of people, who come just before curfew, stay the night, play bridge, and tell stories."

The room they eventually entered, after having been twice identified on the way up the dark staircase by young men who appeared from the shadows, was smoky, and badly lit. The airlessness seemed all the greater because the window panes had been blown out during the initial bombing of Warsaw and replaced by hardboard, as glass was not available.

There were about twenty people sitting, wherever they could find a space, and listening intently to a man reading from a sheaf of papers by the light of a kerosene lamp. A small, thin woman came towards them. She had piercingly blue eyes, which lit up when she saw Tadek, who had walked in first. Briskness and energy emanated from her slender body, around which smart, pre-war clothes hung very loosely, indicating both that she had lost a lot of weight, and that she couldn't or wouldn't have them altered.

"Before you say anything, darling," Tadek said as he embraced her, "remember that my name is Tadek."

"Of course," she kissed him. "And presumably your young friend also has a name."

"Wojtek, meet my aunt, *Pani*[1] Ostrowska."

"I'm delighted to make your acquaintance," Egon kissed the hand she offered him.

"Well, at least this one has been properly brought up. Make yourselves as comfortable as you can. There's plenty of hot water to drink, and if you're very hungry, Marysia will give you some soup, but eat it out of sight. I haven't got enough for everybody."

When they returned from the kitchen, where the faithful Marysia fed them on soup and surreptitiously added a piece of bread and dripping to their supper, they saw that the old gentleman was still reading.

The boys crouched down by the wall and listened.

"The good news from the front and increasingly terrible conditions in the whole of Poland are in a horrific race in which the prize consists not of thousands but tens and hundreds of thousands if not of millions of human beings. The war is now proceeding quickly, but for us it is still far too slow.

The Soviet radio reports advances on all fronts: Caucasus, Kuban, Don, near Voronez and south of Ladoga. This is confirmed by an English correspondent who gives more details.

The German radio says that battles have diminished, and they can be described as a passing phenomenon. They also say that for strategic reasons

---

[1]'Pani' is more or less equivalent to 'lady' although it is not a title, but is used instead of Mrs. It is also customary to use it with the first name.

the Germans left Voronez, and dwell on the heroic battle for Stalingrad, which appears to be coming to an end.

On the 26th January, we have had the first air raid alarm in Warsaw. There was no bombing. It is said that they bombed Radom. We will see what is true.

After the taking of Tripoli, there's not much new on the African front. The Italian press has a difficult job of explaining that it was necessary to leave but say that they will be coming back.

The German press says that Churchill has gone to Washington. Perhaps this means that the allies may be opening up a new front?

We await the end of the terror. People are coming back from Majdanek full of horror. They say that the camp has been enormously enlarged. So is the German quarter in Warsaw. The Vernichtungskommando:[2] has completed the "resettlement" of the Jews. A quarter of the population of the ghetto has been killed in the process. First of all they took the prison, the hospital with all the doctors and most of the officers administering the ghetto. Only three are still alive. The chief of Jewish police Col. Szerynski committed suicide. As you may have heard, Dr. Janusz Korczak went to his death in Tremblinka together with all the children in his ghetto orphanage.

Many of the Jews doing Gestapo work for the Germans have also been killed. Nobody is sorry for them. The individual tragedies are difficult to describe.

Many people have committed suicide. Mothers gave children sleeping pills so that they didn't wake up again. There were also people who sacrificed their lives.

Seventeen SS men were killed and several wounded. A Jewish girl guide threw a granade and killed five of the Gestapo.

Beyond Warsaw it's the same. New actions of murdering Jews in Czestochowa and Radom as well as Lodz.

The paper we call "The Rag" which is published by the Germans in Poland, says that our German Governor, Frank, had various meetings. Somebody opened a new German school etc. etc.

The Polish population in some districts has been replaced by Germans, who are sending looted Polish household goods to Germany.

Food rationing for the Polish people is 800 calories per day, barely enough

---

[2]The annihilation squad:

to survive. In the ghetto it is 184 calories per day , encouraging people to die out. The terror seems almost complete, and nearly everyone had lost someone they loved, but the cafes in Warsaw are full.

And this is the end of my resume of the latest of Mr. Lewandowski's reports on the world situation. How he assembles all the information I do not know, but I've been reliably told that it's pretty accurate."

The distinguished-looking reader stopped for a moment and took a sip of water from a glass which stood on a windowsill next to him. Then he looked around and allowed himself a little smile, which took away the stern seriousness apparent on his face, during his reading.

The whole atmosphere around him suddenly filled with an irrepresible humour, which communicated itself to his audience.

"It is my intention to try and live through this war," he continued. "In order to do so and retain our sanity, we must occasionally try to concentrate our minds on other things than our immediate troubles.

May I therefore add some further news, which I have heard in the aforementioned cafés?" He paused, while everybody exchanged glances and smiles.

"Uncle always collects jokes to cheer us up," Tadek told Egon in whisper.

"There were no Christmas cribs this year," the old gentleman continued in a voice of an announcer, "because of the absence of all the usual participants: Jesus is in the ghetto, the Holy Mother in a concentration camp, the donkey in Rome, the devil in Berlin and the Three Kings in London." He paused for the laughter and applause.

"Jesus and Holy Mary were Jewish, the donkey is Mussolini, the devil is Hitler, but I'm not sure which kings are in London apart from the English one," Tadek explained to Egon in whisper. "It could be the Greek, and the Belgian. All the people here constantly read the newspapers; both the Polish and the German ones, so they understand it all."

When the audience was still again the old gentleman continued:

"Orbis (a Polish Travel Agency) is organising special adventure tours to Berlin under the slogan 'recognise your furniture'.

"According to the latest German orders the minimum penalty for most misdemeanours such as listening to the radio, or the possession of a camera or a pair of skis is death. We look forward to committing some really serious crimes in order to find out what is the maximum penalty." When the bitter laughter subsided a young man stood up.

"There is a special poignancy," he said, "at the present moment in reading Heine and Rilke. The cultured Germans are not allowed to do so. It's up to us uneducated Poles to keep their writings alive."

He then proceeded to read some poems in the original German, which did not seem to present any difficulty to the audience, who then listened with equal ease to some French poetry, but by that time Egon had fallen asleep in his corner.

When next morning Egon finally made his way to the shop and slipped upstairs through the back entrance, he found Otto sitting by the table in the little flat. It was hard not to tell him about Martin Gold and the the trip to Siedlce. He had promised to tell no one, so he had to lie when explaining where he had been, but he tried to keep as near to the truth as he could, because his mother had always preached to them the old Talmudic precept that "the truth is the best lie".

He therefore said that he had spent the night in the flat belonging to *Pani* Ostrowska in order to avoid curfew.

The stories he had heard there found a ready audience in Otto, especially when he heard the name Lewandowski. "His real name," Otto said, "is Ludwik Landau, the economist. He speaks several languages, reads all the official local papers and all the German ones he can get. No doubt he has a good radio hidden somewhere as well, on which he listens to the Russian and English transmissions, collates the information and passes it on to the Polish underground. I have recently been asked to warn him that some Poles knew he was a Jew and were close to discovering his identity. But he said that apart from his wife and daughter, all his family, including his parents, were in the ghetto, and that most of them were already dead. 'If I can do something useful before they kill me,' he told me, 'I'll continue doing it. We all have poison, and they'll not take us alive'."

"Can you tell me how it is that you know so much?" Egon asked, hoping that Otto would tell him that he also belonged to the underground organisation, and that he would then in turn be able to tell him everything.

But Otto said,

"I once knew a Jewish architect. He went to England. I don't know what his role is, but he seems to have been in and out of Warsaw under an assumed name. We accidentally met in the street and he was pleased to see me alive. He must have told somebody about me, because I sometimes get instructions or messages from unknown people. It's all making me jumpy. But here comes our Dr. Meyer again. I wonder what he wants. He wasn't due to come until the end of next week."

Dr. Meyer's pug-nosed, well-fed face looked pinker than usual, making him, Egon thought, resemble a pig. His pale blue eyes under the short, fair lashes looked cross. He came into the shop with a swagger, as if he owned the place, but, when he spoke the usual harshness was absent from his voice.

"I have received orders to leave Warsaw, and will have to carry on my work elsewhere, but I am inviting you all to supper at my quarters, because you're the only non-army people I know. Can you come this evening if I arrange passes for you?"

They could not refuse his invitation without arousing suspicion, so they accepted with as many thanks and expressions of gratitude as they could muster. Punctually at seven o'clock, when curfew reigned over the real Warsaw, which appeared to be asleep behind its darkened windows, they went to the German quarter, where Dr. Fritz Meyer had been allocated a comfortable flat.

Filomena and Otto wore their leather coats; Egon had been cleaned up and his hair carefully combed for the occasion. They looked like a high-ranking German family out for a walk and did not attract any attention. In any case, they had their special passes, which granted them permission to be out after curfew. Otto had even contrived to get a bottle of vodka to bring as a gift, and they were welcomed as honoured guests.

Apart from them there was another visitor, a grey-haired man in Wehrmacht uniform, who was introduced as Dr. Wolfgang Stein. He was taking over from Meyer.

The vodka was quickly used up, and there was no shortage of food to go with it. Egon had been warned not to eat too much, because, after the usual near starvation, he could have become ill. It was very difficult to exercise self-restraint in the face of unlimited bread, butter, sausage, cheese, eggs and other delicacies. There was even chocolate. Apart from the vodka there was plenty of beer, schnapps and wine.

Egon was only allowed a small glass of beer, and Filomena managed to drink little by choosing red wine of which there was a limited supply, but the two Germans drank greedily and Otto had to drink with them in order not to appear standoffish. Their speech became both slurred and careless.

Although originally Dr. Meyer did not tell them where he was going when he left Warsaw, now, he first insisted on drinking Bruderschaft with his fellow guests, so that they could all call each other by their first names, and then held a speech.

"You, Otto, and you Wolfgang, as well as you, charming Filomena, don't know how lucky you are. I'm off to fight the Ruskys, and that's not much fun.

"I've been so happy here," a tear of self-pity rolled down his face, "made good friends and a little bit of money, and now I've got to leave. I've something funny to tell you too. The Gestapo have had a report about the shop where Filomena works. Somebody told them that Jews are hiding in the flat above. I said that I know from my own observations that there could be no Jews there, but once I'm gone, somebody is bound to raid the place. You Poles don't co-operate with us on anything, except finding Jews. That's the only thing in which we've had all the help we need from the population. They're not as stupid, I beg your pardon, as we've been told. Of course, they don't know that Warsaw is to become a small German town, "die neue deutsche Stadt", out of which all Poles will be removed to work in the fields, where they belong." He was interrupted by a loud hiccup. Dr. Wolfgang Stein felt the need to contribute his views.

"First things first," he said solemnly. "I say, 'Juden muss man peitschen'[3] Heil Hitler!"

He made them all stand up as well as they could and "Heil Hitler" with him. He was a good party member.

Otto stood up again, and stayed upright with some difficulty, his shakiness induced as much by the news as by the alcohol, and held up his glass.

"I drink to our good Parteigenosse Fritz, and his well-being on the Eastern front. With his help the war will soon be over, and we'll really be able to celebrate. What I'd like more than anything is to have your home address, so that we can meet again when the war is won."

While writing down the address, which Fritz gave with great pleasure, Otto sobered up sufficiently to start thinking about replacing his hiding place. Fritz Meyer was being transferred in two weeks. After that the Gestapo would be bound to act.

"I hate to bring up business at a party, but, as we happen to be here all together," he said, "I wonder if there's any solution to a problem I have. I'm due to receive a large quantity of bulky supplies from all over the place, and don't want to refuse delivery of the goods because I'm told that the Army needs them, but I've nowhere to put them.

I thought I'd ask now, because you Fritz will by now know all the storehouses in Warsaw, and our new friend Wolfgang has still to get to know the place."

[3]The Jews have to be whipped.

Good friend Wolfgang was having trouble staying awake, but he was feeling happy and murmured something about wanting to help everybody.

Fritz was in better drinking practice, and said that it would be criminal to send back anything at all, and that there was a storeroom in the basement of the Nazi Party Headquarters in the Aleja Roz. It was not being used, and had been offered to him.

"You can have the key tomorrow, and start transferring the stuff. I'll also give you the relevant documents, but now let's drink."

"Talking of documents," Otto's brain continued to work, although he had to keep his drinking level with his host's, and his body did not seem to function properly, "I assume that Dr. Stein will continue to issue stamped receipts for all the goods which he finds it necessary to confiscate. It keeps the books in order."

"Be delighted to," Stein opened his eyes on hearing his name, "everything must have a stamp and a proper document. We'll teach you order!" With that he slumped forward and snored rhythmically for the rest of the evening.

On the way back Egon and Filomena had to support Otto, who slid on the cobblestones, which were wet with rain. Suddenly, as they passed by a soldier on guard duty, whose mackintosh was glistening with rain drops, Otto came to an abrupt standstill.

"Egon," he said solemnly, using the old name in his drunkenness, and pointing an unsteady finger at the guard, "der mann ist bepisst!"

Egon's knees felt weak and Filomena stumbled. They were sure that the soldier would shoot them. By an effort of will they continued walking, waiting for the shots. But they need not have worried. The soldier did not even suspect that they were not German, probably even more so, because Egon was such a typical German name.

When Filomena looked back, still expecting a shot, the soldier smiled conspiratorially at her in full understanding of a drunken condition. She smiled back, and they went home.

"Who could have made the report?" Otto asked Filomena the following morning.

"None of the neighbours, not even Mrs. Piasecka would have suspected," she said slowly, "but I saw the builder who made the staircase the other day. Do you think?"

"I don't think. I'm sure. First of all we must take out the partition behind the cupboard. Without it there's nothing suspicious about the place, and they're bound to find it if they look.

That was made by a carpenter in his workshop, and I put it in and drilled the air holes myself. One thing is sure. We can stay here another couple of weeks – certainly until Dr. Meyer transfers his trading ability to the eastern front. After that it will become dangerous. Egon will have to sleep at the Koronskis. He's registered there anyway, and I'll have to find an alternative for myself."

They dismantled the partition, and put the pieces in the store-room with a label "wood for splints". Then they cleared out the cupboard, and filled it with cardboard boxes containing baby bottles. There was a surplus of those, because there was no market for them. It was both difficult and expensive to buy milk, and if any woman had the misfortune to have a baby, she tried to breast feed. The remainder of the bottle boxes were loaded on to a truck, which Fritz supplied, and transferred to the storeroom at the Headquarters of the NSDAP (Nazi Party) in Warsaw. Otto insisted on carrying some cases full of scalpels and injection needles through the front entrance, and having a chat with the guards.

He told them that he was bringing in vital medical instruments for the hospitals, which cared for the boys out in the front, and that he would have to be checking the supplies daily, so that he could be ready for any emergency. He also introduced his young assistant.

The guards cheerfully "Heil Hitlered", and gravely agreed with the necessity of giving all possible assistance to the wounded.

Egon stood by with, what he hoped, was a relaxed expression on his face. The knot of fear in his stomach had by now become his constant companion. He did not like it being there, and therefore tried to ignore it, making a great effort to appear nonchalant and fearless.

CHAPTER 7

GHETTO

Egon had briefly met Dr. and Mrs. Koronski when his uncle registered him at their flat. Now he really had to live with them and Otto came with him to explain the situation.

The Koronskis still resided in their spacious pre-war flat with their son Andrzej and daughter Susanna. As new rules about the minimum number of people permitted per room were introduced by the Germans, the family had three lodgers registered at their address: an elderly couple, Mr. and Mrs. Witas, who had been their servants, and Egon. Dr. Koronski held a minor post in a German hospital, but still treated many of his old private patients, some of whom could pay for his help. He was a slender man in his early forties, with a deceptively naive look in his pale blue eyes, which hid a formidable academic ability, and an iron determination. Mrs. Alina Koronski was much younger, and was his second wife, whom he had married just before the war. She had worked as a psychiatrist in the same hospital, and had helped him to get over the accidental death of his first wife in a climbing accident. It was no easy task for the pretty "new woman" to win the confidence of her stepchildren, but she had managed it.

Alina was a new woman in every sense of the word, believing strongly in the necessity of independence and higher education for women. She became a good mother to young Andrzej, who was now just ten years old and had only a vague recollection of his real mother, as well as a staunch friend to her step-daughter Susanna, who now, at the age of seventeen tried hard to emulate her step-mother. They did not look alike, Egon thought, as he looked at the two of them standing with their arms linked, waiting to welcome him. *Pani* Alina's dark hair, rounded bosom and hips, contrasted with the boyish slenderness and blonde hair of Susanna. They both had blue eyes, but Susanna's were the pale innocent blue of her father's, whereas *Pani* Alina's were a greenish blue, like a cat's. Egon liked looking at women. Even in their drab wartime clothes they provided a pleasant change from the general hideousness of life. Under normal circumstances he would hardly have spared little Andrzej a look. He was too young to be treated as a friend, and, anyway, little boys were totally uninteresting, but Egon looked at him again, when he heard that he was to share his room, and found himself liking the freckled nose and the impudence in the not so innocent blue eyes.

They were nice people, the Koronskis, and Egon felt happy to be staying with them. He said goodbye to Otto who had to leave.

Otto had an important appointment.

Dr. Wolfgang Stein had arranged to see the Bohemian expert of the medical supplies firm Esculap in order to be shown some of the instruments being delivered to the German military hospitals, which were now working overtime. Otto received him in the little upstairs office where the boxes had been neatly piled up, and the desk tidied up. He offered the German a cup of acorn coffee, which was disdainfully refused, unlike the glass of vodka, poured out of a bottle taken from the desk drawer. When they finished discussing their normal business, Otto poured them another glass of vodka each, and said;

"I am appalled by the numbers of people dying of typhoid, especially as we have received good supplies of vaccine, and it should be easy to eliminate the illness at the source of the disease, which is of course the ghetto. I know that there is a chemist there. There are many Germans who don't want to be vaccinated, because there's a small risk of developing the illness as a result, but the Jews don't need to be told about that."

"It's all very well," Dr. Stein was one of the Germans who had not wanted to be vaccinated, "to talk about getting the stuff to the ghetto, but who is going to do it? I for one wouldn't go, and somebody would have to give them instructions."

Both Otto and Dr. Stein knew that all the doctors and hospital staff from the ghetto had been taken to the extermination camps together with their patients.

"I am also reluctant to go, but I have been vaccinated, and so has the boy who works in the shop. Between us we could carry sufficient equipment to stop the disease from spreading. I have enough friends in Warsaw, both

among the Germans and the Poles not to want them dying of typhoid. I
think I would be safe, but I'd need the necessary papers."

"You sure you want to take the risk? Or is there something in it for
you?" It appeared that Wolfgang Stein could not be sold the idea of pure
altruism. Otto therefore tried another way:

"I do want to take the risk, because it will be small in comparison to the
general gain, but, at the same time I heard that one can buy gold coins at
a reduced rate. I know that the Jews were supposed to have given up
everything of value, but apparently some of them managed to hide something. I don't suppose there is much, but if I get half a dozen I would let
you have half at the price I pay."

"I thought there was something like this," Wolfgang was well pleased
with his astuteness. "It's a deal. I'll get you the papers. After all, we must
do our best to keep the people healthy."

Otto's stock of gold coins was diminishing, but it was well worth while
selling three at a cheaper rate, (and this could still be negotiated not to
make it too cheap) for getting the documents.

Otto and Egon took a rickshaw to the ghetto to make the task of carrying
all the parcels easier. As the Poles were not allowed cars, and the trams
were overcrowded, people made rickshaws out of bicycles. Some were very
elaborate, having car seats fitted in the back for the comfort of the passengers. The more enterprising of the drivers also had taximeters on the
handlebars to avoid arguments about fares. This luxurious transport was
being paid for by Dr. Stein's office for the mercy mission of saving the
Herrenvolk from typhoid. Egon enjoyed the ride, and tried not to think
about his destination.

He was feeling well, because last night he had slept in a real bed for the
first time since he had left the Cracow ghetto. Dr. Koronski introduced
Egon to his family as a Polish boy who had managed to escape a Ukrainian
massacre in the East of Luov, during which his parents were killed. Everybody was very tactful and did not ask Egon anything about his home, which
was just as well as he had never visited the area.

He was treated with great sympathy, because it was known that the
Ukrainians enjoyed torturing their victims, and it was possible that Egon
had actually seen something awful. The two ladies mothered him and last
evening they had given him hot soup to eat. He had not eaten cooked food
for a long time, and still glowed from the warmth it had given him.

His uncle's decision to go to the ghetto had come as a surprise. Otto
had told him that the only thing that mattered was to survive, because the

Nazis were not to be allowed to exterminate all European Jews as they had said they would. Going into the ghetto would draw attention to them, apart from the fact that there were many varieties of typhoid and the vaccination did not cover them all, but on their last night together in the little office Otto explained;

"I knew many Jewish doctors, and most of them landed in the ghetto. You saw Cracow ghetto last year, but the conditions in the Warsaw ghetto have become progressively worse. You can imagine how bad if I tell you that about sixty thousand people died in six months simply from starvation, cold and illness." He was quiet for a while, letting the numbers sink in. And Egon made the calculation: ten thousand a month, two and a half thousand a week. That means about three hundred and fifty every day.

"And those are the ones," Otto continued, "who died by so called 'natural' death. At least as many have been shot or taken to camps. I had the figures from my friend Juliusz. In all this horror he was running a medical school with Professor Ludwik Hirszfeld, whom I had also met. How they could function after an exhausting day's labouring for the Germans and hardly any food, I don't know, but I'm told that both the teachers and the students managed. They had a bit of financial help from the General Sikorski lot. You and I had been vaccinated by illegally made Weigl vaccines, because the ones supplied by the Red Cross are unreliable. I have seen to it that they also had some of the Weigl vaccine in the ghetto. In addition to teaching and fighting illness they were doing research into epidemics and, ironically, into starvation-related illnesses, for which they had unique opportunities. They could have got out of the ghetto and been hidden, but they chose to stay with their patients, and together with their patients they have been taken to Auschwitz." Otto was silent again, and then said matter of factly;

"Now you can see why we have to take the risk."

The rickshaw stopped by the long red brick wall, which separated the Jewish and the "Aryan" sides of Warsaw.

Otto paid the driver, who helped them to take the boxes off the rickshaw. The guards at the ghetto entrance, looked at them curiously. There were both the Gestapo and the Polish police in their special dark blue uniforms.

"Is this some sort of a joke?" the Polish policeman said when he saw the documents, "Medicines for the Jews."

Otto pretended not to understand and spoke in German to the Gestapo guard. "This is an action to stop the epidemic from spreading." The man just shook his head and waved them through.

It was the stench of death, which was the first thing which struck Egon. By now he was used to being cold, unwashed and hungry. He had lived amongst people who could not wash because it was too cold and there was no hot water, whose clothes were dirty because there was no way of getting them clean. There were unspeakable toilets and drains which did not function, but all this was nothing, because here was death. Death naked and unashamed; simply taken for granted as a part of everyday life. As they stood in the street two carts came by pushed from behind and pulled from the front by two men, who themselves looked like corpses, but they were dressed. The limbs, bodies and heads, which were casually hanging from the overfilled carts were naked.

The men reminded Egon of park attendants who cleared the paths of branches and dead leaves in the autumn. These people were just as casual. They were simply quietly doing their job. There was more work for them, because, further along, he could see two more bodies lying on the pavements. They were being stripped of clothing by three teenage boys, whose movements were slow and full of effort, as if they could ill spare the energy required. Their hands were so painfully thin and their clothes so inadequate for the cold weather that it was evident that the lack of energy was due to hunger and the effort necessitated by need. When Otto and Egon walked up to them they saw the boys' feet. They were bare, monstrously swollen and partially wrapped up in torn pieces of paper.

"Ask them the way to the chemist," Otto did not want to speak Polish or Yiddish to them. He had to preserve the myth of knowing only German. Egon obeyed, ashamed of being only slightly cold and only slightly hungry, a feeling so normal to him nowadays that he was used to it. Only one of the boys made the needless effort of raising his head, and Egon saw his eyes. They were large and dark like his own, but all the pain and unhappiness he had known were multiplied in them. Yet through the despair glimmered both thought and defiance, which came out in a shrill whisper.

"He's there, round the corner, but we don't need medicines. We need guns."

"I must deliver these boxes," Egon said, "but I'll come out again and perhaps you can take me to those who may need guns."

He did not need to explain to Otto, who had heard and understood it all. Egon quickly dumped the boxes by the dirty door of the chemist's shop, having only glimpsed the gaunt man who opened it.

"Just one moment," Otto grabbed his arm. "Be back in half an hour. We can't be long. It'll raise suspicion."

The dark eyed boy, followed them. He told Egon that his name was David Blum and led the way between the broken-down houses and the shadows of those who were dead and those who were nearly dead. His movements had quickened as soon as he perceived a purpose. The boys ducked through two doorways and found themselves in a stuffy underground room in which a small candle glowed, vaguely illuminating sunken cheeks and gaunt faces, which stood out like some bizarre black and white pencil drawings of human shapes.

"I've asked him to get us guns," David said pointing to Egon, "and he asked me to take him to those who need them."

There was silence for a moment broken finally by the quivering and querulous voice, belonging to an old man on Egon's right.

"And you just spoke to that child, and led him here, risking exposing everybody? I still say, and I'll say it in Polish not Hebrew, so that even the uneducated can understand it. The Lord said 'Not by might nor by power, but by My spirit'. If He means us to die, it's our duty to die believing in His purpose. Fighting is not a solution."

But another voice, this time that of a young man sitting opposite answered him.

"This may be a good way for those who have already lived, but most of us in this room have hardly known normal life at all, and therefore we have the need to feel alive even if it's to be only for the few days, weeks or months that are still given to us. I say it's better to die fighting than to sit waiting for death."

Sounds of approval met his speech, and Egon had to almost shout to make himself heard.

"I can only stay here for twenty more minutes, and I'm not sure if I can get any weapons for you, but if I manage, how can I get them through?"

"Only through the sewers." The young man who had spoken before sounded very authoritative. "We can pay a little, but not much. Let David show you the way. We don't want to draw attention to ourselves."

He then turned to David and solemnly handed to him a dirty piece of paper.

The two boys walked through the death-filled streets into another cellar where a heap of rubble appeared to have fallen into a corner. David removed a plank which revealed an opening in the ground, leading to a further dugout. Egon followed him, and saw that the dugout led into an evil-smelling tunnel.

"Entrance to the Warsaw drainage system," David indicated proudly.

"Our address here is Karmelicka 4. The exit is in the yard of 49, Zlota Street on the Aryan side. I am told it's possible to get in and out of it there without being seen if one is careful. This document," he continued, handing to Egon the piece of paper he had been given, "is a plan of the Warsaw sewers. You can have it, but even with its help it may be difficult to find us. The only thing you can do at the moment is to memorise this exit, so that you don't go past it. Anyway, there's always someone on watch in the cellar to help you in, although you may not have noticed him."

Egon tried to memorise the shape of the hole, and hoped fervently that he would never have to come there alone. As they emerged back into the large low cellar, they saw that the heap of rags in the corner, covered two human beings, who rose as they passed. It was amazing how the very possibility of action seemed to give them strength.

"We're in touch with some of the Polish underground," David said, "but there are many groups, and the more arms we can get the better. We're making some, but we have no materials . . ," David's voice petered out.

"Why don't you get out of here, if you know the way?" Egon couldn't help asking.

"I'd be picked up in five minutes; if not by the Germans, then by the Poles."

And Egon had to agree. Even if he was dressed differently, the accent of his speech, the extreme emaciation and the arched nose under the almond shaped eyes would have given David away.

"I'll do my best," Egon said when taking leave, "but I can't promise anything, because I don't know if anyone will help."

"Are you a Pole or a Jew?" David wanted to know.

"I thought I was both, but now I know I'm a Jew and have to pretend to be a Pole."

"Good luck. We'll be waiting for you."

Otto was already waiting in front of the chemist and hurried Egon towards the exit. The guards recognised them, but they checked their papers again, and Egon tried to keep calm, ashamed of fearing to remain behind. They walked back to the shop. It was only midday. It had not even taken two hours to pass from the land of bare existence to the land of death and back again.

It was not until they reached the comparative safety of the little office that Egon dared to talk about what he had heard, and only when he had finished telling his story he casually mentioned what he had been planning to say on the way.

"I think that if I asked during my religious lessons, they might find somebody with guns."

"I don't want you involved with the underground," Otto sounded stern. "Whatever we do is a purely private action. I can buy some guns from the German soldiers returning from the front. Many of the convalescents are very happy to sell, but," he relented, "perhaps you can get some help getting them through the sewers. I'm too big to fit into small spaces."

CHAPTER 8

THE SEWERS

Father Michal, the young priest who taught Egon to recite Latin prayers, to say Hail Mary, cross himself and answer questions on the intricacies of the New Testament, met him in the church. Egon had considered him to be boring and colourless. They never talked about anything except the Catholic religion and Egon wondered if it was safe to mention the guns. But Janusz had instructed him to make contact through the religious lessons.

Today Egon's concentration was reduced to nil, and he made one mistake after another. Father Michal was shaking his head in sad disbelief that anyone could have forgotten so much in such a short time, when Egon finally took the plunge and asked.

"Could you possibly pass a message to Janusz for me?"

"And what is it you want me to say to someone called Janusz?" The priest was startled.

"That I need to tell him something urgently."

"If it really is so urgent you'd better tell me. Janusz is not in Warsaw. You can trust me. I know Sergeant Bolek and Tadek as well." Father Michal had evidently decided that Egon could not possibly be an informer.

Egon looked up with interest. The priest's face was pale and colourless as always, but then nearly everybody was pale. At the moment it did not seem as expressionless as he had known it. Was there a hint of a smile at their mutual hesitance? Egon did not have much option regarding himself, but he did not want to involve Otto. The priest must know that he was a Jew, otherwise he would not have needed to be taught elementary prayers.

"I've met a Jewish boy from the ghetto. He told me that the Jews want to defend themselves – at least for a while, and that they need some weapons. There is a way to get in and out of the ghetto through the sewers. He gave me a plan showing how to find it, and I can recognise the exit."

"Why should Janusz take the risk? You know the penalties for carrying weapons. Furthermore, our people are also short of everything."

"They could be paid something."

"All right. I'll pass on your message. You'd better give me the plan so that it can be looked at by someone who can make sense of it. You might just as well go now. Both your understanding of Latin and your memory seem to have evaporated. Come back at the same time tomorrow, and I may have an answer for you."

The following day was more productive. Otto had managed to talk to two German soldiers, who wanted to sell their guns together with ammunition to go with them.

"These are good lads," Otto said. "They're totally fed up with the war generally and Hitler in particular. Furthermore, they have guts. Perhaps there's hope for the Germans yet."

It would have been very foolish to express such views in public. Even Egon thought that they must have been some unusual Germans, because the news at the Koronskis was that more people had been caught in street closures, and two of their friends had been murdered in Pawiak after being taken in the street.

As he made his way back to Father Michal, Egon looked around carefully before jumping onto a passing tram. As was usual, it was jam-packed, except for the carriage reserved for the Germans, and he hung from the steps, before pushing himself into the fetid warmth of the interior, where he paid for his ticket. The tram was always a debating society. This time the subject was the forecast by Poland's most famous astrologer, Jan Starza-Dzierzbicki that Hitler would lose the war.

"He didn't say when," one woman was saying, "though he was sure it wouldn't be this year."

"We won't hear much more from him," another voice said. "The Germans' have got him in the Pawiak."

"It won't help them, they'll loose anyway."

"But will any of us be left alive in the end? Will they continue with us when they've finished off the Jews?"

Egon started to push his way out, giving his ticket back to the conductor as he passed him. This was customarily done, because it enabled the conductor to sell the ticket twice, thus making a bit of extra money for himself, and depriving the Germans of revenue. It was a double good deed. Otto had instructed him about this adding that, "There have to be laws. If the laws are reasonable, reasonable people will obey them. If they're not, everybody will try to break them. The Germans have special carriages and they do not have to pay, so the whole population of Warsaw is doing its best to get some fairness into the system."

Father Michal fetched Egon from the waiting room. As soon as they were alone, he said:

"Well, I've spoken to those in charge, and they said that an experienced man, called Witek, will go with you to the ghetto to see if indeed it is possible to get through, and what their chances are. We can't afford to waste weapons or people."

"Oh. Thank you. When will we go?"

"Get to Zlota Street, number 49 at seventeen hours tomorrow afternoon. You'll see two men talking at the entrance. Walk up to them, and say that you are looking for Janusz."

"But if we start at seventeen hours we'll never be back before curfew."

"That's all I have been told to say. No doubt they know what they are doing."

Egon left Dr. Koronski's flat early the following morning, so that he could become an anonymous unit within the crowd of people going to work. He tried to behave as if this was another "normal" day, and came into the shop as usual. His papers said that he was employed there, so it was a reasonably safe place for him to go to collect the message which Otto had promised to leave with Filomena.

Filomena was unlocking the heavy door locks as Egon walked up the street, but she waited until they were inside before speaking to him:

"Otto said you are to have lunch with him at the Café Sim. He thinks you need some warm food and rubber boots. I know it is wet, but surely you'll be cold in them. If they are big enough, wrap you feet in anything you can find. Even newspaper is better than nothing. He didn't say where you are going, but," she added the unnecessary admonition, "please be careful, little son."

Filomena did her best to be matter of fact. If you allowed yourself to think you became afraid, and then you were lost. Panic set in, which made you say the wrong things, or such black depression engulfed you, that you were unable to cope. She had seen it happen to others and she fought against it. The only way to go on was to dwell on the moment. If the cold was not too severe and the stomach not too empty one had to be content. She knew that something was afoot, and everything one did was dangerous, but there was little she could do to help except being cheerful. Every day they managed to survive was an unexpected bonus. Filomena crossed herself. Lately more and more little altars appeared in the courtyards of houses so that people could pray during curfew. They had no one to help them, except God, and Filomena too prayed for the safety of her Jews. She was not sure if she had done the right thing to have thrown in her lot with them, because if they were caught she would be killed with them, but she could not bring herself to betray them, and betrayal would have been her only way to safety.

Egon walked down Krolewska Street, looking for Café Sim at number eleven. Like everybody else, he moved around Warsaw as little as possible, afraid of being trapped. His shoulders were hunched and his attention was focused entirely on the passers-by.

If there was the slightest indication of people being stopped, if the hateful uniforms of the SS and the Gestapo appeared, he would stop to re-evaluate the situation and decide whether to dive into a doorway, or retrace his steps. In this manner he walked into the cafe without taking in his surroundings, glad to be out of the numbing cold.

The room full of people, smoke, and a most wonderful sound. On a small stage stood two grand pianos and they were both actually being played at the same time, combining and intertwining their music, so that every note had a special emphasis, because it seemed to have been individually considered by two masters.

Egon had never heard such wonderful music before. It flowed and rippled through his ears, overriding his thoughts and filling his body. Suddenly there was something familiar in it, and then it disappeared, only to appear again with another haunting familiarity, to be replaced by a majestic boom. He stood still having forgotten the constant danger, the cold, the hunger, and the purpose of his being there. Otto saw him and pulled him to a side table. Even then, until eventually the music stopped, Egon sat motionless because reality had disappeared and only the sound reigned.

When the clapping finished, Otto managed to order the dish of the day, which was a stew of everything available, and Egon asked;

"Who are these two people? Are they famous?"

"They are famous in Poland. One day they'll be famous everywhere. Their names are Panufnik and Lutoslawski. Speak very quietly and in German. I have to speak German because many Germans come here, though they are not welcome. The clever thing the artists here do, is that they put in snatches of forbidden melodies so delicately that only those who know them well can hear them. The artistic side is run by a man called Mariusz Maszynski, and many people, including the artists owe him a debt of gratitude. I am told that in the evenings before the curfew, he introduces the show and manages to get in various political jokes, without the Germans understanding them. Perhaps one day we'll manage to come and hear him."

Otto could not know that within a short space of time Mariusz Maszynski would join the macabre dance of death at the Pawiak, and there would be no further opportunity for anyone to hear him again. There was little time for idle conversation now.

"Finish eating and we'll go." Otto was getting worried that they would miss their appointments.

Their table was in a corner near the door, and they left as soon as the food was finished. It had been a long time since Egon felt almost full.

The music still reverberated through his head, and he had to make an effort to get up and follow Otto towards the Saski Gardens, which was close to the Café Sim further along Krolewska Street. Otto had obviously planned the outing very carefully.

When Egon realised that they were close to the park, he smiled, and told Otto what he had recently heard in a tram. Apparently a new order had come out permitting only Germans to use the Gardens. From that day on the Polish population started calling it the 'Zoo.' The implication was lost on the Germans:

"Crazy Poles," they said, "there is no Zoo anywhere near the place."

Otto stopped by a loudspeaker at a street corner opposite the park. It was blaring out the usual propaganda, and the majority of the Polish passers-by walked past without listening to it, but a small group stood around. Amongst them were two young men in casual clothes, who could have been either German or Polish.

"How are you, Herr Schmidt?" asked one of them. "Nice to run into you."

"And you, Peter. How are things?"

"Fine, thank you. You couldn't take this small sack to my aunt for me? I've been able to get some potatoes for her."

"Of course. She only lives next door. It's no trouble at all," said Otto picking up the sack, and slipping something into the young man's pocket at the same time.

"Thank you very much," Peter said, leaning against his friend so that he could glance at the contents of his pocket without its being seen. "I'm always happy to help the old lady, but it takes so long to go to see her. Give her my regards, and wish her well."

And with a wave of his hand, Peter walked away with his friend, straight across the road to the Saski Gardens.

Otto limped with Egon to the corner of Zlota Street. It means Golden Street in Polish, but on this February afternoon, with the darkness gathering, the freezing drizzle and wind, there was nothing golden about it. Otto handed over the heavy sack, and watched the small figure disappear round the street corner. He lit a cigarette and wished for his cigar, wished that he could get drunk, like the Poles and the Germans around him, and above all wished that he did not have to send Egon.

It seemed ridiculous to risk two lives for two guns. He should not have come here at all, but he wanted to diminish the distance over which the undernourished boy would have to carry the bag. Perhaps the unknown Witek will help. Peter could have got more guns.

Apparently he had friends, who were keen on getting some money; possibly some who also wanted a Nazi defeat, but Egon could not carry more.

Initially Otto had thought of coming too, but when he considered it coolly he knew that he would be less help than hindrance. Although his arms were very strong, his right leg was getting worse, and his stick was not just a decoration. He had mentioned to the voice on the telephone, which placed "orders" for Mr. Wolf, that he could get weapons if some of them were transported to the ghetto. The man on the phone was very keen and said that he would be able to pay Otto commission because funds were available from the London based government in exile, but Otto told him that he did not need to be paid, provided the ghetto was given priority, if a way into it could be found. There were many underground organisations. Did they co-operate? Otto did not know. He knew only that many political factions existed, and that the Poles were historically unable to work together. They even had to import their kings from other countries during the time Poland was a monarchy, because they could not agree on anyone they knew.

Egon was shivering when he came to the doorway of number 49. His feet were dry, but the newspapers in which they were wrapped did not give them much protection from the cold rubber boots, and he tried to wriggle his toes to keep the circulation going.

There was nobody standing at the door. In fact the door was shut. He tried to open it, and found it locked. Ringing the bell was out of the question, because he could not state his business, and anyone bigger than he could have made him open the sack.

He was in a desparate situation. It was too late to get back to the Koronskis before the curfew. The cold seemed to fill his entire body, seeming to replace the blood drained away by fear. He slung the sack over his shoulder preparing to go away, when the door opened and he saw two men sheltering in the dark archway inside.

"Janusz sent me," said Egon uncertainly.

"It's all right, little one," the smaller of the two men said. "I am Witek, and we'll go down in a minute. We couldn't stand outside the gate chatting in this weather without looking suspect, could we? It would have been asking for trouble. Eh, but you're shivering. It's bloody cold. Here, have a good sip," and he offered Egon the bottle from which both the men had obviously been sipping. The vodka burned its way warmly through Egon's mouth to the pit of his stomach, leaving a warm glowing feeling in its path.

"That was good," he said.

"Eh! One can see that it's one of our own lads," said the big man approvingly. "Go now, and come back safely. I'll have hot water and a bed ready for you when you come back, as well as another sip of vodka."

"He's the doorman of this building," said Witek, as they walked through the courtyard. "Thank God all of Warsaw is in one vast conspiracy, otherwise nothing could be done."

He opened the drain cover so quickly and casually, that even if anyone had been watching, they might have assumed that he was doing a legitimate job. The screws had previously been loosened, and a ladder led into the stinking dark chasm into which Witek disappeared swiftly and silently, indicating to Egon to follow, and holding out a strong hand to help him.

Within seconds the drain cover closed behind them. A feeling of complete panic descended on Egon, as he stood on the shaky ladder in total blackness, with the unspeakable stench filling his nostrils. Witek had withdrawn his hand as soon as both Egon's feet were on the ladder, to which he was now clinging with all his might, clutching the heavy bag at the same time. Just then a light flickered. Witek was down and had lit a small lantern.

"Come on, little one. We had some friends guarding us in case anyone got curious, and they shut the cover for us. Don't worry. I've been down the sewers before, and your plan is quite correct. Here, have another sip of vodka. It keeps the germs away."

There was something absolutely reassuring about Witek, and Egon was grateful for his presence and the feeling of being a part of the great and benevolent conspiracy of Warsaw. He now noticed that the older man had a large rucksack, which he had probably previously lowered into the drain.

"Some home-made grenades for the boys," Witek grinned disarmingly when he saw Egon looking. He could have been proudly talking about a batch of cakes he had baked.

Fortified by Witek's cheerfulness and another sip of vodka, Egon made his first steps into the vileness at the bottom of the drain. It was slippery underfoot and the air was so thick with stench that he wondered whether his lungs would stand it. It seemed to him that he was breathing putrefied excrement. The vodka improved his well-being, but not his sense of balance, and he had to concentrate his entire attention not to slip on the slime under his feet. The guns seemed to have become heavier, bending him on the side on which he carried the sack. He had to support himself by putting out his free hand onto the disgusting, wet walls. Drops of something vile fell from the top, but he tried to re-assure himself that it may just be the rain, as he felt the trickle behind his collar.

The positive thing was that now the fear had left him. He was doing something. He was with somebody who knew his job.

He even smiled to himself, when he thought that, all things considered, this would not be the place where he would choose to die. The melody the pianos had sung in the cafe came back to him, and came out in a melodious whistle.

"Don't whistle, little one," Witek interrupted him. "We may just be passing under an examination hole, and someone could hear you."

And Egon was reminded of the Jewish story Uncle Otto had told him during one of their nights together. "There was a little sparrow," Otto said, "and, like us, it was very hungry. Suddenly it glanced down the road and saw that a horse had left a pile behind him. The sparrow at once flew down to pick out the bits of grain, which had not been digested by the horse. There was plenty to fill the sparrow completely. It made him so happy that he started whistling. A prowling cat heard the whistling, pounced and ate the sparrow. The moral of the tale is: 'Don't whistle when you're sitting in the shit.' "

The story fitted his situation so well, that he smiled again in spite of the misery, but he could not smile for long, because eventually such weariness set in that nothing registered, except the necessity to put one foot in front of the other. It would have been unthinkable not to keep up with Witek, who walked in front lighting the way.

Suddenly Egon realised that they were passing the right exit. A piece of brick had been put there to help distinguish it. He called Witek to stop.

"Well done, little one," Witek said. "I thought we should be nearly there."

There, lit by Witek's lamp, was the hole to the dugout he had seen in the ghetto. They crawled through into the low cellar, where shapes materialised from under the rags in the corner, and one of the shapes was David.

"Some of us are here all the time, in case somebody comes," he said, shaking their hands, and trembling with gratitude. "How was it?"

"If you really want to know," said Witek, who had previously answered such questions, and was obviously pleased with the aptness of his well rehearsed answer, "It was shit."

"D'you think I can't smell it?" David laughed not to be outdone.

The guns and the grenades were concealed under the rubble, and they walked across to the neighbouring cellar, where Egon had been before.

Egon recognised some of the gaunt faces which glimmered in the semi-darkness, glowing with hope, when Witek promised a proper delivery now that the exit had been located.

"But now," Witek was saying, "we must go back. The longer we delay, the more dangerous it becomes."

"Can I ask you for another favour?" A melodious, well-educated voice came from the shadows. "God knows, you've done enough for us, and I will understand if you refuse, but is there any chance of you taking these two little girls with you? We managed to hide them when our parents were killed, otherwise they would have been taken to death with all the other orphans in Dr. Korczak's care. One is my little sister, and the other is David's. They don't look Jewish and their Polish is without an accent."

Two pathetic looking children, aged around five, emerged from the shadows, their golden curls and enormous blue eyes in the pale faces proving that they might have a chance in the Aryan world outside. Egon thought of Rachel who had died clutching her doll, just like one of the little girls was doing, and his head spun, as it always did when he allowed that memory to emerge. He made a great effort to remain conscious, and heard Witek say.

"I can take them to a convent. The sisters will look after them," Witek seemed as relaxed about this as he had been about the sewers.

And the same voice, which had objected to the fighting floated up from the shadows.

"Don't you realise that they'll be lost to Judaism? If God wants them to live, they'll live, and if not, let them die amongst their own people."

"No, Rebbe." The young man spoke with great urgency. "It's the other way round. If God wants them to be Jewish, he'll see to it that they remain so. As long as they live, they will not forget this place, or us, and He has told us that life is the most precious thing."

He turned to the children.

"Remember your names, but do everything that kind strangers tell you. Be good and obedient. Try hard to remember daddy, mummy and us."

The young man and David embraced the girls, who seemed to absorb the scene with their huge eyes, too frightened, or perhaps too weak, to cry.

David and the young man saw them to the odious entrance to the sewers, which gawped more repugnantly than ever in the light of Witek's lamp.

"Bye, little Rosa," David cuddled his little sister. "Be good." He turned to Egon, "We are the last two, the eldest and the youngest. Perhaps one of us will make it."

He tried to sound tough and unconcerned, but his mouth trembled with the effort of holding his tears. The young man did not hold his. They flowed down his thin expressive face, as he gently lowered his little sister into the foulness of the drains.

"Remember, little sister. Remember your name is Helena Ehrenpreis, though you will have to use a new name in the future. Remember that I love you."

This time Egon and Witek had no weapons to carry, but they had the children, who were too weak to walk on their own. In addition the rugs on their emaciated feet were soon permeated by the slime, and gave them no protection. They slid and fell, weeping silently, and had to be first helped, and eventually carried; small bundles of filth and bone, yet so pathetic that Egon's and Witek's own misery seemed like nothing in comparison.

Although his strength was ebbing, and he had to stop every few steps; although the stench-laden air cloyed his lungs, making him choke, the fact that he had to protect somebody weaker than he, gave Egon self-assurance. He knew that he had to make it somehow.

Even Witek stumbled, as he tried to help them all and carry the lamp at the same time, carefully keeping the flame aglow. At last he stopped, putting down the whimpering child he carried, and pushed up the drain cover in the courtyard of 49 Zlota Street, extinguishing the lamp as he did so. A large, dark shadow appeared in the doorway. The janitor had kept his promise. He had been waiting for them.

"Quickly. This way to the cellar," he whispered urgently, and with the last effort of will they followed him.

CHAPTER 9

THE KORONSKIS

When Egon woke up in the morning he was lying on a pallet placed on the cellar floor, and he was stiff with cold. The big janitor was towering over him holding a steaming mug.

"Get this inside of you, young one," he said, "and do a disappearing act. I don't know who you are, but it's better if no strange faces are seen around here. Here's a piece of bread to go with your coffee. My wife has wiped over your clothes the best she could, and they've been airing outside all night, so they don't stink too bad."

Egon thanked the big man, who left immediately. The acorn coffee was hot and had some sugar in it. It failed to warm him, but it stopped his teeth from chattering. Last night, when they had arrived in the cellar the kindly janitor had buckets of hot water waiting for them. He had drained it from the heating system. Although half-conscious from tiredness, Egon had to remember that he must not strip altogether, so that nobody could see that he was circumcised. He was well aware that the friendliness which surrounded him might have been strained as a result of this dangerous discovery, so he had covered his nakedness by washing in stages, and allowing his shirt to cover him, pretending that he kept warmer washing that way.

He fully understood that it was no good trying to ask questions, either about Witek, or about the two little girls. It was always better for everybody to know as little as possible. Egon was not surprised that the janitor had told him to disappear. He also did not want to know too much.

Otto had asked Egon to go back to the Koronskis, and telephone Filo-

mena. He had better hurry; they would be anxious. It proved difficult to
stand up. For some reason his legs refused to obey, and he had to rub them
hard. He was afraid that he was ill, but he managed to walk once his blood
started circulating.

Normally it would not have seemed too far for him to go from Zlota
Street to Marszalkowska, where the Koronskis lived. Now it seemed an
endless journey. In his present condition the grey steps to the Koronskis'
flat on the top floor were almost insurmountable. The worn stone staircase
had had carpet on it in better days, and an elaborate wrought-iron balustrade
to give support to those who used it. Now a part of the supporting railing
was missing, and the entrance smelled of bad drains, general mustiness and
cooking. Still, the Koronskis were lucky to have been able to keep the flat.
Alina Koronski opened the door to him, and asked anxiously:

"Where have you been, Wojtek?" Even she only knew his false name.

He had the answer prepared.

"I'm, sorry," he said. "I went on an errand for Filomena, and had to
stay the night to avoid curfew. I would like to phone her now, if I may,
to tell her I am here."

"Of course, carry on," Pani Alina sounded relieved. "Where have you
got those rubber boots from? Don't they make your feet feel cold? Where
are your shoes?"

"Uncle has them. They hurt a bit. He said he could get them stretched,
and lent me these."

Egon stuck to his policy of telling as few lies as possible, which made
the whole process of lying a lot easier. He slipped off the icy gum boots
and went to the hall to telephone Filomena. It was lucky Mrs. Koronski
had a permanent cold, otherwise she would surely have smelled his clothes.

When he passed the sitting room, Egon noticed that Mrs. Wolynski from
next door was visiting, and Andrzej was with them, because it was the only
room where there was heat. At the other end of the room, he also noticed
Marian Urewicz standing with his back to the room, looking out of the
window. Marian called on the Koronskis from time to time. He had been
a lieutenant in the Polish Army before the war, and had served with Alina
Koronski's elder brother. Like everybody else he was engaged in some
mysterious business of which he did not speak, but which enabled him to
dress very smartly, and always have money.

His brown hair was always sleek over his broad forehead and blue eyes.
He had a neat moustache and particularly white teeth, which sparkled when

he smiled, which he did often. In spite of all this Egon did not like him and slipped through to his room without greeting anybody.

Susanna was out, presumably already at her illegal school, which she attended with enormous perseverance. The very hazardousness of learning, which was, like most things punishable by either death or deportation, made the young particulary attentive and full of respect for their teachers. Egon too would have liked to learn, but Otto had decreed that there was no point in tempting providence.

"Just read anything you can find," he had said. "And I'll teach you business mathematics."

He did just that during the hours of darkness they spent together. It all had to be done mentally, and improved Egon's ability to think in numbers to a remarkable degree.

Fortunately the telephone worked on this occasion and Otto answered almost at once. He sounded much relieved; just like *Pani* Alina.

"Stay at the Koronskis today. Tell them that you have a day off because you are not feeling well. I'll stop by to bring your shoes and collect the boots."

Egon was glad of the rest. He was really not feeling well. He hung his clothes out to air some more, got into bed, hoping to get warm and slept all day. Otto must have told some story to Mrs. Koronski when he came in with the shoes, because she left him alone, apart from bringing him some hot soup and bread. For a little while the food gave him warmth and an illusion of satiety. He ate every drop and every crumb. Everybody ate as much and as often as anything to eat was available. No one was sure of the next meal or the next day.

It was night when the loud knocking on the street door woke him.

"Open up! Gestapo!"

Again the icy fear as the heavy boots tread the worn stone steps up which he had walked early that morning.

*

They stop on their floor. Another knock, but it is not their flat. It is next door. The Wolynskis. Why them? It is a silly question. The Gestapo does not need a reason. Mr. Wolynski works as a translator in a German office, but he had been a judge before the war. Egon had seen his son on the stairs. He heard Mrs. Wolynski call him Wicio and thought the diminutive sounded silly when addressing someone who was nearly grown up.

Wicio must be about eighteen, thin and pale like everybody else, and probably studying illegally. Is that why the Gestapo are there? Will they come to them?

Egon can sense that everybody is awake and afraid around him as the door of the other flat is slammed closed. They cannot hear any more. The house is solidly built and sound does not carry, except, of course, for the shots, which they can now hear quite clearly. One, two, three, four reports, then several more in wild succession: finally silence.

Again the slam of the flat door, heavy tread down the old stairs and the slam of the street door. The strained nerves of many people seem to resonate through the house.

The noise outside, the waking up of the janitor, who has to open the street door, must have also woken some of the people in the neighbouring houses. Many more would be woken by the shots ringing in the silence of the curfew.

The Wolynskis and the Koronskis have been friends for years, and, as soon as the Gestapo leave the whole family rushes across the landing.

Judge Wolynski stands stiffly in the door. The silver of his hair and the greyness of his skin throw into vivid relief the bloody welts on his face and head. He does not seem to be conscious of them and looks as if he was made of stone.

Then he crumples and falls down with all the sinews standing out in his neck and forehead, his teeth clenched with pain. Dr. Koronski has his medical kit with him. He automatically picked it up when he heard the knocking, because he knows that his friend has a heart condition.

The nitroglycerin is a treasure supplied by Otto and he forces a few drops between the judge's teeth.

*

The awful reality returns as the judge whispers.

"Marian Urewicz has been working for the Gestapo at the Aleja Ujazdowskie. He has been blackmailing the Jewish family who have been living with us, but they have run out of money, so he brought in the Gestapo," the old man gasped for breath, "and they kept asking me if there were any more Jews anywhere. They first shot Wicio, then Jadwiga; – each one twice, to make sure. There was no point in telling them anything. They would have shot everybody anyway. Then they went round the flat and found the Rubinsteins. My friend Leo, his wife, and his two girls. They left me alive to warn everybody not to hide Jews, but I only want to warn you against the traitors. They must be punished."

"Surely not Marian. He was a lieutenant in the Polish Army. He couldn't do a thing like that," Dr. Koronski said, cradling his friend's head in his lap.

"He did, and there are others like him. We have real courts working in Poland. They meet secretly. I've reported . . . "

The judge did not manage to say any more before his sinews swelled up like ropes and his teeth clenched again. This time the nitroglycerin did not help; instead it was death that relaxed him. Dr. Koronski rose and walked into the flat followed by his family and some of the neighbours.

The bodies of Wicio and his mother were close together. Egon, who had been following Dr. Koronski, noticed that they held hands. He could not bear to see any more. He had not been aware of anyone living with the Wolynskis and his fear again crystallised his thinking, making him terribly aware. Very slowly he made his way back to the Koronski's flat, where he packed his few belongings.

When Dr. Koronski returned to the flat Egon was waiting for him in the hall. The doctor's face seemed to have borrowed some of the stoniness from the judge's, and Egon hesitated before daring to ask if he could speak to him alone. Dr. Koronski looked up and silently pointed towards the study door.

"Couldn't you wait, Wojtek." Alina Koronski said woodenly, "can't you see that we're all at the end of our tether?"

"It's alright, Alina. I won't be a minute." The husband knew that the boy would not have asked lightly.

"I don't want to take any of your time," Egon said as soon as he was sure that nobody could overhear. "I simply don't want to disappear without saying thank you, and I must go. I can't risk the same happening to you and your family. You've been very kind to me."

"You don't understand," Dr. Koronski said tiredly. "Anyone who's half way decent and has some courage simply has to help you. It's a form of resistance. Furthermore, at this moment, if you wish to survive you can't afford too many principles, though I appreciate them. I must admit that I am worried about my wife and children. That bastard knew the Wolynskis were friends of ours. He may transfer his attention to us. Promise me that if Otto can't find you an alternative hiding place, you'll return here. You don't want to have us on your conscience, and I don't want to have you on mine. Go when you want to and I'll make up some explanation on your behalf."

"Thank you again. It's a deal. I don't need to tell you how I feel about the Wolynskis." Egon wished he could cry to show his sympathy and horror, but his eyes were dry because all he really felt was hatred. He left the flat as soon as he could merge with the crowds going to work.

The family were back in bed and still asleep, having been given some tablets by Dr. Koronski, who thought that sleep might enable them to recover from the shock more easily.

Egon carried his things tied up in a small pillowcase, and went to the little flat above the shop, which he entered without special care, because he thought it was safe to go there. As he came through the door he saw Filomena and a woman, whom he did not know, sitting by the desk and drinking acorn coffee. It was too late to go out again without arousing suspicion. Filomena, as usual, seemed calm and relaxed:

"Hello, Wojtek, come and have a cup of coffee with us," she said, and then turned to the woman: "Let me introduce my nephew Wojtek Romanski. He's really a cousin of a cousin. You didn't know his parents Witold and Helena, by any chance? Her family name was Tobialak. No? I thought you might because they came from your part of the country. The Germans took his parents, and the neighbours sent him over here. He helps me in the shop.

Wojtek, this is Mrs. Zofja Golabek. She manages to bring us food from time to time and keeps us from starving."

"Nice boy," remarked Mrs. Golabek, and Egon immediately recognised the voice of the woman he had heard when hiding in the cupboard.

Very politely he bowed over her hand, and sat down to enjoy a cup of the hot liquid of which he had then been so jealous. Mrs. Golabek charged a lot, but gave good value for money because together with food she carried information.

She sat with her hands cupped round her coffee mug for warmth, her sturdy body covered by an ancient, extremely loose loden coat, under which she could conceal various bags. The heavy walking boots she wore, seemed too large for her feet. All her clothes were reminiscent of the mountains, as was the now empty rucksack, lying on the floor beside her. Had she been a keen walker once? Egon did not ask.

A scarf hid most of her slightly greyish hair, which was still intermingled with the mousy blond of her youth. Round hazel eyes cheerfully lit up an equally round face, made to look almost cheeky by the broad upturned nose and an irrepressible mouth, always turned up at the corners in a half smile, in spite of the dreadful stories which usually came out of it.

Now she was talking not of the routine killings and torture, but food:

"I try to bring food to private customers like yourself, but there's a whole restaurant industry where the real money is being made. Of course, some of my ladies also bake for the restaurants. Those who are still rich say that they've never eaten such delicious cakes as the ones they get now. No wonder. Many of the ladies whose houses in Warsaw were known for their hospitality have to bake cakes for sale. They bring out their secret recipes and keep their families going. Of course, they can only bake at night, when the gas pressure's on, and then they charge high prices, which they deserve. But I hate to see people stuffing themselves while others starve. Don't know what can be done about it. I have bought the *Prawda*, you know the Catholic underground paper, and they suggest a tax. How do they think they'll collect it? And can you blame people for eating when they can? Nobody knows if they'll be alive tomorrow, and there's no other fun to be had. So everybody tries to eat as much as possible, and as for drinking! The Germans want the peasants to drink. That way they think less, so they pay them partly in vodka for the food they take from them, and I'm told that some bars are also given vodka allocations to encourage people to get drunk. Not that they need much encouragement. People drink to forget, to get warm, for medical reasons and simply to cheer themselves up. D'you blame them? I don't. In fact I've been given a little bottle this afternoon, and we could all have a bit. The lad also looks cold. I'll put some in our coffee. It'll do us good."

It did do them good. For a while they felt warmer, not so scared, generally more relaxed.

"Have you heard any more good stories, Miss Filomena? I need them to cheer up the people I see."

"The only one I heard is supposed to be true. A friend of mine was walking near the Church of St. Alexander, when she saw a man dressed in what looked like the remnants of a butler's uniform serving up a meal to the old beggar sitting by the church entrance. Fascinated, she came nearer. The beggar ate half of the food, returned the rest to the servant, and said.

"Thank you, Piotr. Will you now take the rest to her ladyship. She's begging in front of St. Mary's."

They laughed, relaxed by the vodka, and the corners of Mrs. Golabek's mouth were still curved up when she said gravely.

"This could very well be true. Some people manage to have money through trading, or selling their things, but mostly people have nothing. There's no way anyone can make a living through honest work, and the old families are not used to fending for themselves. A lot of them really do beg.

Did you hear that all the food parcels people tried to send for Christmas have been confiscated by the German post office? It really has been the worst Christmas we ever had. They arrested lots of people while they were eating their Christmas Eve dinner, and took them to Pawiak.

They take people from there for torturing at the Aleja Szucha, but I can't even talk about that, because I get too upset, and I must have my wits about me. I must go now. Thank you for the coffee, and the money. See you as soon as I get anything else."

Filomena saw Mrs. Golabek out, and returned at once. "What's the matter, Egon? What have you got in that pillow slip? You look half dead."

Egon told her about the death of the Wolynskis, and his resolve not to endanger the Koronskis.

"I'm afraid you have to think practically," Filomena was unconvinced by his scruples. "Wherever you are you are in danger, and your presence endangers somebody. You have little choice, but we'll hear what Otto has to say."

Egon knew that here he was endangering Filomena, and consciously allowed his hatred to drown his hopelessness.

Otto had, of course, anticipated the possibility of disaster. He was desperately sorry to hear about the Wolynskis, but he did not know them. Nor did he know lieutenant Marian Urewicz, although his action did not surprise him. He did not have as high an opinion of Polish officers as his friend. As far as he was concerned, it was a relief to know that the Koronskis and Egon had survived another night. That was the only way to think.

"But where am I to go?" Egon's voice was tinged with the despair he felt. The vodka had worn off. He was feeling cold and hungry as usual and found it difficult to cope.

"You will now eat your fill of the good food Mrs. Golabek brought. Then you will spend the day here helping Filomena as usual. At about 4 o'clock I'll come to fetch you, and you'll share my residence in the Headquarters of the National Socialist Party at the Aleja Roz. It is not very comfortable, and it will be very boring, because we mustn't make a sound, but it is safer than most places. It's the only place I can think of where they're not looking for Jews. Furthermore, although there is no heater there, it's not too cold, because the building is heated, and our room has no windows."

Otto had devised a routine for moving through Warsaw both for himself and for Filomena. Although they did not dress smartly, because that would have made them stand out in the shabby crowds, they wore old, good quality clothes. They walked with deliberate self-assurance, but constantly watched for any unusual movement of either the uniformed Polish police, or the instantly recognisable Germans. Being tall was good because they could see further. But what helped most of all was the fact that neither of them was thin. A casual observer would not be sure if they were Polish or German civilians. They would never think that Otto was a Jew, because he did not look starved and scared. At least Otto hoped that this was so.

An adult in his late thirties does not need as much food as a growing boy, and Filomena, financed by Otto, could get enough food for them and sufficient for Egon to survive, but not to satisfy his hunger.

Before leaving, Otto gave two bulky cardboard boxes to Egon to carry, and picked some for himself. With a carefully assumed air of importance he led Egon to the entrance of the Nazi building. The guards raised their arms in a Heil Hitler salute. He was obviously a familiar and friendly figure.

"I've to bring in more supplies, and can't carry it all myself. The boy will be coming with me every day. That way we'll be able to get all the goods over. Can't get hold of a car, but I might have some more cigarettes tomorrow," he added in a quieter voice, as he slightly raised his arm in a half-hearted salute.

Otto talked to various people they met on their way, introducing Egon, as they continued walking through the corridors, and down the steps into a courtyard where he stopped in front of a wooden door made of heavy planks in the shape of shutters which were secured by padlock and chain.

He took a key out of his pocket, opened the padlock, took it off, casually putting it in his coat pocket and let Egon into a small locker room nearly all of which was occupied by various boxes stacked on broad shelves. The strip of the floor on which they stood was barely broad enough to accommodate their feet.

"These are mainly milk bottles," Otto said matter of factly pointing at the boxes, "and it would be very difficult to convince even the stupidest Parteigenosse, that the German army has a burning need for them, but today you were carrying genuine surgical tools in case anyone got nosey. All the different guards will have to see you, but I don't anticipate any trouble. They're beginning not to feel so safe in the streets of Warsaw, but here, of course, they feel completely secure. The guards are changing about now. The new ones have not seen us come in, so they'll not expect us to come out, but very soon the offices will be closed and they'll make a tour of the premises to make sure all is safe. After that we must not make a sound. The place is supposed to be empty, but one never knows who could hear us."

While he was speaking Otto was clearing the boxes from the lowest of the shelves, putting them into slots obviously intended for them, and in the one corner of the floor not occupied by their feet. When the shelf was empty he told Egon to lie on it and cover himself with his coat. He put a flat box under his head to make him more comfortable.

It was Otto's next action which made Egon sit up and stare, banging his head on the next shelf as he did so. His uncle had threaded the chain through the shutters so that both ends were inside. He then put the padlock through the metal rings and started pulling it back through the shutters. A neatly and inconspicuously carved out opening between the planks of the shutters allowed the padlock to slip back to the outside of the door giving every appearance of it being locked from the outside.

"I did the bit of carving when I was adjusting the shelves. At that time I could make as much noise as I liked, because it was during the day, and, as everybody knew I had been given the locker for storage, I could keep the door open and see if the coast was clear."

Otto was trying to be modest, but was clearly proud of himself.

"In the morning, we have to listen carefully, and if there's nobody around, we can pull the lock in, unlock it, and go out. I've taken out a milk bottle for our use in case of emergencies. A chamber pot might arouse suspicion. It's a good job we're both men. I hate to think how a woman would cope, but it's better to try and last out. Whatever you do, don't speak. Even a small creak could be dangerous, but a sound of human voice when nobody is supposed to be about, would be sure to give us away."

He was now trying to lift his large body next to Egon's. They could just manage to fit on the shelf if they both lay on the same side; Egon's smaller shape curled into the hollow between his uncle's knees and chin.

"If you want to turn over, prod me with your finger and then count to three. We can then turn over at the same time. Otherwise I'll fall off. Should I make any sound in my sleep give me two or three prods at once. I'll do the same for you."

They giggled nervously as they practiced: one prod, two prods, three prods, turn! One had to laugh, in spite of, or, perhaps because of the danger, and the situation was sufficiently ridiculous to merit anyone's mirth.

"Not a sound from now on." Otto whispered. "They'll be locking up soon."

They listened in the stuffy darkness of the room to the steps of the staff leaving their offices on the floors above. Voices were saying goodnight. The employees were going home. It was difficult to imagine that people had real homes, but were they real people? What sort of reality was theirs which allowed them to do their "work"?

Egon tried not to think about the wounds on the face of the old judge, the swollen veins of his neck and forehead, and above all about the mother and son holding hands in death.

The sound of heavy footsteps outside made him tense up again. The guards were checking the doors.

They passed their door and Egon heard them giving a routine pull to the lock and chain. It was in their nature to be thorough. Several minutes passed before his heart stopped trying to come out through his throat.

That night he was so exhausted that he slept in spite of the discomfort and the airlessness, but in the nights that followed neither of them managed to get a lot of sleep.

CHAPTER 10

STACH

"Hello, little one. Where've you been keeping yourself?" Egon recognised the voice, rather than the person of Witek, standing next to him in the tram which, unbelievably was empty. "I was hoping I'd run into you," Witek continued. "Come with me and I'll buy you a cake. We're near the Plac of Three Crosses. There's a place I know, called 'U Marka', where they know me."

There were several reasons why Egon was delighted to come, apart from the fact that he had a great respect and liking for Witek. It was a long time since he had eaten a cake and he hoped that Witek might find him something useful to do. Furthermore, he was trying to spend as much time as possible away from the shop, because Mrs. Piasecka from the second floor had been asking too many questions.

She confided to Filomena, that she had "sniffed out" three Jews. "Three heads, I collected today," she told her. Apparently she received money on a piecework basis from the Polish policeman, who had visited Otto and Franz Mitke.

"It would be twice as awful if you were reported by this odious woman," Filomena remarked. "First of all we would all be killed, and secondly we would enrich her. Keep away from her when at all possible."

"Now that you have gobbled up your cake," Witek said in the cafe, "Tell me, how would you like to come on another jaunt with me? I need somebody small with a bit of experience, and you know your way about the sewers. There's lots of young ones who'd be only too ready to come, but who can tell how they'd behave when there. Also, you seem to know what you're doing and can keep your mouth shut."

The very thought of the sewers filled Egon with horror. Even as a small child he liked to be clean, which had greatly impressed Fraulein Hedwige, but the possibility of positive action outweighed his disgust. Also, the nights spent at the Nazi Headquarters were extremely uncomfortable in addition to making him nervous. But more than anything the bantering tone and the complimentary nature of Witek's invitation made it irresistible.

"There's only one snag," Egon said, having nodded his agreement. "I couldn't possibly return to where I live at the moment smelling of . . . "

"That's enough," Witek interrupted. "I was told you were an orphan, and I dare say it's not easy for you living with others. You can tell them that you've been invited to join the scouts. I'll meet you here tomorrow at the same time as now – about twelve. Bring your things with you."

Egon returned to the office, carefully using the back door, but it was the friendly voice of Franz Mitke that he heard as he came in. As usual, he was speaking German, and telling Otto the latest news.

"They've brought thousands of Ukrainians to Warsaw to do their dirty work. I am told that the Wehrmacht doesn't like killing unarmed civilians, and the SS and Gestapo have their hands full with the attacks on trains and on anyone in Nazi uniform. They are doing more and more street round-ups, but the papers say that their most important task is looking for and exterminating the chief enemy, the Jews, of whom, of course, there are practically none."

"Yes," agreed Otto. "You'd think they would concentrate on defending themselves. I suppose they hope to get the sympathy of the population by playing on their natural anti-semitism, but they don't endear themselves to anybody when they catch thousands of innocent Poles. They've kept people out in the cold for hours before taking them to Pawiak. I met somebody, who was released, and he said that the only thing that kept him alive while he stood for five hours at a temperature of minus twenty degrees was the thought that it must be still colder for the Germans on the Russian front. I don't know how he got out, probably a relative knew whom to bribe, but he said they were pushed into cells with gun handles and jammed in so tightly that they couldn't move.

Did you hear the shooting in the ghetto? That's probably why they brought the Ukrainians. They're supposed to liquidate the ghetto."

"I've heard some shooting, but mostly I have to sit around with people and hear the most awful things, without being able to say what I think."

Franz was getting it all off his chest now. "The worst I've heard was from a new SS man, who came into my office. He told me that the Jews are being humanely liquidated and enjoy the new sweet gas."

"Yes. It is the total callousness that makes it all even worse," agreed Otto. "The street round-ups are carried out totally at random and so many have been caught and either killed or sent to Majdanek, that people have stopped going to work."

"That's why the trams were empty," Egon whispered in the silence, which followed. It was lucky that they were silent, because in the stillness they managed to hear the sound of furtive steps outside. Whoever it was had stopped to listen outside the office door. Exactly on cue Otto said in a businesslike voice.

"If you'll kindly read through those documents, Herr Mitke, and tell me what I'm to do about them."

"I'll let you know tomorrow, Herr Schmidt." Franz Mitke was not slow on the uptake, and was holding a handful of papers when Mrs. Piasecka came in, after a quick knock on the door.

The two men looked questioningly at her as she said in Polish to Egon. "Oh! I'm sorry. I didn't know the gentlemen were here. I was looking for Miss Filomena. Anyway what are you doing here when these gentlemen are having a meeting."

Before Egon could answer, Otto said in German.

"Fräulein Filomena is downstairs. Please don't bother us here."

They listened to Mrs. Piasecka's steps this time quite openly descending towards the shop.

"It's getting more and more difficult to survive," said Otto heavily, "and sleeping where we do is also not easy."

"I've been asked to stay with some boy scouts." Egon butted in, deciding that it was a good moment to tell them that a friend asked him to join the scouts. The two men discussed the proposal and decided that he would be safer with the scouts than anywhere else and that he should accept the offer. It was a good camouflage. If you were arrested as a Pole you still had a small chance, but if you were a Jew you had none.

"Keep in touch when you can," said Otto, "but don't get killed trying to do it. Whether or not I hear from you, I shall assume that you're alright. We'll all try to continue living. The war can't last much longer."

He said no more, but put some money in Egon's pocket, patted him on the shoulder, and loudly blew his nose.

Filomena was not so stoical. She cried, made him a parcel of food, helped him to put together his few belongings and made a sign of the Cross over him.

"God be with you, little son," she said. "You'll now be a soldier defending his country. May the Holy Mary, mother of Poland, look after you."

This patriotism was echoed in the group of boys Egon encountered in the noisy cellar to which Witek led him. Witek explained that they were being trained in warfare and acts of minor sabotage by older scouts and young army officers. Beyond this their enthusiasm had to be curbed, otherwise they would all have been killed as a result of foolhardy attacks on the occupiers. These children had seen their families, friends and neighbours butchered and their houses burned. They themselves had escaped only through luck, their knowledge of the back streets of Warsaw and the fleetness of their feet. All they wanted to do now was to retaliate. In the meantime, they acted tough, laughed and joked amongst themselves, and showed off about the number of German weapons they had managed to steal or acquire by killing their owners. Egon stood on the steps relishing the vitality and optimism which, in spite of their tragedy, emanated from people of his own age. But he felt alone and strange, when suddenly he recognised a familiar face.

"Tadek!"

"Wojtek, you old member of the Hitlerjugend. Nice to see you here. Come and meet my brother Stach. You must be about the same age. Shake!"

The two boys shook hands, looked each other over, and liked what they saw.

Tadek, watching them, thought that they made an interesting pair with their contrasting colouring Egon being so fair and dark eyed, and Stach so dark with the bluest of blue eyes in his finely shaped face.

Many of the boys had homes to which they returned at night, but Stach and Tadek, stayed in the cellar when their only relative, their aunt, *Pani* Ostrowska, had guests. Their father had been a high ranking army officer, and had left Poland with a group going out through Rumania to fight on. Their mother had looked after them alone, giving language and piano lessons to those who could still afford them. That had been at the beginning of the war, until, one day, the boys returned from school to find that their mother was not there, and the house had been burned down. They did not know whether their mother had engaged in any political activities, or if it had simply been done as a punishment for trying to provide education. She had told them nothing.

It was fortunate that her sister, *Pani* Ostrowska, happened to arrive at about the same time as the boys, and took them home with her. Later she introduced Tadek to Janusz. Now *Pani* Ostrowska also had to be careful, and the boys spent most of their time in the cellar being trained for action.

"Tadek is training us. Very soon we'll be able to really fight for Poland," explained Stach obviously very proud of his brother.

"And a good Poland it will be too," said a voice behind them, "free from the Germans and the Jews."

Egon looked up and saw a large-boned boy, who towered above both of them.

"This is Piotr," Stach introduced politely, but with no great eagerness. "He and his friends go through the streets hunting Jews. You'd think those poor bastards had enough trouble." He tried to sound tough in spite of the mildness of his remark.

"You're too young to understand these things," Piotr sounded instructive. "When we have our own new Poland we'll run it ourselves. We'll not be told what to do by those smart Alecs."

Fortunately his attention was attracted by somebody at the other end of the room, and Stach continued hotly, totally ignoring Piotr's remarks.

"We're all fighting for Poland and will continue until it is free. I'm sure it'll be very soon. There's already lots of things we've done, and it's the Holy Mary, the Queen of Poland who keeps us going. We will never be anything else except Polish. When we want to let each other know our whereabouts, we whistle the opening bars of the national anthem, and if a friend is about he continues with the following ones.

I'd start with 'Poland is not dead yet,' and you'd continue with 'while we are alive'. And we know that's true. When we were learning the words as children at school we didn't really understand them, but now we do."

Witek, who had been talking to some of the young officers made his way back to the boys.

"Tadek told me that you must have already taken the oath to go on your last job with him. We've got to be on our guard all the time. You and I will be leading a party who are making a delivery tomorrow. We will then make a little exploration. I'll tell you about it in the morning, and give you some proper clothes. Be at the same place as before at eight o'clock. It's still busier then than at other times, though not many people are going to work right now. Even so, we'll have a better chance to get through without being caught in a round-up. Have a good sleep. You'll need your strength."

Egon shared Filomena's generous food parcel with Stach, and four other boys who had no homes. There was bread, sausage, apples and milk. The other boys contributed acorn coffee heated on a primus stove, and they all had a feast. One of them, called Jasiek, proudly placed on the table a bunch of radishes and a few wrinkled apples.

"I managed to get out into the country early this morning, and scrounged these from the peasants," he said in a gruff accent of the countryside. He had a turned up nose covered in freckles, and a mop of blonde hair, which fell on his face, giving it an impudent look. It was re-enforced by a broad grin of satisfaction as he proceeded to take a knife out of his pocket to clean the radishes.

First they ate and then they talked about fighting, about the end of the war and about the things the scouts were doing.

"We've been making incendiary bombs, and Jeremy's lot have thrown some at a train and at a lorry. They work!" said the smallest boy, whom they all called Bronek. He was pale and colourless, like a little mouse, and his high-pitched voice heightened the similarity.

"Some of the scouts have helped in big things," a tall, dark boy, named Jurek said seriously. "You may have seen the placards on the walls about the Polish Special Court judgment on Ossowski and Swiecicki. No?

Well. Ossowski worked in the German employment office and helped them to cart off a lot of good people for work in Germany. As you know, it's not work, but slavery. But in addition to being simply helpful to the Germans, the swine blackmailed people, telling them he'd get them transported if they didn't pay up. The Polish Court sentenced him to death.

Swiecicki was a pig who, not only worked with the police co-operating with the Germans, but also blackmailed people, threatening to have them arrested if they didn't part with all they had. He helped the Germans to catch Poles, and would keep some people locked up specially to collect a ransom. The underground army managed to carry out the sentence and shot both of them. We helped as look-outs."

"There are many groups like ours," piped up Stach. "There are also girls and some of them are very pretty. They act as couriers, because the Germans stop women less than men. Most of the girls with whom we work are from the ballet school."

"And we all know which one you particularly like," grinned a sturdily built, but painfully thin lad, called Wacek, who completed their party. "Her name wouldn't by any chance be Marylka?"

"You leave Marylka out of your chatter," Stach blushed furiously. "As I was saying, there are many of us and all of us are training. We'll pay the swine back.

For the time being we mainly write slogans on the walls to show people that Poland is fighting back. To give them hope. We will win, you know. It might take a little time, but we will," and Stach smiled his charming warm smile, which brought a return smile to Egon's lips. He suddenly realised how unaccustomed his lips were to smiling, and made a conscious effort to continue.

"You had better take that grin off your face, and go to bed," said Stach, watching Egon curiously. He was very perceptive, and wondered about the duration of that smile.

Tadek had gone to sleep somewhere else, leaving his bedding for Egon. With a full stomach, in the comparative safety of the cellar, and the warmth of the developing friendship, Egon slept very well, but nervously, worried about oversleeping.

But he did not oversleep and at the appointed time found himself slipping once again into the sewer entrance ahead of a party of dark shadows, which seemed to materialise out of nowhere in the familiar courtyard at 49 Zlota Street. Witek said that the large crates they helped to lower down on long ropes contained some home-made grenades, a few machine guns and shotguns, as well as some revolvers.

"I want you to lead, holding the lamp," Witek said. "That way you'll remember better, and it'll give me two hands to carry the stuff. I'm stronger than you. Don't worry. I'll be right behind you, and will not let you lead us astray."

But Egon did not lose his way. He was thinking of David, and hoping that he was still alive, of Stach with his hope and warm smile, and feeling that he was doing something important. The slime and stink became secondary. He did not think about the cold drops behind his collar, but about the vague outlines of the tunnel. Anyway, it was no longer so cold. It was April.

This time they were expected. Somehow a message must have been smuggled through to the ghetto. A number of young people were waiting for them. They looked so emaciated that it was surprising to see them smile, shake the filthy hands of the drains party, and help with the crates. And among them was David.

"Did little Rosa make it?" he asked Egon immediately he saw him.

"Both girls made it, and were being washed and fed last time I saw them," Egon was quick to reassure him. "I was told they were going to be taken to a convent, but I don't know which one. It's better if I don't know, but I'm sure they'll be alright."

"That's wonderful. And you see I'm also still alive," David grinned. "Though it's not easy. My other two friends didn't make it. One became ill and died, and the other got shot by a fun-loving SS officer.

I want to live just a little longer to have a go at them. If you die fighting you die with some honour. You die like a human being, protesting against inhumanity, and you show the Poles that you too can die for Poland."

Much later Egon heard that David died throwing petrol bombs under a tank. But by then it had become a commonplace sort of death for the young boys and girls of Warsaw.

"The Rabbi said that tomorrow is *Erev Pesach*[1]," David said. "All the family used to come to our house for the Feast of Passover. There were white table cloths and stiffly starched white napkins. White candles in tall silver candlesticks. Beautiful china and glasses, and lots to eat and drink. Apart from Rosa, who was still a baby, and was not allowed to stay up, I was the youngest of the family and had to ask the special questions in Hebrew. There were up to thirty of us at the table, and I think I'm the only one left alive. Do you remember Passover?"

"I do," Egon said, "but I must be careful what I say, because the others don't know I'm a Jew. I do wish you'd come out of here. Perhaps you could get through to the forest and the partisans."

"Not any more. I really haven't got much strength. Just enough to shoot and throw a grenade if I have one. As I told you before, I want to die with some dignity, to die fighting against the inhuman. It's difficult to say things like that, but you must know what I mean, although you may think I sound pompous. I am sixteen, probably quite a bit older than you, and I've done a lot of reading when there were books and a lot of thinking since I've been here."

Egon understood. He could imagine his brother Kurt speaking like this. It surprised him to hear, however, that David, who was hardly as tall as he, was so much older.

"Come on, Wojtek! We have to go," Witek was calling.

"I know. Good luck," Egon whispered, "Next year in Jerusalem."

"Next year in Jerusalem," David whispered back the ancient Passover greeting of the Jews.

The rest of their group was staying for a while to explain the working of the weapons they had brought, but Witek and Egon were going to explore. The "exploration" consisted of looking at the canals.

[1]The eve of Passover

Witek made Egon crawl into narrow connecting links, where even the
boy had to bend down, and found himself up to the waist in the stinking
water, but he was beginning to understand the network.

"I want you to grasp the way in which the sewage system works," Witek
said, "If and when it comes to fighting in Warsaw this could be the only
way to get around and people will be needed who can do the guiding. It
was a chance that brought you to me, but you're good for this work and
you must learn."

Eventually, their time was up. They had to return and lead their party
back. Egon was completely wet, cold and exhausted, but it was unthinkable
to even mention it. The honour of being able to help in preference to all
the others was so great, that he used every last bit of his strength to appear
steady; to combat the giddiness, which plagued him, and eventually made
him retreat into semi-consciousness.

*

*He is aware that their party has grown. Three women and four children are
being taken out of the ghetto. They are all weak and the small children need to
be carried. There is a girl about the same age as Egon, and he pulls her along
with his free hand carrying the lamp in the other. The men carry the children,
and have to bend over to avoid the low ceilings of the tunnels. They have to
stop from time to time to straighten their backs, and their progress is slow. It is
just as well, otherwise the women could not have kept up, because they are
overcome by weakness and dizziness.*

*The journey seems endless. Hours appear to pass, and Egon tries to keep hold
of the girl, whose poor skeletal feet slide helplessly in the unspeakable grime
below, and at the same time hold up the lamp, without falling down himself.
Every muscle hurts, as he dully puts one foot in front of the other. His
thoughts are still with David, and his mind takes him back to the Pesach celebrations.*

*He remembers the special Passover china being taken out; all the dishes that
had never touched bread.*

*Only unleavened bread, the matzo was allowed for a week. No ordinary
bread at all! He remembers the fun Kurt and he had following his father, who
carried a symbolic candle round the house, looking for imaginary bread crumbs,
which could have remained in the corners. Of course there were no crumbs. A
ritual spring cleaning preceded the holidays. Every cupboard and every drawer
had to be cleaned out. All Jewish households were busy.*

The cheerful flowered Passover cups suddenly gleam in front of his eyes, until he manages to focus them on the lamp.

*

"Come on, Wojtek! Hold the lamp up!"

*

He puts the lamp in the other hand, which is less cramped, and catches the falling girl with his free arm. They settle again into the mechanical step by step motion.

Like David, he had also been the youngest, and had to ask the questions, which he had learned by heart in Hebrew when he was three. They float into his mind, and he walks in time with the tune in which he had to sing them. He hears it clearly, without uttering a sound:

"Wherein is this night different from all other nights?

For on all other nights we may eat either leavened bread or unleavened, but on this night only unleavened.

On all other nights we may eat other kinds of herb, but on this night only bitter herbs.

On all other nights we need not dip our herbs even once, but on this night we do so twice.

On all other nights we eat either sitting upright or reclining, but on this night we all recline.

We were Pharaoh's bondmen in Egypt; and the Lord our God brought us out therefrom with a mighty hand and an outstretched arm."

Why did God perform miracles then, and not now? Was there going to be a miracle in the Ghetto?

According to the Jewish law, this year he would become a man, and have to read a portion of the Torah in Hebrew in front of all the members of the synagogue. But there was no longer a synagogue and all its members were dead.

*

The stench of death in the ghetto seemed more pervasive than the stench of the drains, which he no longer registered.

"Hold the lamp up, Wojtek, we're nearly there!"

Witek seems to be the only one of the party to move and react normally. All the others have become robots, motivated only by will power.

Egon held the lamp high, trying very hard to behave like Witek.

CHAPTER 11

THE GHETTO UPRISING

" . . . The worst crime in human history is taking place. We know that you are helping the tormented Jews as much as you can. Thank you, my countrymen, in my own name and in the name of the Government. I beg you to give all possible help . . .

Every Pole who in any way co-operates with the murderous German action, whether by blackmailing or denouncing Jews, or by taking advantage of their tragic situation, commits a heavy crime against the laws of the Polish Republic and can be assured that the time is not far when he will have to face the judgment of a Reborn Poland."

From a proclamation by the Polish Freedom Organisations.

Quotes from some of the Polish underground papers:

POLAND LIVES mentions that "The Warsaw ghetto is fighting . . . These things do not concern us."

VOICE OF POLAND communicates that "The Jews fear the Germans more than death. When they are caught they show in many cases where they spent the night. As a result whole Polish families are caught for one Jew."

GREAT POLAND expresses the opinion that "The fight of the Jews in the ghetto has not the slightest relation to the Polish question. There is neither heroism there nor danger."

Head of German Police in the area of Warsaw, Karl Eberhard Schongarth on the 20th April, 1943.

"Einen solchen Druck, wie ihn das polnische Volk erleide, habe noch nie ein Volk erleiden müssen".

No other nation has ever suffered under the sort of pressure that is suffered by the Poles.

*

Szymon Datner, a Polish/Jewish writer:

"A society with a noose round its neck attempts to save another society with a noose already tightened round its neck."

*

Julian Tuwim – Polish poet – a Jew (a partial free translation):

"Such a flood of martyr's blood has not flown since the beginning of the world . . . We Polish Jews . . . we, who are an endless family grave . . . a funeral cortege, the like of which has never before been seen; we, suffocated in gas chambers and melted into soap; we, whose brains bespattered the walls of our beggarly hovels and the walls against which we were shot only because we were Jews. We are a scream of pain: a scream so protracted that the remotest aeons will hear it."

* * *

When Egon woke up, having again spent the night in the cellar of the kindly caretaker at 49 Zlota Street, he found that Witek had slept there too. They had been warned not to go back in the evening, although they might have made it before the curfew. Apparently the indiscriminate street round ups all over Warsaw, which had been going on during the last few days, had further intensified, and thousands of people had been caught. Those who were not killed on the spot, were being taken to Majdanek.

Egon listened to the two men talking about the events in town, and a terrible anxiety filled him. It sounded as if nearly everybody had been caught. The awful possibility of Otto and Filomena being amongst them came to his mind. He asked Witek if he could go to see whether his people were safe. Witek reluctantly agreed, but told him to return to the cellar as soon as possible.

Egon half ran and half walked all the way. He avoided the main streets, and did not use trams. Most of all he tried not to think about all the terrible possibilities, or how he felt about them, but concentrate on his actions only. Instinctively he knew that this was the only way to preserve his sanity.

Dwelling on one's feelings is the luxury of those who have the time and detachment to analyse all the nuances of their reactions or of the people who are unfortunate enough to be unable or unwilling to act. Sounds of shooting reached him, and he thought that they came from the direction of the ghetto. He wondered whether his imagination was playing tricks on him, connecting the shots with the weapons they had taken there.

But it was no trick of imagination, because it was on that day the 19th of April on the first day of Passover, while he was running through the fear-filled streets of Warsaw, that the ghetto uprising started. The Gestapo troops walked in to perform the final liquidation of the pitiful remnants of humanity which still managed to survive, and were astonished to meet with armed resistance. The walking dead decided that, as there was no hope of life, they would defend themselves and die fighting.

Egon approached the premises of Esculap cautiously, but he need not have worried. Filomena was alone in the shop, and looked as if she had been crying. She cuddled him silently, and answered his unspoken urgent question:

"Otto is alright. He's upstairs."

"Then why have you been crying?"

He picked up a sheet of paper which had fallen on the floor, and handed it to him.

"Read for yourself, little son," she said. "A kindly German, though to us here it appears to be a contradiction in terms, posted it to him. You've never met my little brother Henryk. He will be eighteen in May. They caught him during the winter of 1941, and we've not heard from him since."

"They caught me," Egon read, "in the street in Warsaw, on my way home from work. As soon as we arrived here (we are in a small town not far from Berlin) we had to stitch on a big letter 'P' on our clothes, and we are not allowed to be seen without this, so that people know we are Poles.

"It was supposed to put off the other workers in the factory, but many of them tried to treat us well, so notices were put in their pay packets, saying that the Poles are sworn enemies, spies and should be constantly watched and reported. We were also forbidden to meet local people.

"But the locals are not the sort of Germans we have. They all listen to the English radio. We are working in an aeroplane factory, and the local Germans are not keen on the war work. They meet in toilets where they have meetings and write anti-Hitler slogans on doors. We have had some superb British bombing, which we are not allowed to watch, and we all look after one another.

"Our only recreation is news from the big world outside, and various attempts at running away – twenty four people got away in one day. Give my best regards to everybody. Henryk."

"So why are you crying?" Egon asked having finished reading. "He seems better off there than here."

"It's the relief," Filomena said. "One never knows if it's really work or a concentration camp. You'd better go and see your uncle."

"Right," Egon said and ran up the stairs. A sudden glimpse of a Germany, where the Germans were people like any other went through his mind. Otto was always telling him that all the German papers were full of lies. Ludwig Landau, whose writings he managed to read from time to time, always pointed out the lies, but he listened to foreign radio transmissions and had a means of comparison. The German people would not know what the reality in Poland was, and would believe what was written in their newspapers.

Egon dismissed these thoughts from his mind, replacing them by understanding that one could cry from relief. It would have been unbearable if Otto had been caught. He was Egon's last link with normality, the imperturbable source of clear thinking and immediate action. But Otto's nerves were stretched as far as they could go, and he nearly jumped into the air when Egon rushed into the room.

He tried to conceal his nervousness, but Egon felt the trembling of the arms, which held him, and knew renewed fear, because he suddenly realised that Otto could no longer maintain his cool detachment. He was soon reassured by his uncle's next remark:

"Tell Filomena to close up shop. It's lunch hour. *Pani* Zofja Golabek has been, and there's food to be eaten. We don't see each other every day. Let's eat while we may. Today is *Pesach*. We can't have the real celebration, but let's gather as much family as we can and eat."

They had all the wrong things to eat, but the very fact that sufficient food was passing their lips was itself a cause of festivity. Otto did not attempt to say prayers. It seemed blasphemous to utter them while eating bread and butter with pork sausage instead of matzo. Bread would not have been allowed during a Passover meal, eating butter and meat together was not allowed at any time, and eating pork was forbidden.

While satisfying their first hunger they had no thoughts for anything but food, but then Filomena voiced their thoughts.

"It seems wrong to eat one's fill when people are dying from hunger."

The pictures of the emaciated figures in the ghetto rose in front of Egon's eyes, although those were not the ones to which Filomena referred.

"It will not help anybody if we also die, and in any case we may be killed at any time. It would be worse if we were killed leaving the food behind." Otto could always be trusted to view life pragmatically.

They all relaxed somewhat with the food inside them and the sudden ring of the telephone, which was covered by the debris of the meal spread on the desk, startled them. Otto answered and listened carefully, said goodbye and turned to his little family:

"That was Franz Mitke. He's seen ambulances going to the ghetto. There's been shooting. They'd not be sending ambulances for the Jewish injured. Some resistance must have started in the ghetto."

They looked at each other, and found that words would not come. They felt a mixture of excitement and hopelessness.

"May God help them," Filomena said at last.

"Amen," Otto answered with feeling, "but He doesn't seem to have done much so far."

Egon said nothing, but thought of David.

They helped Filomena to clear up and Egon lingered after she went down to the shop. Then he turned to Otto and said:

"I've to go now, but I've been given a copy of the plan of the sewers, and told to hide it in a safe place. I don't want to leave it here, because it would be dangerous for you if anyone found it. I don't want to incriminate you. Where d'you think I should put it?"

"I know of a very safe place," Otto grinned. "The very safest. Give it to me and I'll put it within the unholy walls of the Nazi Headquarters. I'll put it under the furthest case of the baby milk bottles in the store. If they find out that it's mostly bottles that I have there, I'll be so incriminated that a little extra danger will make no difference." He stopped and continued more soberly, "I can't stop thinking about the ghetto."

Neither of them could stop thinking about it, but there was nothing they could do. The whole of Warsaw watched and listened to explosions as, day after day, the Germans methodically rolled barrels of petrol into the entrance of every house they reached within the walled-in area of the ghetto, and then ignited it. Wild rumours circulated round Warsaw, of battles in which the Polish underground also took part, but no one really knew what was going on. Egon returned to the cellar, where life went on as usual.

Stach came back from an errand one day with a leaflet from the ghetto which said that "we are fighting for our freedom and your's". He was excited because he had been told that the red and white flag of Poland was flying over the ghetto together with the white and blue Jewish one. Even Piotr seemed affected.

"I'd never have thought that the bloody Jews had it in them to fight," he said carefully. "At least they'll kill a few of the Krauts. But all the Jews will be killed anyway, so there's not much difference."

The night sky over Warsaw glowed red as the houses burned, incinerating all who lived within them. A strong wind blew during that April and spread the fires, creating a horrific theatrical backdrop accompanied by a macabre concert of shooting and explosions.

Egon lived in a curious state of unreality; of suspended animation. He was desperately, but vainly looking for Witek, hoping that he would be able to do something to help.

Tadek introduced a strict routine of schooling, and people came to give them lessons in the Polish language, literature, geography, and arithmetic. It was as dangerous to be learning these things as taking guns apart to see how they worked, or training in shadowing people. The danger concentrated the minds of the pupils, who paid maximum attention to their teachers. Egon mechanically and perfectly did whatever was asked of him, but his mind was on the Jews fighting in the burning ghetto. He knew how few and pathetic their weapons were.

The only time his attention was completely caught, was when a new history teacher was introduced to them.

In the dim light of the cellar he looked just like any other of their instructors, but his voice was compelling and his diction so clear that every word seemed to acquire an importance of its own.

"My introductory lesson," he started, " is on the history of Warszawa (Warsaw), which has been our capital for the last three hundred and fifty years, although as a settlement and a town it has existed for much longer than that.

"Legend has it, that a young man called Warsz and a young woman called Sawa fell in love and were married. They left their home village to look for a beautiful and peaceful place to live, and built themselves a cottage on the bank of the Vistula. They combined their names to call the place

Warszawa and were often known to say to each other 'we have to work
hard, but at least we have found a place where we can ensure a beautiful
and peaceful existence for ourselves and for our children and grandchildren.' The peace may have lasted during the life of their children and
grandchildren because they prospered and a settlement grew around their
cottage. In 1262 it became sufficiently prosperous to merit the attention of
the Lithuanians, who came to pillage.

"But the villagers must have been pretty hard working, because they rebuild to such an extent that in 1282 Warsaw was given the status of a town,
though the first brick houses were only built in the middle of the XVth
century. Very sensibly, instead of continuing to fight each other, the Lithuanians and the Poles united in 1386.

"All this time the Kings of Poland governed from the ancient capital
Cracow, but Cracow is far in the south of the country and it became more
convenient for the Diet (a sort of parliament) to meet nearer the centre of
Poland and nearer to Lithuania, in Warsaw. They did that for the first time
in 1569. Some years later, in 1595, there was a big fire at the Royal Castle
of Cracow, and King Sigismund Vasa III (who was a Swede) moved to
Warsaw.

"There was a strong Italian influence in the enlarging of Warsaw to
become the capital of Poland. In the XVIIIth century Warsaw became
known as the City of Palaces. Almost every Polish noble (of whom there
were many) had a large palace with a park outside the city walls, and each
accommodated smaller gentry so that it had small satellites around it. The
main principle of contemporary economics was that the rich must spend
very much very quickly to enable the poor to earn money. In order to do
this, they had constant feasts and balls, and lived in extravagant luxury.
Linen was sent by some of them to Paris to be specially laundered; others
had tea brought from England in special coaches. There was a police force,
but no prison in Warsaw. All this may sound wonderful, but it was only a
short period in the history of Warsaw. In the three hundred and fifty years
of its being capital

"Swedes captured it three times.
Germans also three times.
Austrians also only had one go
but the Russians did it four times.
And, of course, the French came in as allies on one occasion.

"It survived six insurrections, two sieges and was four times taken by storm. When in 1659 Poland was cleared of invaders, only about three hundred and forty houses were left standing, and it was after that that the city achieved its magnificence.

"I hope to have the opportunity to teach you the history of Poland through the history of Warsaw, a city, which has never given up and never will."

The teacher caught the children's imagination. They listened spellbound, and afterwards Stach said.

"If our mother had lived, she would have told us all this. She knew about everything. Perhaps, after the war, I'll be able to study like both of my parents did." He stopped for a while, allowing himself to dream, and then said briskly.

"He's a super sort of chap, and we'll learn a lot from him, but first we have to learn how to fight to get rid of the latest plague that overcame Warsaw."

And Egon thought how much Kurt would have enjoyed it, but he could not tell Stach what he thought. Nobody could be told that Kurt had existed.

However, they were never to learn any more from their new history teacher, because the following day a frantic Piotr came back from the town and screamed out,

"They caught him! They caught our history teacher in a silly lapanka! I saw him and managed to scram!"

Sometimes, very rarely, it was possible to organise an escape, but this time the time was too short. It was also probable that the teacher's fighting ability did not match his teaching, and it was not deemed right to risk other lives for his.

"I hate them. I hate them all," Stach said with a passionate stubbornness of total conviction. "Every single one of them is bad and has to be killed. A good German is a dead German."

Egon tried to remember Janusz's warning about indiscriminate hatred, but he felt the same as Stach.

"Yes," he said, "a good German is a dead one," but then he thought of Fräulein Hedwige.

Easter came and people had two days free. Warsaw had been adorned by the Germans with Nazi flags to honour Hitler's birthday, but the population totally ignored the celebrations.

Instead, crowds gathered behind the German cordons which surrounded the ghetto, and watched the spectacle of the enormous conflagration which was consuming its inhabitants with flames and smoke.

Egon and Stach mingled with the people. It had been a milder winter than the one before, and the spring was warm.

"They have cut off their water supplies," said a tall, gaunt woman in a scarf, "and have asked for guides to the sewers, so they can stop them running away. My husband works for the water company, so he knows what's going on," she added importantly.

"I saw people being taken away from the ghetto workrooms. Mostly women and children, but also some men in chains. Some say they are being taken to Majdanek, but others said that they are shooting them on the spot at the Jewish cemetery behind the Citadel," the shorter, younger woman contributed.

"One thing is sure," the gaunt one said authoritatively, "The Germans will leave no one alive there. It's only a question of how and when they'll die."

With an odd detachment Egon looked on as a gust of wind blew the heavy clouds of smoke towards them, making the crowd recede, leaving himself and Stach in the front. Then the smoke dissipated, and he could see the nearest burning house quite clearly. Helplessly he watched what appeared in front of him like a horrifying slow motion film.

A window opened; a woman with a child in her arms climbed onto the window sill. She hesitated for a while until a hand appeared and pushed her. Silently she fell, still clutching the child. Was she really silent, or did the roar of the fire camouflage her screams?

He thought her face looked composed, but the distance could have deceived him. It was impossible to accept it all as reality. The owner of the hand now followed. Egon could not exactly discern the man's features, but he thought that his face looked calm. His dark shape was silhouetted against the bright flames behind him and framed by the partly dark, partly crimson-lit wall surrounding the hole where the window had been.

Then, almost casually, the man stepped forward, and fell into the inferno below. Egon stood dazed watching the houses disintegrating in front of him, and thought of David's desire to die with dignity. That is what these people were doing.

Suddenly the sound of music reached him. A merry-go-round had been set up close to the burning ghetto. The sound of children's laughter mingled with the cheerful tune providing a grotesque musical background to the picture.

Stach brought Egon back to reality. He was pulling his sleeve and pointing to a new notice from the chief of police, which had been stuck on the lamp post next to them, and reminded the general public that helping Jews was punishable by death. It also cautioned the citizens of Warsaw that anyone found in "the past Jewish district" would be shot on the spot.

"As if they needed any excuse to shoot anybody on the spot," the gaunt woman, who now returned and stood next to Egon, said to her neighbour.

"I live in Leszno," the other woman said, "and I saw the chief of water supplies with his clerks waiting by the sewer cover with the Gestapo. About thirty people came out of the sewer, and they shot them all. All the clerks and their chief also took pot shots. They enjoyed it. It was as if they were on a hunt."

"I live nearby," the first woman was not to be outdone, "and I saw them killing children by putting guns in their mouths and shooting."

"I don't really like Jews, but this is too much."

Slowly the boys walked back through the neglected but still beautiful streets in the centre of town, so lost in thought that they forgot to take the usual precautions, until they became aware of a minor commotion. A woman with a pram was pointing out a dark-haired man on the other side of the pavement to a group of Gestapo officers.

"I'm sure he's a Jew," she was saying. "Just look at his nose, and the shape of his ears. He must be one of those who escaped from the ghetto."

Shots rang out before the astonished man could say anything, and he lay in a gathering pool of blood which glistened in the spring sunshine. It was all so quick and casual that the horror of it took time to register.

The boys did not wait to find out if the man had really been a Jew. Quickly and silently they returned to their cellar, where a pillow was being thrown about, provoking screams of laughter every time it hit a target. Stach dived in first, and Egon joined in, successfully ducking an assault aimed at him because he had stood still outlined by the light behind him.

News came all the time of particularly evil Gestapo officers and Polish blue policemen being killed as punishment by the Polish underground.

The street loudspeakers, "the barkers", were now giving names of the hundreds of hostages shot by the Germans in reprisals, and red posters stuck on the lamp posts listed their names.

The boys kept in little groups, and Egon stayed mostly with Stach and Piotr, who had attached himself to the two younger boys. Tadek, of course, was a much superior being, and was mostly away on some mysterious errand.

Piotr was a pleasant chap, when he was not indulging his virulent anti-semitism, and he took a particular liking to Egon, because they both enjoyed fiddling with electrical systems and telephones. They did not have much opportunity to do this in the cellar, but one of the teachers found them some old books with diagrams, which they could follow.

The 3rd of May, Polish national holiday, was approaching and rumour had it that the underground was planning to do something to give hope to the people of Warsaw and show them that resistance to the occupation was active.

"It should be possible," Egon and Piotr decided, after carefully studying their diagrams, "to connect one of the German public radio transmitters to a telephone, and broadcast something useful instead of the garbage they normally spout forth."

When they told Tadek about it, he looked at them suspiciously and asked.

"Who's been talking to you?"

They convinced him that the idea had come to them when they tried to find an application for their newly found knowledge.

"Alright, I believe you, though some wouldn't. Anyway, somebody else thought of a scheme like yours, though I don't know how it is going to be done. Don't know if your way would work. As you've managed to think all this out, I'll tell you where you can listen on the day, but mind you skedaddle before any trouble starts."

So they were present when the loudspeaker on Plac Wilsona, which had been out of action for a while, presumably having had its cable cut by an underground electrician, suddenly came alive during the beautiful sunny afternoon on the 3rd of May, 1943.

It was nearly six o'clock and people were hurrying home, when unexpectedly the hated "barker" instead of spouting forth propaganda, or the names of hostages executed by the Germans, burst forth with Polish marching songs, followed by an announcement.

"This is the station of the Leadership of the Civil Struggle. We are transmitting a special audition on the occasion of the National Holiday of the 3rd of May."

Then the majestic, measured notes of *Rota* the hymn with words written by the poet, Maria Konopnicka, sounded over the square.

WE WILL NOT GIVE UP THE LAND OF OUR BIRTH,
WE WILL NOT ALLOW ITS SPEECH TO BE FORGOTTEN.
WE ARE THE POLISH NATION, POLISH BREED,

THE ROYAL TRIBE OF PIAST.
EVERY DOORSTEP WILL BE OUR FORTRESS.
SO HELP US GOD.

People cried unashamedly, and stood listening to the words of hope and defiance, which poured out of the normally hateful loudspeaker.

"Poland lives!" a man's voice proclaimed clearly and loudly from the loudspeaker.

The bewildered German passers-by did not know how to react. Hearing the solemn music they too stood to attention and took their hats off, not even recognising the final sound of the Polish National Anthem, which followed.

The sight of them made the boys giggle. It was always a relief to see something ridiculous. It helped them to hide the tears which stood in their eyes. They were not supposed to cry. Sentimentality was frowned upon.

They ran away before any German investigation commenced, and bumped into a radiant Tadek.

"It was my friend Lech, who was speaking," he said proudly. "Of course, he was not called that when I trained under him."

The Germans now set on fire the area called the Small Ghetto and it seemed to burn even more brightly than its larger neighbour. They had probably benefitted from their earlier practice. In any case it gave sufficient illumination for the first Russian raid on Warsaw, and enabled the Russians to concentrate their bombing pretty accurately on the railway network. They had timed it well, because three days later Jurgen Stroop, in charge of fighting the Jews in ghetto, announced that "the action" has been satisfactorily completed, and there was no more illumination.

Stroop crowned his achievement by blowing up the Great Synagogue on Tlomacki, and creating another gaping ruin in an area which had become a macabre cemetery, where the mausoleums and tombstones consisted of piles of rubble. It was said that people were still hiding in some of the mounds and that shots came from there well into June, but then all was quiet.

Franz Mitke did not take shelter when the alarm sounded and the Russian planes appeared. He stood on the balcony of his comfortable flat watching the bombs falling on the station, and on the roofs of the city he loved, clearly outlined against the angry red sky. Though it was long after midnight, he would not have been asleep anyway. He suffered from a persistent and awful feeling of being afloat on a sea of wretchedness, which lapped at him from all sides. Precisely because his mind was not always preoccupied with the necessity to find food and shelter he had time to think, and his thoughts were such that he longed for death, which was vouchsafed to him during that May night by the courtesy of the Russian pilot, who slightly misjudged his aim. Franz Mitke lived conveniently close to the main station and the bomb scored a direct hit on his block of flats. His body was never found, but Otto saw the ruins and never heard from his friend again.

Dr. Wolfgang Stein took the business over on behalf of the Third Reich, but retained the services of Herr Herman Schmidt, who asked him for a proper receipt on behalf of any heirs of Franz Mitke, who might survive the war. He also said that the work would demand his permanent residence in Warsaw, which was granted to him.

With these papers he found a room in a flat with a family called Tulipski. They were so ardently anti-semitic that his conscience did not trouble him. He felt that it would be divine justice if they were shot for hiding a Jew. Nothing happened to the Tulipskis, however, because they left Warsaw shortly after he moved in.

They said that they had got used to the lapanki, but the bombing had scared them, though they did not hold it against the Russians, calling it a "justified war action."

Egon heard about all this only later, when he went to say goodbye, before leaving Warsaw.

In the meantime he was living with the scouts, and all the original group became his close friends, but Stach and he were inseparable. They were all training keenly and longing to be used in real action, which was taking place in the streets.

In the background of their life the ghetto was continuing to fight, the explosions went on, and the black smoke rose to heaven, while on earth the hunt for Jews continued.

It became a sport in which the Germans, crowds of local teenagers, the Polish police indulged. They were frequently helped by passers by, like the woman with a pram whom Egon and Stach had seen, and by people who felt they were doing their duty when betraying those who had managed to hide. However, the immediate executions also provoked sympathy amongst some of the population, especially as mistakes often occurred and some people were killed who were innocent of the dreadful and sinister crime of being Jewish.

*

"You mentioned that you had met Marian Urewicz," Tadek said to Egon one day. "The man who gave away the Wolynskis. Could you recognise him again?"

"I could recognise the bastard anywhere. Why?"

"There's an order out to liquidate him. He's been sentenced to death by the Polish Court for, among other things, blackmailing and betraying Jews. Somebody needs to stand guard, and it's just as well if it's someone who knows him and someone who can pretend to be a German. Others have followed him and have done the research, but he seems to have become aware of them, and it's better if somebody else provides the final cover."

"Nothing would give me greater pleasure."

At last something real to do!

"We'll need to move around after curfew, so we'll get you a Hitler Jugend uniform, and a Stabsunteroffizier again for me. I've got them here.

We also have two hand guns. You have plenty of room to conceal yours in your trousers, and I hope you've been paying enough attention to Sergeant Bolek's and my lessons so that you can use it if necessary, though you've not had much practice."

*

It was eerie walking through the dark streets of Warsaw, lit only by the glare of the ghetto fires.

The carvings on the handsome buildings stood out against the red sky, and the imperfect light hid the general dilapidation, conjuring up the past. Warsaw had been a beautiful city.

Tadek led the way confidently and stopped in front of a cáfe, which they entered. It was full of uniformed Germans and people in civilian clothes.

"The shit should still be here," he said very quietly, but in German to match his uniform. "I've been told that he usually begins to say his good-byes at about this time."

They sat down at a table not too far from the door.

"All we have to do, once you've located him," Tadek whispered, "is to follow him. We'll get further instructions when we get to his place."

Egon looked round the room, and easily spotted the handsome Marian sitting at a corner table, wearing a well-cut suit and tie and smoking a cigarette in a long holder. His perfect teeth shone white for a moment when he laughed at something the pretty girl next to him was saying. Then he rose and bent to kiss her hand. As Tadek had predicted, he was preparing to leave.

Egon was just about to tell Tadek that their prey was there, when he sensed that somebody was looking at him. The feeling was so strong that he felt compelled to look up, but he did it very slowly, so as not to meet the eyes, which he thought were watching him.

He succeeded, and managed to avoid the stare of Thomas Braun, the stationmaster of the station in Siedlce, who was even now rising from his seat with a smile of uncertain recognition. Fortunately they were standing in a badly lit part of the room.

Egon fought his initial panic, and turned his back on the stationmaster trying to do it as casually as he could manage. He then walked out ahead of Tadek and before the man they were to follow. Tadek, astonished, followed him out.

"What d'you think you're doing?" he said. "I didn't see anyone leave. Wasn't he there?"

"He was there, and he's just leaving. But our friend, the stationmaster is also there, and was just making up his mind to come over to talk to us. I thought we shouldn't give him any opportunity to reminisce. He didn't seem sure it was us, so, with any luck, he'll give up if we disappear in time."

"What's that son of a bitch doing here, I wonder," Tadek started saying, but Egon kicked him on the shin, because just then Marian Urewicz came out of the door. He looked up and down the street, and obviously did not feel threatened by two people in German uniforms, because he nodded to them and went on his way.

They followed him at a distance, as they had been trained to do.

It would have been difficult to do this without being noticed, as there were very few passers by, but they could stay well behind because Tadek knew their likely destination and Marian suspected nothing. He lived very near the café, and let himself into the modern, uncompromisingly stark block of flats without looking back.

A shadow materialised from the darkness. With a sudden thrill of excitement Egon realised that it was Janusz.

"I want you both to come in with me," Janusz said. "I need cover."

He had a key to the block of flats, and led them up the dark staircase, using a torch he took out of his pocket. They stopped in front of a door on the fifth floor.

"Don't let him see you and don't follow me in," Janusz said, "but don't allow this door to close after me, and listen. Shoot if it's necessary. Use your own judgment."

He rang the bell. Egon could hear the thumping of his heart as they waited in silence, pressed to the wall, while listening to steps coming towards them on the other side of the door, and the sound of the safety chain slipping in.

"Who's there?"

The expected question seemed to come suddenly and too quickly in Polish.

"Dietrich has asked me to pop in and have a chat with you about future plans. I'll be taking over from him next week," Janusz said in German. Egon noticed that he too wore a German uniform.

"Come in then," Marian said undoing the safety chain.

Janusz walked in without closing the door behind him. There was a gun in his hand. Tadek soundlessly, and barely touching it, put his shoulder and foot against the door. Egon, equally quietly, slipped to the unilluminated part of the wall, which faced the small gap by the door frame from where he could watch.

Marian's handsome face was now pale. He had a gun in his shoulder holster but he had not had time to take it out.

"It can't be you," he said. "You're dead. All of the Jewish professors were caught in the first action."

"As you can see," Janusz spoke Polish now. "I'm not dead, and don't try to use your gun for the moment. There's a firing squad outside the door, authorised by a Polish Court to execute you. But as we were both Polish officers once, I would like to allow you to die like a Polish officer who admits to being a traitor. Keep your gun, go to the bathroom and shoot yourself."

"You don't understand what you're saying! What about my immortal soul? I can't die without confessing! I'm a practising Catholic!"

"You're going to die now anyhow. This is hardly the time to think about the doubtful purity of your soul! If you promise on the honour of a Polish officer that you will kill yourself, I'll give you five minutes to say your prayers."

"On my honour as a Polish Officer," Marian whispered, turning towards a door on his left. Janusz followed him and peered in to make sure that it was one of the windowless bathrooms, common in the modern buildings, then closed the bathroom door and stood still in the softly lit hall, holding his gun, and looking at his watch.

It was an endless five minutes.

All Egon could see was Janusz silhouetted darkly against the light coming from the living room beyond, and a hatstand. Hanging on it was a soft velour hat, a handsome umbrella with an ivory handle and an elegant fur-lined coat.

Suddenly, through his satisfaction with the knowledge that justice was being done, and through his burning hate, he had a fleeting feeling of the waste of the handsome young man, who would never again wear his beautiful hat and coat, carry his umbrella or laugh with a pretty girl. He put the thought away with disgust at his own stupidity.

How many men, women and children did this monster help to kill? What about Wicio? He had not even had the chance to grow up.

When the shot came Egon's relief was absolute and he felt no pity when they went to the bathroom to check that what was left of Marian's honour had helped him to shoot himself. The handsome face had been undamaged, though Marian had shot himself through the temple. The bullet had gone cleanly in and out of the other side of the head, and there was only a gathering pool of blood on the floor. But the expression on the face was of such terror, that it contrasted sharply with what Egon had seen, or had thought he had seen on the faces of the man and the woman in the ghetto fire. Was it all a trick of imagination? He did not know. He was conscious only of great excitement and satisfaction.

They all had a feeling of a job well done, when Janusz put the sheet with the court sentence on the body and they left as silently as they had come in. Nobody in the neighbourhood seemed to have reacted to the shot. There was nothing unusual about it, and it was better to keep out of trouble.

They went to *Pani* Ostrowska's to change. She looked even thinner and more frail than before; her living room seemed bare without the crowd of people. Most of the ornaments were missing. She must have sold them to buy food.

The apartment had been searched by the Gestapo the week before, but fortunately they had been careless and not found the so called *bibula* – tissue paper, which was used for illegal printing. Although the search had upset the household, *Pani* Ostrowska's spirits were high because of her lucky escape, and she brought them hot water with sugar and vodka to warm them up while they changed.

"I don't know how much you heard," Janusz said to the boys, while their hostess was out of the room, "but if you have heard him saying that I was a Jew, please do not tell anyone else. Unfortunately, one is never sure that somebody might not use this sort of knowledge badly."

"You can rely on me, Sir," Tadek said at once. "And I'd personally break every bone in this young one's body if I so much as heard a squeak out of him."

Egon could not help smiling and hoped that Tadek would think that it was his turn of speech that amused him.

When they told Janusz about seeing Thomas Braun at the café, he thought for a while and said:

"I think the time has come for both of you to have some practical shooting training anyhow. I'm going back to the forest myself tomorrow, and you can come with me. I don't want Thomas Braun finding you, and if he has recognised you your usefulness here is gone."

He turned to Egon: "I'm sorry to tell you that Witek was killed leading people out through the sewers to Leszno. He liked you, and said you might be useful in the next battle. He didn't want to use you in his last job, because he thought it was easy enough for one."

They were silent for a while, thinking of Witek, who was never flustered and never afraid, and of the death which was always so close to them all. Eventually Janusz said,

"Go and say your goodbyes first thing in the morning, immediately the curfew is over. You can bring Stach with you Tadek, and report to your superiors, but I don't want anyone else. Meet me outside the bar Zywiec by the main station sharp at midday. I'll have permits to travel and tickets for you."

When Egon arrived at the shop to tell them that he was going away for a while, Otto was not there and Filomena was once more in tears. She told him about Franz Mitke, but she was not crying for him.

"Yesterday," she told him through her tears, "was the 15th of May, St. Zofja's name day and our Zofja Golabek decided to have a party at the café Fuchs in the Filtrowa street. There were many such parties going on there at the same time. Every second woman in Warsaw is called Zofja. She invited me too, but I couldn't go. There was a raid, and they took about two hundred people to Pawiak.

"A friend just phoned me. She was late, saw the horrible Krauts, and didn't go in. Poor, poor Zofja, and what shall we do for food?"

But Egon was too elated to sympathise.

"*Pani* Zofja is sure to find somebody to bribe, and Otto will find a way to get some food. Say goodbye to me. I'm going to the forest!"

He was very proud to be going, and nothing was going to spoil it. Not the imprisonment of *Pani* Zofja, or the death of Franz Mitke. There were too many dreadful shadows, and he was not going to allow them to overwhelm him. Only . . . how could anyone as vital and sure as Witek be dead?

CHAPTER 12

FOREST

The sky was a bright blue with just a few clouds to emphasise its
blueness, and the sun shone as brightly as it did on those holiday
beaches which presumably existed in some other world, taking
notice neither of the ruined, burned out houses, nor of the suffering
humanity on which its rays rested. It was a lovely late May day.

Tadek, Stach and Egon made their way separately, so as not to attract
attention, to the bar called "Zywiec", carefully avoiding any possible
German traps. Egon walked along Zlota street, and remembered how cold
and scared he was on that rainy night when he approached it for the first
time, carrying the two guns. He thought about Witek, as time after time
he dived into a doorway, just in case . . . He could not resist looking into
the courtyard of No.49, but there was nobody there. The cobblestoned
street was long. He walked down it without looking at the tall three storied
houses with their graceful, ornamented windows, and the mostly empty
shops, which lined the pavements. Everything looked shabby anyway, and
he concentrated entirely on getting to the meeting place safely, but he
noticed that the Skoda car repair workshop seemed to have some life in it,
and he knew that the Uciecha Cinema still functioned.

Like all other cinemas, it was only allowed to show either German
propaganda, or trivial films and most Poles considered it wrong to go there.
Egon remembered the patriotic slogan "only pigs see the flicks" and smiled
to himself.

He felt happy and excited. Every one of his friends would have given
anything to be in his place. Egon knew that he owed this privilege to Janusz,

and wondered how it was being justified. Tadek must have some special assignment and did not want to be parted from his brother. They were the only survivors of their family and had resolved to live or die together. Egon saw them approaching from different directions almost at the same time as he saw that Janusz was already waiting for them. He was wearing inconspicuous oldish clothes, and stood, leaning against the wall at the entrance to the bar, ready to disappear if anything suspicious occurred. Though the station, the main one in Warsaw, had been bombed, most of the rail repairs had been quickly carried out so that the trains were able to move. As he had promised, Janusz not only had all the necessary papers but also the tickets for the train going out of town.

"It's fortunate," he said, "that most of the railway workers are our friends."

The slow train took nearly three hours to take them to the small station, where they got off. They left with the other passengers. Janusz crossed the dusty road to a street where an old man with a horse and cart was trimming trees by the roadside, the boys following at a distance. They saw Janusz approach the man, say something to him and help him to pick up the branches. When the boys came close, Janusz gestured to them to climb onto the back of the cart, having himself joined the man in the front, and they drove off. If anyone was watching them he would not have noticed anything which would appear to be furtive about any of their movements. The man started the horse without looking around, and they trotted off in such a natural way, that the German soldiers on duty at the station evidently assumed that they were a part of the local village life and ignored them completely. It was only after they had gone some distance, that the old man turned around and winked at them. There was something young and mischievous in his sunburned wrinkled face, in the angle of his squashed hat and in the way he smiled.

"They're afraid to interfere too much these days," he said, "and justly so. I had them covered. We, the old foresters know how to shoot. I've ten guns under the straw here.

They've been buried until now, but I was told you're collecting them in the forest.

You'll be able to carry them between the three of you from where I drop you."

He and Janusz evidently knew each other and talked about common acquaintances, but after about an hour the old man stopped the cart under a tree, moved the branches and the straw in his cart and produced the guns of which he had spoken. They were sports guns. Someone had lovingly greased and polished them, as well as making sure that each one had some ammunition, packed into heavy rucksacks which Janusz and Tadek took as they were too much for the youngsters to carry. The old man made a sign of the cross over them, cracked his whip and drove off, leaving them alone at the edge of the forest.

They walked briskly and silently under the shade of the trees following Janusz along narrow footpaths. After a while the foothpaths disappeared, and they had to make their way through the undergrowth, diving under the branches of overhanging bushes and trees. The guns, and their few possessions became heavy; the rucksacks cut into the men's shoulders.

Eventually Janusz gestured towards a little spring of fresh water trickling from a rock from which they gratefully drank, and rested for a few minutes, still not speaking a word.

They did not want to be heard by any German patrols which might be prowling through the forest.

Egon felt the pleasure of the grass under his feet, and smelled the fragrance of the wood. It reminded him of holidays before the war, and the pleasant thought brought with it a terrible sense of loss, because those times would never come back, and the people with whom he had shared them vanished into an unknown limbo. His senses became extremely alert, and he thought he could hear a sound from the rocks forming a small hill opposite to where they were sitting, but he listened again and all was still. He did not raise an alarm. The others had heard nothing. Perhaps it was just his fancy.

*

However, there had been a movement. A creature of about Egon's age had moved in the cave behind the rocks, dislodging a stone. Adam Weiss could only with difficulty be described as a human being. His growth was stunted, his body shapeless and covered with grime, his eyes wild and his hair matted.

Adam and Tina Weiss had been taken to the cave in the rocks by their parents, who had for some time been filling it with basic foods, and hoped to hide their little Jewish family until the madness died out. All had seemed reasonably secure, until little Tina became ill.

The Weiss's were both doctors, but there was little they could do when the aspirin they had brought with them ran out. The child's temperature was rising, and they decided to risk going to a nearby village to get some more. Rational thinking became difficult in their circumstances, otherwise they would have reasoned that the danger outside outweighed the child's right to live. But then logical thinking is a lot easier when your body is properly nourished, healthy, warm and well exercised, if a sea of fear, violence and death does not surround you, if your children are safe and your future assured. Even under those circumstances how many of us think clearly?

The mother insisted on going, because a woman was less conspicuous. She kissed them all, even the unconscious little Tina. Two days later, when she had not returned, the father decided to try. He could not bear inactively to watch his child die, while wondering what had happened to his wife.

Perhaps she had just got lost in the forest, she never had a very good sense of direction. He convinced himself that she must be somewhere near, just wandering through the woods, and he would find her and bring her back. He could see her quite clearly in his mind, looking puzzled and not being able to make up her mind which way to go. Being alone with the two children in the silence of the cave made him hallucinate.

Relieved to be able to take some action, he instructed Adam never to leave the safety of the cave, to bury their faeces, go back at once after drinking the water from the spring, and wait.

Then he too kissed the children and went. Neither the father nor the mother ever returned though, for a long time, Adam was sure they would. That was while he could still think properly. Later it all became blurred, and he only mechanically continued doing as he had been told. He had tried to feed his sister and give her water, but she had stopped moving and looked at him with still, glassy eyes, which seemed to sap his strength and hypnotise him into a state of unthinking existence. All he could remember was that he must not leave the cave, and that they needed to eat, drink and bury their faeces.

Still, like an animal, he sat next to the decomposing body of Tina, and watched the three people drink, pick up their things and go. He knew he must stay in the cave, and the others continued on their way, unaware of the eyes that had watched them. Somewhere at the back of Adam's mind, thought came into being provoked by the unaccustomed sight of human beings. He wondered if these were the last people he would ever see, and then, for no reason at all, he saw a long table at which both he and the youngest of the strangers were dining. This picture was so clear and so re-assuring that it brought him hope.

*

Finally, at dusk, they arrived at a forest clearing, which looked no different from many others they had crossed, but Janusz stopped.

A large, skinny, multicoloured, shaggy dog appeared out of nowhere. He did not bark, but wagged his tail, having recognised Janusz and Tadek. Very carefully he sniffed all over Stach and Egon, as if trying to memorise their smell.

Egon recognised the short, dark man who followed the dog, also seemingly materialising out of thin air. He was the one whom he had described in German at the Church of Three Crosses.

"Wojtek, you can now be properly introduced to Sergeant Bolek. He teaches us all our tricks, and maintains discipline. Tadek has learned a lot from him already."

"Heel, Maniek!" the sergeant obviously thought that the dog merited primary attention, but then turned to the newcomers with a warm smile on his dark face and led them deeper into the forest.

Not much further away, they saw a scattering of tents, and heard voices. They were among the partisans.

Egon looked around noticing the assorted clothing of the soldiers. Some wore pre-war army uniforms, some German ones, others looked English. There were also uniforms of the forestry corps, as well as ordinary civilian suits. His attention was quickly diverted by some baked potatoes offered to him by a cheerful, dimply girl, called Basia. Her blonde hair was severely tied back and over her flowered dress she wore an old Polish soldier's jacket, which was much too large for her, but of which she seemed very proud, because she had kept it on in spite of the warm weather.

"I advise you to collect some branches and some moss before it gets dark," she said. "Make yourselves a bed. Tomorrow will be a busy day for you."

They did as she told them and slept hard, but woke up early, and tried to tidy themselves up. Some hot acorn coffee and a chunk of bread were available from the kitchen which consisted of two buckets hung over a thick stick. A small fire burnt under each bucket.

The training with Sergeant Bolek commenced almost at once and was very hard work, because he insisted on absolute discipline, and perfection in all they did. He explained that being totally sure that they knew what they were doing could often save their lives.

"Shooting with a revolver is only good for the cinema and at close range. Otherwise forget it," he told them.

"Here, take this revolver, stand by that tree and shoot me in the arse," the sergeant stuck his posterior out at the other end of the green.

"What if I hit you?" Egon asked doubtfully.

"You can't".

Very carefully Egon took aim and shot, but the sergeant had been right. Although the direction of the shot was correct, the bullet fell a long way short. Normally they trained with guns. Both boys tried hard, but Egon proved to have a natural aptitude for marksmanship, because his eyesight was unusually sharp.

The difficulty lay in the great variety of guns they had. Some were almost antique, some came from the original equipment of the Polish army, and the remainder were German, taken in assaults on German patrols, stolen from factories, requisitioned from criminals, or bought. Later, from the spring of 1944, there were also English Sten machine guns, dropped by parachute.

They had to learn to take each type to pieces, clean it, and only then use it. The shooting practice was not very frequent, because of the noise and the scarcity of ammunition.

The partisans made their own explosive devices, and some weapons. In order to be able to do this they had to have saltpeter and metal parts. These were ordered by fictitious agricultural co-operatives from German suppliers, and then smuggled into the forest.

The men regarded the two boys as mascots, but they had to train like everybody else. Fortunately, they were both very strong, though their bodies were small and undernourished.

They tried to be together whenever possible, and were assigned to the same platoon. Egon's fluent German and his dexterity with electrical devices made him a natural candidate for the group assigned to blowing up trains. One of the main aims of the Home Army was to disrupt supplies to the front, and if possible get guns and ammunitiion from the guards as well as from the freight being transported, though they seldom had much time to look. Egon now had his own Hitlerjugend uniform, but he never again went into a station to get a timetable. He would simply chat with the soldiers and guards. It was surprising how much information could be gleaned from a seemingly innocent conversation.

Then there were the nights Stach and Egon spent with their platoon laying mines under the railway tracks and waiting for explosions.

The boys were useful wherever sheer physical effort was not required, because they were less noticeable than adults. Stach was stronger than

Egon, and therefore excelled in grenade throwing, but Egon's reactions were unusually fast, which served him well when they were told to train with Felek.

"What will that little monster teach us, I wonder," whispered Stach, as they approached the clearing where they were told Felek was waiting for them.

"Probably ballroom dancing or hand-to-hand fighting," Egon giggled back.

They could hardly contain their smiles, as they came nearer. There was no doubt that Felek looked very odd. He was not old, but his body was bent, his nose broken, and his ears misshapen. His mouth looked sunken, because there was a gap, where his teeth should have been. Only the silky brown hair and the blue eyes looked almost normal. Almost, because above the eyes, crossing the forehead there were scars, which pulled the lids out of alignment. But the eyes burned with such strength and seriousness that the grins died on the boys' faces.

What Egon had flippantly said a few moments ago proved to be true. Felek taught the partisans how to fight using just their hands or any object that happened to be lying around. His crippled body moved with incredible speed. He only needed one movement to topple anyone, and he showed them how a small boy could knock down or kill an adult. Their attention remained constant, although he made them repeat every movement many times until it became a reflex action. The training required patience and perserverance, but Felek and his pupils had both.

They were learning all the time. Janusz encouraged everyone to learn what they could, but he insisted on the two young boys also having proper lessons with Basia, who had been a teacher before her school ceased to exist.

"When the war is over you'll want to go to school, and you don't want to look stupid," Janusz said to them. This encouragement added to the fact that being with Basia was fun, made them attend their lessons whenever it was possible. She communicated to them her love of learning, but even more her love for her country.

Her patriotism was absolute and was completely intertwined with her Catholic religion. She was most impressed with the knowledge of prayers displayed by Egon as a result of the hours spent with Father Michal.

"Your mother must've been a good Polish Catholic," she said. "You must never let her down, and always remember to say your prayers. Holy Mary, the patroness of Poland will look after all of us if we do her bidding. The Mother of God loves our country."

As Basia was also teaching them Polish history and geography, drawing sketchy maps on the damp earth, Egon could not help thinking that either the Mother of God did not have very much power at her disposal, or it was all just too difficult, the Good Lord having placed Poland in a very bad spot. His scepticism extended only to the efficacy of religion; he felt as patriotic as Basia and Stach, and was ready to fight and die for Poland.

"I wish we were allowed to do some real fighting," Stach would say whenever they were alone.

"We're lucky to be here at all," Egon would answer. He was beginning to feel safe, a feeling which he had not experienced for many years. Even the constant danger, which hung over them all in the forest did not worry him. They were all in it together, and they were fighting back. The various actions of sabotage, collecting weapons, and explosives were conducted by a limited number of men at a time. On many occasions some did not return, but in the immediate preoccupations during the first days of their new life, the boys were too busy to be aware of the general activities.

Whenever the outposts reported that there were no Germans in the vicinity, fires were lit, and the men sat around singing softly. They sang all the old songs, but also new ones, written specially about people like them. The songs were sentimental and the melodies tuneful.
They haunted them for ever after:

> A heart went from a young breast out
> And flew after the soldiers like a dove;
> Full of great pain and doubt
> Somebody's heart in love.

> A soldier marching on his way
> On the little heart too pity
> Stowed it in his knapsack away
> And marched on singing this ditty:

> This very very special song
> I sing for you as I march along.
> Perhaps your heart is also confused
> Totally in love suffused
> Perhaps you also love without hope

And every night cry without stop
Oh, this very very special song
I'll sing just for you
As I march along.

The soldier went the war to fight
Far away he carried his shot
He always walked with death in his sight
For that is ever a soldier's lot.

He was often made to stop and start
By the bullets when attacking he went
But he laughed while running forward hellbent
Because in his knapsack he had a spare heart.

When the fires died out and people's faces became invisible in the night, they would stop singing, and talk. "You only know me as a semi-monster," Egon recognised Felek's voice, and wondered whether their supressed giggles did not provoke this outburst.

"I was in the first year of medical studies in Warsaw when the war broke out, but my hobbies were judo, gymnastics and wrestling. I competed in various events and did quite well.

"I shall never know why they arrested me. Perhaps they were looking for someone whom I resembled, or somebody took a dislike to me and made some kind of a report, but two Gestapo men simply came into the house and got me out of bed. My mother tried to ask them where they were taking me, tried to give me food, but they told her nothing, waited for me to get dressed and bundled me into a car. We arrived at a beautiful building in Aleja Szucha, where, they told me, I was to be interrogated. They took me to a room where they asked me a lot of questions which I was unable to answer. Clearly, they thought I was somebody else.

"If you don't want to answer when we ask you civilly," my interrogator, a senior Gestapo officer said, "you'll be made to answer unwillingly."

"I'll not go into details of what his team of young Gestapo men, almost children, did to me, carefully watched and supervised by their seniors, but what was particularly monstrous was the inventiveness, and precise manufacture of some of their complicated instruments of torture. Some highly educated person must have concentrated their mind on producing modern tools for inflicting maximum pain. They did not look hand-made, but were obviously made in a factory. People have been cruel to each other throughout history, but for a country's manufacturing industry to concentrate a part of its ability on making such things is surely unknown. They had special 'swings', electrical tools for burning off areas of skin and different ones for running electric current through parts of the body, adjustable springs for crushing testicles, etc. etc. What an enormous 'progress' since the Middle Ages! And all this machinery was used by the handsome young Germans in the Aleja Szucha. That was of course in addition to what their sadistic instincts dictated. They also had ordinary whips, and liked to break people's noses, fingers and fingernails, while looking their victims straight in the eyes.

"It was comparatively simple for me, because I could not tell them anything anyway, but there were people who withstood all the torture and did not betray their friends. Oddly, some of them had a spiritual strength which increased when they had to withstand pain.

"At the end of my 'cosmetic' treatment I looked even worse than I do now. But I was still alive, because the constant physical training I used to do before they caught me made me extremely healthy and strong. The doctors did not offer any treatment, but were simply there to judge whether there was any use left in a tortured body. They decided that I could probably still manage to do some work, so they sent me to Auschwitz. There were a hundred and twenty of us in the tightly sealed railway carriage. The journey lasted two days during which we had no food, or water and no possibility to move or use a toilet. Eighteen of us died. You may well ask why they didn't kill them straight away. But this is the illustration of the German sense of legality, the awful moral degeneration of the Gestapo, who feel that what they do is not a crime against humanity, but their duty to their Fuhrer.

"We arrived in the side camp of Birkenau for the so called quarantine. Here we were put into the charge of long time prisoners, who pushed us into an enormous bath house, together with women. They shaved us and tatooed numbers on our left arms and gave us the rags previously worn by Jews who had already been burned in the ovens. Those were our first activities in the camp. It was all accompanied by casual beatings, knocking out of teeth, kicking and an occasional killing. This introductory exercise was being done by 'Haftlings', long time prisoners, who had been reduced to bestiality by the system, through threats of death, pain and hunger. It is possible that once they had been perfectly normal decent people. Until one has experienced all this one doesn't know how one would react. I was

very ill at the time and semi-conscious, which was just as well because we
had had no food for three days.

"Some kind soul had put me on the top of the three layers of bare planks
– no blankets, not even straw – which were our living quarters in the
baracks. From there I watched the arrival of our supervisor. He was a
German aged about twenty, named Franz, who could speak passable Polish
and made a pleasant impression. His number was low, so he had been there
for a long time. I wondered why.

"Franz arrived with a group of boys younger than himself, and started
arranging the newcomers on the planks, seven to a bunk. There wasn't
enough space, and all the people were exhausted. Those who fainted were
declared unsuitable for work and killed on the spot by Franz and his
helpers. Franz had a handle from a shovel, and the others simply kicked
them to death. The people who could not find a place were pulled to the
middle of the room where there was an iron stove.

"Without any sign of excitement and with a pleasant smile on his lips
the handsome young man proceeded to murder the group gathered in front
of him. He enjoyed the fear and the pain of his victims. He hit people with
his fists and with the stick, while conducting a pleasant conversation with his
adjutants and pausing from time to time to rest and light a cigarette. When
a man could no longer stand and fell on the floor they finished him off by
dancing on his belly and throat with their heels. When they thought that
the screams were too much for them to bear, the young helpers put the
victim's head inside the iron stove. After having finished off the first three
persons, he turned to the fourth and asked him politely:

"How do you want to die? Like they, or on the wire fence?"

"The fences had electric current running through them. Watch towers
occupied by SS were placed in intervals of fifty paces along them. An old
man, past chief of police, whom I had met in the train, chose the wires.
He did not reach them before several SS bullets found him, but he did not
die at once. Franz could not deny himself the pleasure of finishing him off
by kicking him to death. He killed the next eight victims slowly, working
till midnight.

"That was just the reception. I'll not tell you any more, but eventually
I was lucky. For some reason they took a group of us to Mauthausen,
another camp where we were set to work in a quarry. There's no point in
telling you how many died and how. The important thing was that, as soon
as I found myself in a detail outside camp, I looked for an opportunity to
escape. It came when one of the guards bent down near me to tie his

shoelace. He was big and well fed. I was ill, broken and starved, but my training allowed me to kill him soundlessly, and that, by the way is why it is so important for you all to learn my skills. You never know when you might need them. Anyway, I first of all put on his hat so that it could be seen from behind the rock by the other guards. I then managed to strip him and put on his uniform. It was getting dark, and the other guards, who were widely spaced apart, were not taking much notice anyway. They assumed that the starved, terrorised wrecks they watched would not be able to do anything out of order. I crawled up to all five of them and dealt with them one by one. In this way no warning was given, and we all went in different directions to reduce the chances of being caught. I managed to get here. I don't know if they caught the others. If they did they hanged them in full view of the rest of the camp. That was the routine." Felek stopped exhausted by his own tale.

Egon had listened to the quiet pleasant voice, telling the horrific story in the middle of the ancient forest, and the words which he kept hearing were "the rags taken from the Jews who had already been burned in the ovens." Was it where his family were? Hatred and loathing filled him to the exclusion of everything else, until he heard Basia's sweet voice singing another song:

> The weeping willows trembled, so fierce,
> And the girl wept aloud in their shade
> Lifting her eyes shining with tears
> Looking at a soldier's fate.
> Don't tremble willows for us
> With pity that breaks the heart,
> Don't weep my love for us
> The partisans don't have it so bad.
> We dance to the music of grenades
> And the clang of army gear
> Death scythes us like blades,
> But we don't know the meaning of fear.

The haunting melody continued and, as more couplets were sung, it lulled the hatred and the pain.

CHAPTER 13

WINTER 1943

The winter came to the forest like a beautiful foe. It covered it with the white softness of snow, but brought such hunger and cold that they thought that they had reached the limit of privation which human beings can survive. That was until Tadek's patrol returned from action a long way out to the east and brought with them a Russian soldier who had escaped from the Germans.

He was nearly dead, and had weighed so little that they managed to carry him through the forest without difficulty, but he had been a very strong man and revived when given hot, watery soup and some of the scarce food, not to mention the universally beneficial sip of the precious vodka, a small supply of which they still had for medicinal purposes. By the time the evening fire was lit, he was able to talk and someone was found to translate for him. They all listened, and for a while forgot their own suffering, which became insignificant in comparison with his.

"Before anything else, thank you," the Russian said. "You've been good to me, and as soon as I'm better I'll fight at your side, if you'll have me. My name is Alexander Ivanovitch Yegorov. I was a corporal stationed in the Ukraine when the war started. I think I can tell you the truth, because you're not a part of the Red Army.

"My platoon and I were quite happy to surrender to the Germans. We were fed up with the way things were in the Soviet Union. Many of us had friends or relatives who had been sent to labour camps without any good reason, and we thought that nothing could be much worse than the life we had, but we were mistaken. The Germans gave us the option of joining them. But it is one thing to surrender, and quite another to shoot your own people, so most of us refused. We were then made to walk to Eastern Poland. As you can imagine, it was a long walk, and in our exhaustion we lost count of time, so I can't tell you how many weeks it lasted. It seemed an eternity during which they did not give us much rest, food or drink, and beat us with rifle butts when we slowed down, so that many died on the way, but the Russian peasant is used to hardship, and there were still thousands of us left when we arrived. We were divided into smaller groups and herded into barbed-wire enclosures in open fields. There was just about enough space on the bare ground to lie down, but no more than that, and they stopped giving us food. Sometimes they even forgot the water. Certainly we were given no water for washing and had to relieve ourselves where we stood. I don't speak German, but those who could understand said that our guards were telling each other that we're nothing more than animals.

"We are strong people and it took us a long time to die and those who died were eaten by their comrades. Many were crazed by hunger, and it became dangerous to sleep, because somebody might try tearing pieces out of you to eat. Eventually the few of us who were not dead decided that it was better to die being shot, and we started digging under the poles of the fence. Your doctor has bandaged my hands, but they were so frozen that I did not feel much pain when I used them for digging. It was easy to cover any traces of digging with excrement and what was left of the dead bodies. Anyway, the Germans thought quite rightly that we were nearly all dead. There was a surprisingly large number of those who eventually managed to break out. The Germans had machine guns, and of course shot a great number of people, but we kept going at them and killed them with our bare hands. We then crawled and dragged ourselves off in different directions, because as a group we would have been too conspicuous. I don't know how long it was before you found me."

He stopped talking, and silence fell, when the translator finished. The fire had died down, and they were too cold to sing.

By the morning the branches of the forest had frozen into a beautiful white lacework, which gave no shelter and hunger made the cold even more difficult to bear.

Sleeping on mosses and branches, which had been fun in the summer, became almost a torture in the cold weather. Janusz understood the importance of keeping everyone as busy as possible so that they would not have too much time to think of how cold and hungry they were, and insisted that all learning should go on regardless, and all duties be stringently adhered to.

Everybody had different methods of fighting privation. Stach was a great one for finding frozen potatoes in the fields, and one day found so many that a soldier gave him some cigarettes for the extra ones.

"You'll not feel the hunger pangs when you take a few puffs, and inhale deeply," the older man advised Stach wisely, and Stach brought the precious palliative to Egon, because they always shared everything. Egon thought that it was worth trying, and they retired behind a large tree where they could practice without interruption. To start off they only coughed, but very soon they inhaled as instructed and did not feel too hungry for a while.

"It is a good thing you've done," Egon told Stach, feeling comforted by the warm smoke which filled him, and Stach swelled up with pride at his achievement.

Later that day, when they had finished their lessons Stach, as always full of enterprise, went to see if Tadek had something to eat.

Egon and Basia stayed behind. Hunger brought on a lassitude, and for a while they sat in silence, watching some dark birds whirling over the tree tops. Egon felt Basia's warmth next to him, and wanted to prolong the moment:

"How did you come to the forest, Basia?" he asked quietly.

Her eyes filled with tears, and he put an arm round her shoulders to comfort her.

"You're a nice lad," she said at last, "and it'll do me good to talk."

And indeed her eyes lit up as she talked about her mother, Jadzia Bujak, who had been a nanny before the war. Her husband had died, and Basia was already at school, but her grandmother lived with them, and could look after the house and Basia. Jadzia worked for a family called Fisher. They had the famous antique shop, right in the Sukiennice in Cracow.

There was only one son, called Stefan, and Jadzia adored her charge. She also enjoyed being in the Fishers' apartment. Sometimes she would take her little daughter along.

"It was a great treat to go there," Basia told Egon. "You can't imagine how wonderful it was. Every piece of furniture, every painting and every carpet had a story to it, and both Mr. and Mrs. Fisher never minded answering questions about it.

"Mrs. Fisher played the piano beautifully, and there were always flowers about. The whole place smelled of newly waxed parquet floors and flowers. They were always very kind to us too. I never went away without some sweets, but most of all, my mother loved little Stefan. I was a little jealous of Stefan, but he was so nice that I could understand how she felt. He could be naughty, but if he thought he had upset her, he would be more worried about having hurt someone than about any punishment he would be given. By the time he was four, he could read but not write properly, and when the war broke out he was already ten, a big boy and going to school, but mother still kept in touch with the family, and we stayed at the flat with Stefan when they were travelling abroad."

In fact both Basia and her mother thought that the family had left Poland and Jadzia took a job in a brush factory in Plaszow (a suburb of Cracow). To her astonishment and horror, when she saw a group of ghetto Jews being brought in to work in the factory, she recognised Mr. Leon Fisher and Stefan amongst them. Mr. Leon saw her too.

"I'll try to repeat to you what my mother said happened after that," Basia continued, "because I can still hear her words, as she told me, and it's easier for me just to repeat it all as I remember her telling me."

"Please, Jadzia," Leon Fisher had whispered. "Get in touch with Ania. See if she can help." Jadzia nodded, and said nothing, because her heart was breaking to see "her" child so pale and thin, his clothes insufficient to keep him warm in the freezing weather. Next day she asked for sick leave and went to look for Miss Ania. Ania was Leon's younger sister. She had married a non-Jew, who had been lecturing in London when the war broke out. He had not officially returned but people were saying that he had been seen. Jadzia had recently met Ania in the street in Cracow, and they exchanged addresses. She was at home when Jadzia called and listened intently to her story.

"I can get them "Aryan" papers in two days," she said quietly. "Time is of utmost importance. They must disappear on their way from Plaszow as soon as you have the papers. I'll have to organise something else for my sister in-law, if women are kept separately."

"They can stay with me," Jadzia said staunchly.

"You're marvellous," Ania smiled gratefully, "but it's too dangerous both for you and for them. Everyone knows Leon in Cracow, and I'm going back to Warsaw. I can make arrangements for them there. You shouldn't come here again, but meet me the day after tomorrow at seven o'clock at the Phoenix Cafe."

"It all went well. I didn't hear how they did it, but they managed to slip away from the column returning from work, and mother brought them home to us. We had a lovely evening with Mr. Fisher and Stefan in our little flat talking about the past, and working out how Mrs. Fisher was going to get out. Ania had insisted that they should only stay overnight. My boyfriend Jozek worked on the railways and promised to get the Fishers through to Warsaw if I brought them to the station by 2.30 in the afternoon. I took them, gave Jozek an extra kiss for helping me, and was coming home feeling very pleased. It had all been like the sort of adventure you read about in books. Walking through Cracow in the sunshine is always lovely, and I remember smiling to myself, when little Henio, the neighbours' son, ran up to me.

"Don't go home, Basia," he sobbed, "The Germans have shot your mother, because she had been hiding Jews, and they're waiting around to shoot you. It was Mrs. Marusiewicz next door who told the Germans. She was paid for it too. Don't go home, Basia. I don't want them to shoot you." And the child cried. Basia had been about to rush back, but she bent over automatically to comfort the boy, as she had done many times in the past. This time they wept together. She kissed him goodbye, and went back to Warsaw to Ania, and Ania sent her to the forest to the partisans.

"And here I am," sighed Basia, and wept again, because she had loved her mother, and had wanted to be happy.

All through her narrative Egon found it most difficult not to say that he had also been in the Cracow ghetto, and that his father and older brother had also worked for a while in the brush factory, but he only nodded in deep genuine sympathy. He knew how she felt. At the same time he couldn't avoid noticing the swell of Basia's round bosom, and wondered if it looked anything like Filomena's. He chased that unworthy thought away, and asked.

"Is your boyfriend, Jozek, also here? And did the Fishers get safely to Warsaw?"

"Jozek is still working on the railways, but I haven't seen him since. He sent word that he is alright. Perhaps they'll leave him alone. He is a good mechanic," she added proudly. "I don't know about the Fishers. I'm afraid even to ask anyone about them. But d'you know, there's something about you that reminds me of Stefan. Not the looks. He was quite different, dark you know, but you have the nice ways that he used to have, though, of course, you're a good Catholic and he's a Jew. I'd like you to be one of those who survive. Perhaps the Holy Mother will protect you. I've a little amulet I'd like to give you. Here. Take it," and she thrust a small object into his hand, and ran away.

Egon tried to run after her, to protest, to thank her, but she had mingled with the others, and obviously did not want to speak to him any more for the moment. He returned to the tree stump, where they had been sitting and looked at the amulet. It was shaped like a tiny silver shield, a rounded triangle on which the shape of the Polish eagle had been traced. Superimposed on it was a minute, perfectly carved out figure of the Holy Mary, wearing a crown and holding a baby. Her delicate right hand was pressed against her chest, and her face was beautiful. Egon kept and treasured it for the rest of his life.

One day when Egon was returning from a turn of guard duty he smelled the wonderful fragrance of meat being fried. His hunger had sharpened his sense of smell to such an extent that he thought he could discern that not only meat, but also liver was being cooked. He had a particular liking for liver, so he dashed towards the fire and asked:

"Where did you get the meat? Can I have some?"

There was silence while somebody started putting some pieces on a plate, but Egon no longer wanted any. He saw a black tail lying by the bushes.

It was the same tail which the dog Maniek wagged in recognition and acceptance of the group.

"How could you?" He turned to the sergeant. "He was your friend."

The small, deep-set eyes of the sergeant were red and angry as they looked out of his wrinkled, thin and hungry face. "He was dying of starvation anyway. His death a few days early may save lives. Now eat and that's an order."

But Egon could not bring himself to eat, and the sergeant did not waste either energy or meat by trying to make him.

Things were getting bad in the forest, not only because of the lack of food and cold, but also because the cover, provided by the foliage in the summer, had deteriorated in the winter months. A lot of the trees had shed their leaves, and people left footsteps in the snow, betraying their presence.

In spite of the fact that the Germans tried to confiscate all the crops, the peasants managed to keep some back. It was quite easy to assure the Germans that the Poles were so inferior in their food production, that all the German estimates were naturally much greater than the reality. The peasants smuggled most of it for sale in towns, but they seldom refused the partisans, when they came asking for help. In the summer it was possible to sneak into the villages unobserved, but in the winter it was much more difficult.

It was Basia, and the other girls who mostly went, because a woman did not arouse as much suspicion as a young man, who, according to the Germans, should have been deported for work in Germany.

Basia enjoyed her outings to the villages. With a scarf on her head and a bundle on her back she looked the very image of a peasant girl, and she loved the general appreciation of the food she brought back. One sunny day, when Basia went to the village on one of her routine outings, Egon and Stach walked with her to the edge of the forest. They waited in the bushes for her return to help her carry the food, and, with any luck, get a bit of something to eat for their trouble. After a short while they saw her in the distance returning towards the place where they lay hidden. Suddenly, a group of German soldiers came into view behind her. They called out to her to stop. Basia saw that she was now not far from the forest, and decided to run for it. She forgot to take into account how weakened by hunger she was, and how heavy the bundle she carried was. The Germans were young, well-nourished, and full of fun. They ran a lot faster than she, and could have caught her, but then stopped and decided to have a shooting practice. It was a lot more exciting than hunting deer.

Basia continued running even after the first shots hit her. Did they miss on purpose? Egon and Stach never knew. Helplessly they watched as Basia eventually staggered and fell very near them, still clutching the precious bundle of food. They saw the Germans walk up and kick the body face upwards.

"Pretty girl." One of them said. "Perhaps we should have used her first." The others laughed.

Horrified and silent the boys returned to the camp to tell what had happened. The peasants also reported to the partisans, and warned them not to try to recover the body, because the Germans were watching it, hoping to find those for whom the food had been intended. Basia's body lay in the fields for a whole week, a trap for the unwary. Eventually the local priest was given permission to bury her, because the Germans were worried about infection.

Egon had thought that nothing could make him cry again. He had not even cried when Maniek was eaten, but he could not stop himself from crying now. He went to the tree stumps on which they had sat when Basia had taught them, and where he had listened to the story of the Fishers. In the summer the stumps had been covered by velvety moss. Now the moss had shrivelled and became brown. Like Basia.

Dimply, smiling Basia, who also lay shrivelling.

Except that the moss will be green again, but Basia?

Perhaps there was a heaven about which the priests spoke so eloquently. If so, Basia would be sure of a place in it. Dutifully, Egon knelt down, and holding the amulet she had given him, recited all of the prayers he had learned, which seemed appropriate. In his heart he did not think it would do much good, but that was all he could do for her now.

He felt better, when he finished, because he knew that this was what she would have liked him to do.

Basia had been everyone's favourite, and Janusz led the prayers for her soul. Where, Egon wondered, had he learnt them? It did not matter. What mattered was that the grief was expressed in the way which seemed right.

After the prayers Janusz called him to the headquarters tent.

"Tadek and Stach are being sent to Warsaw. We have accumulated some weapons, and have concealed them in the forest. There is a possibility of action in town for which these weapons will be needed, and Tadek will be responsible for arranging transport. I want you to return with them. We've been very successful in blowing up trains, and the Germans are looking for us, although I've taken care that all our actions were carried out at a distance from here. However, they have planes, and now that the cover is not so good, they may find us."

Janusz strolled round the tent, making sure they were not overheard.

"I want you to live," he continued at length, "and bad though the chances are in Warsaw, the odds are now better there. If we don't see each other again and you do live, try to grow up into a decent man. Create a life where people know how to love, and clean yourself of hate. It'll not be easy, but it's worth trying. It is important that those of us who survive can represent real human values. I know you don't understand everything I say, but I know that you feel it, and remember that the right feeling is more important than everything else." They were both silent for a while. Janusz had finished, and Egon did not know what to say. He was also afraid that if he tried to speak he might cry.

Eventually he saluted, as Sergeant Bolek had shown him, did an about-turn and started to walk off with his head high, then he turned round and saw that Janusz was smiling. He suddenly became aware of how funny he must look, so small and thin, in the short soldier's jacket, which he and Stach found in Basia's bundle, and wore on alternate days. He did not mind looking funny, because he saw the tenderness in Janusz's smile, but the awareness made him turn round impulsively and run back. Solemnly Janusz offered him his hand, and they shook hands man to man.

That was the last time he was alone with Janusz. Later that day Tadek told the boys to collect their few belongings, leave behind the precious jacket, which could betray their connection with the partisans, and be ready to leave when darkness fell. He thought it would be safer to move through the forest during the night.

They were sitting with Tadek on their usual tree stump a little outside the camp, when a formation of small aeroplanes appeared over the horizon. It happened so suddenly that the tents could not be folded up in time and the Germans saw them. Methodically they circled the area, dropped their bombs, shot out their ammunition and flew off to get ground support.

The three boys fell to the ground when the bombing started and raced back when the planes flew away. The torn bodies of their comrades lay scattered on the ground.

Janusz lay on his back. His face was untouched, but his body was a mass of bone and blood from the waist down. The boys were seized by an attack of nausea, until they heard Sergeant Bolek.

"Don't just stand there puking. Get as many weapons as you can carry and skedaddle. Hide them somewhere, but remember where so you can find them again. The planes'll be back as soon as they get some more ammunition and bring the Kraut soldiers with them."

He made everybody concern themselves with the weapons and the wounded, who had to be left behind. In moments the clearing was empty except for the medical orderlies, the dead and the maimed.

The young men moved silently through the frozen thickets, carrying the precious guns, which hindered their progress.

"If we start digging holes, it'll take a long time, and any freshly moved soil will draw attention," Tadek said when they stopped to catch breath.

"You know where we stopped for water when we first came," Egon said. "There were a lot of stones and rocks there. Perhaps we could move some and fit these in between."

"Let's try."

They found a large rock which they managed to pivot. Underneath it, packed in dead moss they stored the guns. Then they moved a fallen tree over it and carefully cleared away all traces of their presence. No footprints showed on the rocks because they had been sheltered from snow by the tall evergreens.

Again, they were watched without knowing it. Some memory stirred in the dormant brain of Adam Weiss, as he watched their feverish work, but this time he was careful not to move at all until they were out of sight.

Again the picture of a long table, covered with a white cloth flickered in front of him, and he sat there with the boy who was busy putting guns under a rock.

The sound of shooting and explosions reached them when they were quite near the road, and it was coming closer. Egon's typical Weiner brain worked fast and effectively, like Otto's.

"We'll never manage to outrun them," he said. "Our only chance is to hide. We have the advantage that we are light. The tree branches will support us, and there are many strong evergreens here."

They looked at each other, nodded, and each one found a tree he thought he could manage to climb.

"I've found quite a comfortable place for imitating a monkey, but I thought that monkeys lived in a warm climate," Stach whispered shivering with cold. Both Egon and Tadek smiled but remained still. They were right. Slowly, looking behind every bush, a German patrol was advancing through the forest.

Egon worried that the chattering of his teeth and the beating of his heart would attract their attention, but they passed underneath them without once looking up.

"Can we get down?" Stach was impatient.

"No. They'll be coming back this way, and they'll have posted guards at the edge of the forest. Make yourselves as comfortable as you can and stay put."

Tadek was taking charge.

Egon climbed further up his tree to a thick forked branch, which he could not reach before in his haste. They were freezing, but they were used to being out in the cold, and knew that discomfort could be survived. Egon touched his amulet, and settled to wait. After a short while, the sound of motorised vehicles could be heard. They were coming up the road, and soon the boys could see the shape of armoured cars making their way through the bushes.

Then they heard more shots coming from the direction of the camp, and eventually saw the German patrol pushing in front of them those of the wounded who could still move and the orderlies who had looked after them. They were tied up with thick ropes. The soldiers painstakingly attached the ropes to the armoured cars, which then drove off full speed pulling the partisans on the ground behind them.

"Now see if you can find any more," the officer in charge told his men, and they obediently spread through the forest again.

The three young men were stiff with horror, cold and fatigue when eventually Tadek judged it safe for them to come down, and spent some time rubbing their limbs before setting off.

"We can't make it to Warsaw in our present state," he said. "Some of this part of the country used to belong to our family, and I know a farmer not very far from here, who might let us sleep in his barn."

It was getting dark when they reached the isolated farmhouse. Tadek told them to stay in the bushes, and they fell to the ground thinking that they will never be able to get up again. He himself slipped into the shadow of the fence. One never knew. The Germans may have set a trap for anyone escaping, but all was quiet and the dogs obviously knew Tadek, because they let him through.

The boys thought that they had waited for an eternity until they saw a woman waving to them from the door. Surprisingly they found that they could get up again and carelessly, helter skelter they ran into the house towards the woman whose weathered face was full of pity, as she showed them to the table.

"I've just made a pot of stuffed dumplings," she said, "but eat slowly, otherwise you'll feel sick if you've not eaten for a while."

She tried to give them a few at a time, but it only slowed them down a little. Nothing ever, as far as they could remember, had tasted as good as the dumplings made of thin dough and stuffed with mashed potatoes, cream cheese and onions. There was even some hot pork dripping sprinkled over them.

Their host was a leathery old man. His hands were gnarled like tree branches through a lifetime of hard labour. He sat at the table watching them silently until they finished eating.

"Now go upstairs into the loft and sleep in the hay. Nobody will disturb you, even if I've to stop them with my wood chopper. I'm glad that the lady, your mother, never saw you in this state."

The luxury of the soft hay, unfrozen because of the warmth of the house rising through the ceiling, was wonderful, and later, when he could think again, Egon felt ashamed that he could so much enjoy food and sleep while Janusz lay dead and their comrades were dying in pain.

CHAPTER 14

BACK IN WARSAW

"In Prague . . . . . . they hung out big red placards stating that seven Czechs had been shot. I said to myself that if a placard had to be hung out for every seven Poles shot, then all the forests of Poland would not be sufficient to produce the paper for such placards."
Hans Frank – German Governor of Poland.

*

Coming back to Warsaw had proved easier than they had thought. The German army was retreating from Russia in trains steaming back to the Fatherland through Poland. The trains were overcrowded with wounded and frostbitten soldiers, and the Gestapo was afraid. It was therefore less efficient, though no less vicious.

Tadek led them cautiously back towards the cellar, but on their way they heard the "barkers" going full swing, and saw people gathering round them. The boys mingled with the crowd and heard recitations of names of those executed for the assassination of the chief of the Gestapo, a man named Kutschera.

"They never gave the names of the first hundred they killed," a woman next to them was saying to her neighbour.

"Nothing much has changed; they've been killing people all the time. At least now they're getting a little of their own back," answered her friend.

"Look at this placard!" Stach liked a giggle, when things were so bad that they would have wept otherwise. The others looked round, and saw a long list of extremely strict rules and regulations, threatening death and/ or imprisonment for every trespass. They were now so used to these edicts, that their contents made no impression on them, but this one was written in such execrable and funny Polish, that they could not help smiling.

The Germans had placards pasted on all available walls. Some of the notices proclaimed that "England and America work only for the Jews". The Polish of these notices was even worse and again they giggled, but then Stach asked,

"D'you think that this could be true?"

Egon's heart missed a beat, and then he heard Tadek answer:

"It's about as true as the fact that this placard was written by a professor of Polish grammar. Just imagine, though, how almighty the Jews would have had to be if it was true."

Further along there was another placard, this time written correctly in both Polish and German warning the Germans about the consequences of their behaviour and promising death penalty for anyone taking down the notice.

"Now that one makes me feel proud," announced Stach again, and the others nodded. That was what they also felt, but found it difficult to say.

They were now walking along the Nowogrodzka Street not far from the corner of Aleja Jerozolimskie and Marszalkowska and suddenly saw ahead of them a group wearing the hated uniforms of SS and Gestapo. In an instinctive and well practised manoeuvre they entered the nearest doorway and ran up the stairs. Tadek hesitated at the first floor and then led them up one more flight.

"Gives us more time if we hear them coming in, " he whispered as he pressed the bell.

The door was opened by a dignified old lady, who looked at them questioningly without saying anything.

"We think that there's a lapanka in the street," Tadek said. The lady waved them in before he could continue.

"Please come in," she said showing them into the room beyond the hall.

"May we look out to see what's going on? We don't want to inconvenience you any longer than necessary."

"Make yourselves at home," she answered returning to her desk, where she had been busy writing.

The three boys pressed themselves to the side of the windows so that they could not be seen from the street.

Egon's window contained a cage in which a pretty yellow canary jumped about happily pecking at some seeds. He found that the cage presented a useful screen from behind which he could see what was going on below.

In front of the ornate facades of the elegant buildings the Germans were lining up a large group of people dressed, in spite of the bitter cold, only in what appeared to be white paper bags. Their eyes were bound and their hands were tied behind them.

The canary chose this moment to burst into a cheerful song, jolting them all because of its unexpectedness, and making them grin inanely for a second, only to return almost at once to watching the macabre scene below.

When the white ghost-like figures had been neatly lined up to the Germans' satisfaction, the commanding officer gave an order and the first batch of ten fell under a salvo of shots. He then checked them painstakingly and finished off anyone who still moved by carefully aimed revolver shots. What amazed the boys was that not one of the victims made a sound.

"They fill their mouths with gypsum," the quiet voice of their hostess said behind them.

She was now also standing at the window, and, like Egon, was concealed by the canary cage. The canary had stopped singing in mid-note when the shooting started. Egon's eyes turned to the bystanders.

There was the usual group of Gestapo officers, but there were also some Germans in Luftwaffe uniforms.

Groups of ten continued to be executed. After the first ten salvos a lorry came up to remove the corpses and a limousine drew up. Its door was opened with a flourish by a chauffeur and two obviously important personages emerged. The man was tall, slim and ascetic looking. His face was devoid of warmth, although his skin was tinged with sun. As if he had been on holiday, Egon thought. Did it only seem so to him, or did the face really light up after every salvo. The woman with him was fat. The fat spilled into her overfed broad face, covered the square chin, and stopped only at the edges of the large mouth, which was open, revealing what looked like excessive rows of big teeth. Her smile was of almost sensuous pleasure, as she watched the dead prisoners being driven away in piles, like tree trunks. They looked on as the next seven salvos proceeded unhurriedly, after which no human ghost was left standing.

Then the VIP shook the officer by the hand, evidently congratulating him on a job well done, got into the car with the woman and drove away.

The executioners marched away, and soon there was only some blood left in the street.

The canary resumed singing.

"We'll pay them back," said Stach through clenched teeth.

"Yes, there will be revenge," Tadek agreed thoughtfully.

"What kind of revenge can there be?" the woman whispered. "Surely death is only a release. Everyone dies in the end. How could you pay back for the years of fear and for the torture. These poor souls could hardly stand. Death was the least of their suffering."

Egon said nothing. He agreed with the woman and looked at her carefully, noticing the dreadful fear in her eyes and wondering whether like him she was Jewish. He dropped his eyes, afraid that she might betray herself or him. They murmured their thanks and walked downstairs.

When they found themselves in the street, Egon realised how close they were to Otto's shop, and begged Tadek to allow him to see how things were "at home". Tadek gave his permission, provided that Egon reported at the cellar before curfew.

As Egon furtively climbed the stairs to Uncle's office, he heard the voice of *Pani* Zofja Golabek, which stopped, as soon as even his quiet step sounded on the staircase.

"Dear God, but you're thin, little son!" Filomena welcomed him. "It's a good job *Pani* Zofja is back and we can feed you up a bit."

The women asked no questions, but put a little bread, cream cheese, and coffee with milk in front of him.

They were careful not to give him too much, or anything too heavy to digest, knowing that it could kill people who had starved.

"You're just in time," *Pani* Golabek said, "we were about to have coffee ourselves." Then she turned to Filomena, obviously resuming her usual report.

"It's dangerous to move around the streets, but people seem to have got so used to the lapanki, that now they worry more about the bombing. They stop to read the red placards to see if anyone they know is listed, but nowadays a head is cheaper than a potato. If you tell the Germans that anyone's a Jew, they'll believe you, and kill him, but they execute hundreds of people as hostages for no reason at all. Just before Christmas they shot six young boys. Didn't even bother to tie them up. People say they were so beaten up they couldn't have run away in any case. The only thing that cheers people up is the news about the bombing of Berlin and other German cities. Let them taste some of their own medicine. The Good

Lord and the Holy Mother of God know that they can never be bombed enough," she added piously.

"Yes," agreed Filomena. "I hope that before the war is over all German cities become piles of rubble, but even that will not be enough. With God's help we will pay them back."

Egon wanted to ask how *Pani* Zofja managed to get out, but did not. He knew that such things could not be discussed. In the meantime, having sipped some coffee, *Pani* Golabek resumed.

"The Germans are so scared of the underground that they have decided that everybody wearing riding boots is a part of it. So now it's dangerous to wear riding boots, because you're likely to be arrested, beaten up and asked who's your leader.

You know that all of us in Warsaw had to collect a hundred million zlotys to pay a fine for the death of Kutschera? Well, thank God, that people can still laugh. Somebody said that. 'We've paid you a hundred million for Kutschera, and will willingly pay two hundred for Himmler. How much do you want for Hitler?' "

Otto came in soon after *Pani* Golabek and Filomena went home and hugged Egon quietly for a long time.

"So you're back from the wars?" he said at last. "Do you want to sleep at the Nazi headquarters again? They've got so used to me going in and out, which I keep doing, just to have this option open, that it would be no problem."

"No, thanks. I'll be going back to the scouts."

"Perhaps that's safer," Otto nodded. "This war can't last much longer. I have just been to see our mutual friend, Dr. Wolfgang Stein, who has, by the way, asked after you. I told him that you had gone to relatives in the country. Our dear Wolfgang is scared stiff. He keeps his door double locked, and doesn't go out unless he has to. He has also asked if I'll testify that he, personally, has not killed any Jews, or Poles. I said I could, but did not remind him of his remark that 'Juden muss man peitschen.' I hope we will live long enough to tell him that we are Jews.

"That's all very well, but the situation for us seems worse than ever. I've just heard that Ludwik Landau has disappeared. Some Poles had been trying to blackmail him for money, and he truthfully told them that he had none. They didn't believe him, and said that he was lying, because Jews always had money. I've been told that his wife and daughter managed to take poison before the Gestapo got them. Another of the people who have tried so hard to serve their country has been lost. He wrote a daily report for the Polish underground. If his writings survive, they will represent one of the most valuable documents of this war, but our Poles don't think in that way."

Otto did not consider himself to be a Pole. His education had been completely German, and German was his mother tongue.

Though he had come to hate the Germans, he was so like them himself, that he could understand them better than the Poles.

"Dr. Martin Gold has also been killed," Egon felt that now he could share his sorrow. "He was a leader in the conspiracy, and helped me, but he asked me not to implicate you."

Egon paused, because tears tried to work their way into his eyes and constricted his throat, but underground army fighters do not cry, so he said instead.

"He was a very nice and a very wise man. Once, during the night, we talked about anti-semitism."

Otto saw Egon's distress. The death of another old friend hurt him too, but he had already buried them all in his mind.

"Do you know how he died?" he asked gently.

"He was hit by a bomb during an attack in the forest. He was fighting." Egon added as an afterthought. The difference was important to him.

"And what did he tell you about anti-semitism?"

"Oh, lots of mainly historical stuff, but it was very interesting. He said there were good and bad amongst all people, Jews included."

"Yes. It's a subject we discussed many times. He and I were at school together, you know. We talked about it again when we accidentally met in a restaurant in Paris about a couple of years before the war I was with some German clients, who were absolutely squirming, because a group of Germans at the next table were rowdy and rude. My clients were quite mortified to see that their compatriots could behave in such a way. At another table there was a noisy group of Italians, but their noise did not disturb my friends. Italians, they said, were expected to be noisy. Incidentally one of my German clients landed up in Dachau for saying what he thought about the Nazis. The other two learned to keep their mouths shut. Remember, there are Germans and there are Germans, though we seem to get the worst scum over here.

"Martin and I arranged to meet again that evening, and we talked about the phenomenon of being sensitive to the failings of our own kin. We too were most upset when we saw 'our' Jewish people behaving badly. Filomena used to get terribly worked up when she saw drunken Poles abroad. The answer is that nobody is perfect, but we feel particularly responsible for those with whom we identify ourselves, simply, I suppose, because we fear that some of the image they create will rub off on us. I've known a lot of Jews from whom I wanted to distance myself, and a lot of quite wonderful ones. Somebody once said that Jews are just like other people, but more so. It's probably right, and it's our history, of which Martin talked to you, that made us like this, perhaps more extreme that others. The only thing is that this does not merit a death penalty. People have always been killed in wars. Civilians were injured, murdered and robbed; property destroyed. That's the senseless stupidity of war, but never before has there been a systematic extermination, done in cold blood, without any feeling, except of a job well done. Everything is being efficiently documented, and people are regarded not even as cattle, but some kind of inferior goods."

They were silent for a while.

"I must go now," Egon said at last.

He felt guilty that he was glad to be leaving his family. Their main concern was survival – whereas he and his young friends were fighting back. In both cases lives were at risk, but their lives would be more dearly sold. Suddenly he remembered the sewer plan. Surely the fight for Warsaw could not be far off, and he did not know when he would have another opportunity to get it back.

"Could I come with you to the Nazi Headquarters, and collect my plan?"

"Yes. I suppose the time may soon come when it might be of use. Be careful, Egon. I want you to survive." The old name came out with the anxiety and memories of the past swept over both of them.

The guards at Aleja Roz stretched their arms smartly in the Hitler salute, which was returned with somewhat less vigour by Otto and Egon, as they walked past them into the building.

Casually greeting some of the clerks, Otto slowly made his way to the store.

"Who have you got with you today?" Suddenly asked a voice behind them.

Egon looked back in terror, which he did his best not to show, to see a man in the black uniform of an SS officer.

"Ah! You haven't met Filomena's nephew, Romek, who comes to help me occasionally. I need to shift some boxes around today. I might come round later. It's possible that a bottle may come my way."

Otto sounded so relaxed that he could have been talking about help to carry picnic baskets, Egon thought, but it helped to conquer his fear, and he clicked his heels and bowed as Fraulein Hedwige had taught him.

"Do you also speak German?"

"I do my best," Egon answered, "but, of course, I'm not as perfect as Mr. Schmidt, especially in writing."

"But the boy speaks totally without a foreign accent!" exclaimed the officer. "You must see if you can't get him accepted into Hitlerjugend. He's just the sort we need."

"Thank you." Otto sounded pleased. "We can perhaps talk about it when you have time."

They did not even allow themselves an obvious sigh of relief when they could continue on their way.

Otto opened the store-room door, and made Egon help him shift the large boxes around, leaving the door open so that people could see them working.

Having made a great show of re-arranging the boxes, they put them back exactly where they had been before. When they had finished Otto removed the plan from under the furthest pile, and handed it to Egon.

"What documents are you using at the moment? " he asked, reminded by the paper in his hand.

"I've been given new ones," answered Egon. "I'm now called, Zbigniew Baranski, pseudonim Zbyszek."

"What have you done with the old ones?"

"I've still got them, but they would be difficult to find unless I was stripped. They're pinned in my underpants. "

"Give them to me," Otto said. "It would be stupid for you to be caught with two lots of documents, and I can keep them with mine. Everybody here knows that you are with me, and I am entitled to hold them for you. You never know when they can come in handy. By the way, if they had caught you, they'd have found the papers. Don't fool yourself. They're nothing if not thorough. Be careful," he said again, as they parted company further down the road, where the saluting guards could no longer see them.

When Egon returned to the cellar he at once became aware that preparations for some special effort were going on.

As summer progressed, their training intensified, and the Russians drew nearer. The Soviet radio broadcasts, which, towards the end of July were transmitted about four times a day, appealed to the population of Warsaw to rise, accused the resistance leadership of lack of courage and generally inflamed the ever present desire of the people to act violently against the violence being inflicted upon them.

On the 29th of July a Polish voice from the Russian radio station proclaimed:

"The hour of action has struck for Warsaw. The Germans will surely want to defend themselves in Warsaw, creating further destruction and further thousands of victims.

"Our houses and gardens, our bridges and stations, our factories and buildings will be changed into centres of resistance. The city will be changed to ruins, and its population annihilated. Everything of value will be taken away, and all they leave behind will be turned to rubble. That is why, a hundred times more now than ever, one cannot forget that in the deluge of hitlerite destruction all will be lost, which will not be saved by action.

"By active fight in the streets of Warsaw, in her houses, factories and warehouses, we will not only bring nearer the moment of the final liberty, but will save the national wealth and the lives of our brothers."

Further broadcasts were even more definite, calling the inhabitants of Warsaw to arms, telling them that the Russian army is already within shooting distance of Warsaw, and explaining:

"The Germans, when pushed out of Praga[1] will try to defend themselves in Warsaw. They will want to destroy everything. In Bialystok they spent six whole days destroying the town. They murdered thousands of our brothers. We must do all we can so that they cannot manage to do this in Warsaw."

The broadcast asked the Polish population to help the united Red Army, and Polish divisions under Soviet command, to cross the Vistula, which the Russians had already reached.

In fact, by the 1st of August, the Russian army was stationed in a large arc within shooting distance of Praga, which they now began to enter.

In the earlier days of July, near the main railway station, German soldiers established a market, where they sold things looted in Russia, but the main thing they brought with them were lice. Some wit put up a sign:

"Good fat lice for sale."

But it was not just a joke, because the soldiers were allowed two weeks quarantine if they had lice, and by now they all wanted to stay away from

[1]Praga is a suburb of Warsaw.

the war they had started, and which their leaders were determined to continue.

Suddenly, in the third week of July 1944 the excitement grew to a fever, because the Germans started evacuating their army and office staff. The underground press wrote jubilantly that it looked as if the occupation would finish within days if not within hours. People walked about pretending to enjoy the beautiful weather, but in fact relishing the sight of the beaten Germans.

But then, just as suddenly, on the 27th of July, there was a change of plans. The German leadership decided to defend Warsaw. The columns of soldiers ceased to withdraw, armoured cars appeared in the streets, and, in the middle of the day at one o'clock the "barkers" broadcast the latest German order.

All the population of Warsaw, regardless of sex, between the ages of seventeen and sixty five was ordered to report on the following day at 8 a.m. to build fortifications. Out of them a hundred thousand people would be selected for work digging trenches, and the rest, it was rumoured, were going to be taken for work within Germany. Warsaw was to be depopulated.

Hardly anybody obeyed. The capital ignored the order.

People wanted to fight back, and the Polish government-in-exile agreed that the uprising, which had been so long awaited, had to take place. Polish General Bor Komorowski, who was in Warsaw at the time, was empowered to determine the time of the beginning of the uprising, and decided that further delay was impossible.

He fixed the date for the 1st of August at 17.00. The Polish Prime Minister Mikolajczyk went to Moscow to inform Stalin personally about the need for the insurgents to have immediate aid, just in case the Russian army did not manage to cross the river at once, because the underground army in Warsaw did not have the strength for more than a few days' battle. At the back of it all, there was always the hope that, if Warsaw managed to liberate itself by its own efforts, the world would see that it did not want Soviet type of freedom.

The Polish Home Army had found that the Russians did not want to co-operate with them when they entered Poland. Instead they arrested the officers and soldiers of the Polish Underground, or incorporated them into General Berling's Polish Army, which was in effect a part of the Soviet forces. It therefore seemed important to play the host to the Russians when they entered a free Warsaw, rather than be liberated by them.

There was an heroic, and possibly naive hope that the conscience of the world would be stirred. In any case, it was assumed that the uprising would not last more than a week or ten days, and that its success was assured, because both the Russians and the Allies would help.

The boys, of course, knew little of all this, but were aware of the increase in the numbers of underground fighters in the capital, and saw the signs painted on the walls by some unknown hand. The signs proclaimed ominously "The day is coming close". The Germans also knew that preparations for an uprising were going on, but felt sufficiently strong to deal with it.

At daybreak of the 1st of August 1944 an excited Tadek appeared in the cellar.

"I have with me special orders," he said solemnly, "which need to be distributed as soon as possible. The 'W' hour is today at 17 hours, and you will all serve as messengers at the Headquarters company."

It was as if a lid was taken off a fast-boiling pot. The boys threw their caps in the air, and had to be prevented from rushing out at once.

"Where's your discipline?" Tadek exclaimed angrily.

"Wait until you have been given proper instructions."

It was pouring with rain, but the streets were full of young people, moving purposefully about the city.

Egon and Stach were among them in a delirium of happiness. Many of the shops were shut and empty. It seemed to the boys that the whole city was aware that something special was going to happen. They felt the general excitement, as they went from one house to another distributing the orders entrusted to them.

"You two will be permanently attached to the Headquarters' company," Tadek had told them, as they patiently waited to be told what to do. "When you've distributed all the orders, go to Jasna 22. Sergeant Bolek ought to be there, and I'll try to get there too. I'm pleased to say that, although you're almost the youngest, you're the top of your group and rank as qualified scout instructors and marksmen."

CHAPTER 15

WARSAW UPRISING

Why do you sing such mournful choruses in London,
When the long awaited festival has arrived?
Here, girls and boys are fighting side by side
And little children fight, and blood gladly flows.

Zbigniew Jasinski.

*

When in people love became death,
And thundering the burning heavens fell upon us,
Blessed are those for whose hands and hearts
Fear was too small a consideration.

Krzysztof Kamil Baczynski.

*

All week, night and day,
We dragged sacks of sand to doors and windows.
Ahead of us – the Germans.
Our home will be a fortress,
We will last out.
On the seventh day at daybreak
A plane flew very low over the roof
And only the sand remained.

Anna Swirszczynska.

*

Himmler speaking at the outbreak of the Uprising to a group of German officers and Area Commanders:
(Quoted from "Civilian Population and the Warsaw Uprising").
"When I heard the news about the Uprising I went straight to the Fuhrer. You may take that as an example of how such news should be calmly received. I said, 'Mein Fuhrer, the moment is unfavourable. From an historical point of view, however, it is a blessing what the Poles are doing. In five or six weeks it will be all behind us. Then Warsaw will have been extinguished, the capital, the head, the intelligence of 16 17 million Poles, the Volk which has blocked our way east for seven hundred years and had always lain in our way since the first battle of Grunwald. Then the Polish historical problem will no longer be a great one for our children and for all our descendants, yes, even for ourselves.'

Apart from that at the same time I ordered that Warsaw should be totally destroyed. You may well think that I am a frightful barbarian; I am, if you like, when I have to be."

*

1. CAPTURED INSURGENTS OUGHT TO BE KILLED REGARDLESS OF WHETHER THEY ARE FIGHTING IN ACCORDANCE WITH THE HAGUE CONVENTION OR NOT.

2. THE PART OF THE POPULATION NOT FIGHTING, WOMEN AND CHILDREN, SHOULD LIKEWISE BE KILLED.

3. THE WHOLE TOWN MUST BE LEVELLED TO THE GROUND, I.E. HOUSES, STREETS, OFFICES – EVERYTHING THAT IS IN THE TOWN.

Hitler and Himmler's orders reconstructed after the war by General von dem Bach, who had been put in charge of crushing the Uprising.
(Quoted from "Civilian population and the Warsaw Uprising".)

*

The state of euphoria, which overcame Egon in the very early morning on the 1st of August, when he left the cellar with Stach for the last time, also increased his consciousness; he became suddenly more aware of everything around him. The sky, which almost palpably hung over them; the heavy clouds, which seemed determined to tumble down to earth but only managed to produce a heavy rainfall and the nervousness of the city around him. The air was sultry, heavy and oppressive. Artillery shots could be heard from beyond the Vistula, filling the boys with hopes of swift success. Surely, if the Red Army was so near, it would be over in no time.

Tadek had given them orders to take to various destinations within Warsaw, instructing people to report to their commanders and telling them about hour 'W' – the appointed time for the start of the uprising. They were to distribute the orders as quickly as possible, because time was short. So they sped through the city, elated and happy, ignoring the rain, tiredness and hunger. Later, when it was all over, Egon remembered certain events with an incredible clarity for as long as he lived, while others became one endless nebulous canvass of fire, noise, death and deprivation.

But, in any case, the beginning was wonderful, in spite of the ceaseless rain. Giving over the orders was like sparking off fireworks.

Light appeared on the faces of the men and the women, the boys and the girls, who were given them, and they sprang into immediate action – almost a controlled hysteria. Many of them vigorously pushed their feet into riding boots (perhaps the Germans knew something when they started arresting people who wore them) and those who had them unearthed guns, which they hid under summer raincoats. Then they hurried through Warsaw trying to reach their various destinations.

Public transport did not seem to be functioning properly that day, and all rickshaws appeared to be busy carrying some unspecified loads, so that the streets suddenly filled with smiling young people striding hastily along. They had for so long been the victims, that the permission to hit back released only joy, and having become accustomed to living with terror, they did not think that anything worse could happen to them than had already befallen so many of their friends and family. All the pent-up resentment and fury was allowed to bubble over, and they set forth with delighted determination and, at last, a purpose.

The rain stopped in the late afternoon by the time Egon and Stach distributed the last orders. Although they had moved as fast as their legs could carry them, it was not far from seventeen hours, the time the Uprising was to start, when they finished.

Their last batch of documents was delivered near the Powazki cemetery, and utterly exhausted, because they had been running since dawn and had had nothing to eat, they managed to get on a tram.

As soon the tram reached Powazkowska Street, it came under machine gun fire, but there were no casualties, because, showing great presence of mind, the driver accelerated and did not stop for a long time. Why the Germans were firing on the tram, nobody knew, but it was a narrow escape, as Stach said when they managed to scramble to the windows, which had been prudently abandoned by most adults as soon as the shooting commenced.

"I wonder if any of our people were hurt," Stach said conscious of his responsibility.

"I hope not," Egon answered, "It should start any minute now," he added in a whisper.

Almost as if to confirm this, they heard the first salvos, which changed into a continuous firing noise by the time they left the tram, and continued moving towards the centre of the city. Somehow they found themselves on Plac Bankowy, where bullets flew from all directions. Pressed hard against a house wall the boys saw people being wounded and killed as they tried to make their way across. The fire came from Ogrod Saski, where the Germans evidently had gun emplacements.

It was impossible to help the wounded without being killed or injured as well, and the people, who were now coming out of various office buildings, moved along the walls, with their hands up, making a desperate attempt to get to their homes.

Progress was difficult. Because of the firing, the boys had to run from doorway to doorway; stop to catch their breath, judge the situation and continue again. Like the passers-by they had observed before, it was now their turn to move slowly, pressing their backs to the walls, and the short distance they covered took a long time. When they finally reached the central district, they were stumbling with tiredness and hunger. The many years of undernourishment had lessened their endurance.

"The Koronskis live in that house just across the road." Egon pointed it out. "They're old friends of our family. I'm sure they'll give us something to eat, and let us rest for a while. If we keep going in our present state, we'll only get ourselves killed, and will be of no use to anybody."

"Are you sure they'll not mind?" Stach seemed doubtful. "Especially if you turn up with a friend."

"No. They're the sort of people on whom one can rely in trouble," Egon answered positively, remembering his stay with them. "I have great respect for them."

Once again Egon climbed the long staircase to the Koronski's flat in a state of exhaustion and looked longingly at the lift which had not been working since the outbreak of the war. This time, of course, he was not ill, as he had been after going through the sewers. The heady excitement still filled him, as he pressed the bell. They could hear it ringing somewhere far in the flat, and thought that there was a movement, but nobody came.

Disappointed, Egon pressed the bell again. This time they heard the sound of somebody slowly approaching, and Susanna's voice called out through the door.

"Who is it?"

"It's me, Romek, with a friend."

The door opened while Stach glanced at Egon somewhat puzzled. He knew him as Zbyszek Baranski, which was the name on the papers he had seen Egon carrying with him, but then everybody had pseudonyms for safety, and Stach turned instead to look at the girl, who stood at the door. Her blonde hair fell to her shoulders, and shone in the dim light of the single electric lamp, which still burned in the hall. She was taller than the boys, but as slim as they were. Stach's eyes stopped at her right foot, which was covered by a lump of plaster.

"You may well look," she said, catching them both staring at it. "What a time to have a broken ankle."

Then, remembering her manners, she showed them in and added, "Do introduce me to your friend."

"Please forgive us barging in like this," Egon said apologetically. "My friend's name is Stach. We have been delivering uprising orders all day and are supposed to report to the Headquarters company, but it doesn't look as if it is possible to get there tonight, and we are terribly tired and hungry. I'm sorry to be so blatant, but I have regarded this place as home for so long, that I took the liberty to come, as we found ourselves just across the road."

It was a great relief not to have to be secretive; after all, everybody now knew that the uprising was on, but, as soon as Egon returned to any normal surroundings, his speech became formal and polite. He spoke, as they had spoken at home. Susanna too played her part of the hostess.

"I'm delighted you came. It's now a week since I slipped, creeping up the stairs in the dark, after curfew, and broke this stupid ankle. There's no way I can do anything useful. My parents are on duty at the hospital, my brother, my fiancé and all the others are somewhere out there fighting, or building barricades, and I'm stuck here alone with all this excitement going on. But don't let me keep you standing in the hall. There's lots of food in the kitchen, because my parents have been storing it all the time, and I think there's still some soup. You can warm it up on the primus."

The soup was thick and nourishing, and they ate it ravenously with some sliced bread and dry sausage, which Susanna produced from somewhere. Stach's eyes were beginning to close while he was still chewing, and his head nodded over the half empty plate.

For some reason the food seemed to have increased Egon's excitement, which was still sparkling inside him, and, anyway he felt that Susanna needed company, so he readily agreed to stay for another few minutes with her, after they had put Stach into Egon's old bed.

Stach fell asleep in his clothes as soon as his head touched the pillow.

"I've a brilliant idea," Susanna said, as she hobbled into the sitting room, and stretched out on the sofa. "Daddy said that there's lots of wine in the cupboard, and, if my foot hurts me I can have some. It'll help me to sleep and stop me feeling too miserable. I didn't feel like drinking it on my own, but now you're here we can have some."

"Let me do it," said Egon, jumping up. He was not a boy-scout for nothing. His pride and joy, the faithful penknife his father had given him, had a corkscrew attached to it and he was delighted to be able to use it. This was the first time he had an opportunity to do so.

Neither he nor Susanna had drunk wine before, and initially they found it to be too sour for their taste.

"Let's swallow it quickly, like vodka," Egon said wisely. "Perhaps then the second glass will taste better."

They were using tea glasses, as the vodka ones seemed too small.

"After all," said Susanna, who had studied chemistry at her clandestine school and knew about such things, "wine is only fermented grape juice, almost a soft drink, and you need to drink something after eating all this dry bread and sausage."

Egon admitted to being very thirsty, and remarked that the stuff was beginning to taste much better.

His hand was not so steady, when he opened the third bottle, but he put it down to tiredness. He turned round to look for Susanna's glass, and saw that she was slowly unbuttoning the front of her blouse. Her face was thoughtful and concentrated.

"My mother said," she told Egon, "that I've become impossible since Lech had to report for duty. You don't know Lech. He's super and I'm engaged to him. Now, my mother said that it's her considered opinion, as a psychiatrist, that once a young girl starts having sex her body keeps demanding it, and I agree with her."

Susanna spoke gravely, but was interrupted by an occasional hiccup, which somewhat diminished the seriousness of her speech.

"My mother also said that you're going to be a very handsome man, and that you were very well developed for your age. I always thought that you were a beautiful boy. Pity, . . . so young."

By now her speech was becoming blurred and she was beginning to be bored with talking, but was determined to finish explaining what was on her mind.

"Now you've come back," she continued gravely." In this light you look very grown up, because your moustache is beginning to grow." She began to giggle, wrinkling her nose as she laughed. Then she became serious again. "But you probably don't know what to do."

As she talked she managed to finish the difficult task (her fingers for some reason did not want to obey her will) of unbuttoning her blouse. She was not wearing a bra, and Egon saw her breasts. It was the first time in his life that he had seen the breasts of a young girl. They were not the large, soft, droopy things that Filomena had, but the most delicious looking, pointed cones, standing up proudly from the dark folds of her open shirt.

He knew exactly what to do. He had seen Filomena and Fritz Myer many times, but the body lying on the sofa seemed to him to be so fragile and beautiful, that he had to touch it with utmost gentleness, at least while he was still reasoning. After he very lightly put his hand and mouth over the hard tips of the pale cones, a great urgency filled his body, and he managed to enter her by simply opening his trousers and pushing aside her underwear. A great storm swept over him, and then he realised that he had left her unsatisfied. He had heard Fritz saying this to Filomena when things happened too quickly, but Susanna seemed to doze and they lay silently for a while. Red light came through the window. Warsaw was burning, and the sky above it, which had been so dark, had now turned crimson, painting Susanna's breasts a soft pink.

There was heavy shooting outside, but they paid no attention to it. He helped her to undress: she had difficulty, because of her foot. Now all the rest of her was a surreal pink, only the hair between her legs shone pale. This time and the time after he moved gently and slowly until she moaned, and only allowed the storm to come after that.

"Why didn't you get properly undressed?" Susanna whispered, as she ran her fingers over the smooth breadth of his shoulders and felt the smallness of his buttocks through his underpants.

"I didn't think of it," lied Egon. Even in his drunken condition he had considered it wiser for her not to know that he was a Jew. He knew that nothing would really be safe until the Germans had gone. They dozed for a while, and quickly became sober.

"They're fighting, the city is burning, and we make love. It doesn't seem to be right, but it's the most wonderful thing that's ever happened to me," Egon said quietly cradling his head in the hollow of Susanna's neck.

"It's alright," Susanna whispered. "Tomorrow we may no longer be able to." Then she laughed, and started singing the old song:

"Let's enjoy ourselves and have no fears,
We shan't be here in a hundred years."

Egon sang on with her, their young voices coming together as happily as their bodies had done.

"What we've enjoyed is ours my dears,
We shan't be here in a hundred years."

"Except, in our case, it could be a lot sooner," Susanna said, her mood suddenly changing.

"Yes," Egon agreed. "Nothing really makes sense. I've seen so many people die, and one doesn't know why the one on your right is wounded and the one on your left is dead, and you yourself stay alive. It's as if some of us were meant to live and the others to die. Sometimes it's the careful ones that go first. I think it's fate. So many of those who said that they want me to survive are now dead, that I think they're up there somewhere, watching me, and helping me along, otherwise I should've been dead long ago."

Neither of them voiced the exact thought which was in their minds; it was quite possible that even tomorrow they will not be alive.

"Stay and sleep here next to me," Susanna voice was now steady, almost motherly. "You'll not be able to find anybody in this chaos anyway during the night."

And all three of them slept soundly, while heavy guns fired, people died and the rain put out the big fire the excited populace of Warsaw lit in the market square to signal to the Russians that the Old City district was free.

Egon felt wonderful when he woke up in the morning. His elation had grown further, and he decided that he would love Susanna for ever. He told her so, when Stach was in the bathroom, and she laughed her tinkling laugh.

"You're young and you're sweet, but remember, I'm an engaged woman.

However, at this moment, I love you too. We were very happy last night. After the war it will all get sorted out."

In her youthful wisdom she forgot that the war had its own ways of sorting things out. She saw them off, having given them breakfast, and was again furious that she could not join the fighting herself.

"Thank you," Stach had said. "We shouldn't have stopped but it is wonderful not to feel tired and hungry. I'm sure we'll be of much more use because of you, so you've already done your bit."

And Egon thanked her too.

"I'll never forget your hospitality," he said solemnly, as if swearing an oath. "Regardless what happens, I'll always remember."

Stach looked at him with surprise, because the words seemed to him to be excessive, but Susanna said quietly,

"We will all remember this night. It was the first night of the uprising."

Then they went off briskly towards Jasna 22 to find Sergeant Bolek. It was still very early morning, but people were already out in the streets building barricades. The sound of shooting came from all sides. Paving stones and tram lines were being ripped out, old furniture was brought down, and everything was piled up high at street intersections. The boys stood, somewhat bewildered by all the activity and unsure which way to go, when they heard a familiar voice:

"Zbyszek, Stach over here!" And there was Piotr in charge of taking a heavy table down from No.28, the house on the other side of the street.

Delighted to see a familiar face, they ran over to him and joined Wacek and Jasiek who were helping Piotr to take the table to the barricade. All their friends were there. Little Bronek was carrying the lighter pieces, his pale face flushed with effort. Tall Jurek stood by the barricade helping to pile things on top of it.

"Tadek has been here," Piotr told them when eventually they managed to wedge the table into the base of the barricade.

"Our scout group here is called 'Gustaw', but he's gone to another, called 'Wigra', who are somewhere in the old city, which seems to be ours.

"He said that if I happen to see you I should tell you to try and join him instead of going to Jasna, but I must run. These barricades have to be up quickly, before the Germans arrive."

Piotr was right. The Old City was in Polish hands and the enthusiasm the boys saw as they entered it, was overwhelming. People were out in the streets delirious with the pleasure of being able to speak freely to each other and not seeing the hated German soldiers and police. Here too they were building barricades, singing national songs and hanging red and white Polish flags, which seemed to have appeared from nowhere.

The soldiers of the A.K.[1], many wearing adapted German uniforms with red and white arm bands, were being given flowers. It was as if a great festival was taking place uniting all the participants in a wave of goodwill and shared happiness.

The boys noticed that large openings were being made in courtyard walls and the walls of ground floors of houses in order to create alternative passages when there was shooting in the streets. They dived through some of those in order to move more quickly, and unexpectedly found themselves in a room full of women who were stitching together red and white strips for armbands. Egon was suddenly seized with the necessity of having one, and purposefully walked up to the woman, who appeared to be in charge.

"We're on our way to scout group Wigra, madam," he said. "We have not yet been able to get any uniforms, but need to have some armbands to allow us to move more quickly, without being stopped for identification."

"You don't have far to go," she laughed. "Some boys from Wigra are building the barricade across the road over there, but you can certainly have a couple of armbands."

Proudly wearing the armbands and feeling at last that they belonged Stach and Egon ran towards the barricade, and to their enormous delight found Tadek in charge.

"Ah, so here you are," Tadek tried to sound casual, but Egon noticed the relief and happiness in his face, when he saw his younger brother. "Come on, give us a hand."

All that day they worked hard and happily, building the barricades and making petrol bombs in a cellar. It was extremely simple to make them. All you needed was a bottle full of petrol, some grey packing paper, a little powder in between, and then the whole thing was tied with a string. They had learned how it all worked in the forest. You threw the bomb, the breaking of the bottle ignited the powder, which, in turn started off the petrol. Sergeant Bolek had told them that this kind of bomb was surprisingly effective. They had trained with bottles full of water, but throwing the real thing was going to be much the same. In the meantime people brought them food. A woman carried a basket of cakes and biscuits which she distributed to the fighters. Everybody felt needed and important. It was wonderful.

[1]The Polish Home Army

They managed to get some sleep that night, although shooting could be heard from other parts of Warsaw and German search-lights lit the streets from far away, but on the third day, the attack on the Old City began.

At first heavy guns opened up, and then the bombing started. Bombs fell close-by on Plac Krasinski. Tadek, who had been patrolling the area with his superiors, said that the Germans must have had spies because they concentrated on the buildings which housed soldiers, but later they noticed that it was the houses with flags which received unwarranted attention, and the flags began to come down.

And then Sergeant Bolek appeared with a group of eight soldiers. Out of the whole group he selected the boys he had trained himself. Egon and Stach were, of course, among them.

"Come on, boys," he said. "At last we can show them what we can do. Keep calm. German tanks are advancing down Miodowa on Plac Krasinski. We are going to take them out."

Hardly containing their excitement the group stood in a doorway on Plac Krasinski watching a tank coming nearer, its guns firing as it went.

"Now," said Sergeant Bolek, and they all ran headlong, bent low, as they had been taught, each carrying their bottles, and only throwing them when they could judge that the distance was right. Nobody knew which bombs hit true, but the tank stopped its tracks damaged and was overwhelmed by the soldiers throwing grenades. Three tanks in all were destroyed by various groups on the Plac Krasinski that day.

"It'll be all over in a week, and we will win," said Stach happily, as tired, dirty and happy they curled up to sleep for a while on a cellar floor.

"You're right," said a voice from another corner of the cellar. "I've just come back from the river, and last night a Russian captain landed with a group of thirty people to maintain liaison with us. If he could get through, the others will come too."[1]

HISTORICAL NOTES:

In November 1943 Stalin, Roosevelt and Churchill met in Teheran, where they discussed various policies including Poland. They agreed on moving the Polish eastern border approximately to the so-called Curzon

---

[1] It was commonly believed by most Poles that the Russians were waiting across the Vistula until all those who could oppose them were dead. This certainly appears to have been Stalin's policy.

line compensating them by a chunk of Germany as far west as the Oder Neisse line (see map). Great Britain and the USA recognised the Polish government-in-exile in London and Churchill hoped that the Russians would accept it too in exchange for his backing for letting them have the eastern part of Poland. He might have succeeded if the Poles had agreed to his proposals, but they did not. General Wladyslaw Sikorski, who combined the offices of Prime Minister and Commander in Chief of the Polish Armed forces, was a much respected statesman. Sadly, he had been killed in an air crash in July 1943.

He was succeeded by the Peasant Party Leader, Stanislaw Mikolajczyk, who was not able to get his government to agree to any territorial sacrifices. His job was not made easier by the fact that the Polish under-ground was not likely to recognise his government if he too easily accepted the Curzon line.

Mikolajczyk's position was further weakened by the establishment in July 1944 of a Committee of National Liberation sponsored by the Communist-dominated National Council of the Homeland, which was set up in Lublin, the first indisputably Polish city occupied by the Soviet army. This committee claimed to be a coalition of genuinely democratic and patriotic forces, and was friendly towards the Soviet Union. They accepted the Curzon line, as well as any other reforms proposed by the Russians, who promptly recognised them as the only lawful authority in Poland. The Soviet armed forces were instructed to co-operate only with them.

Mikolajczyk decided to approach Stalin personally and his arrival in Moscow coincided with the outbreak of the Warsaw uprising. He was daily advised of the progress of the uprising and constantly informed the Soviet authorities of the terrible struggle and of the necessity to help.

The following are excerpts from a chapter called "The Martyrdom of Warsaw" in Volume VI of Winston S. Churchill's "*The Second World War*":

"General Bor therefore decided to stage a major rising and liberate the city. He had about forty thousand men, with reserves of food and ammunition for seven to ten days' fighting. The sound of Russian guns across the Vistula could now be heard.

The Soviet Air Force began bombing the Germans in Warsaw from recently captured airfields near the capital, of which the closest was only twenty minutes' flight away . . . . "

*

"On July 29th, three days before the rising began, the Moscow radio station broadcast an appeal from the Polish Communists to the people of Warsaw, saying that the guns of liberation were now within hearing, and calling upon them as in 1939 to join battle with the Germans, this time for decisive action. 'For Warsaw, which did not yield but fought on, the hour of action has already arrived.' After pointing out that the German plan to set up defence points would result in the gradual destruction of the city, the broadcast ended by reminding the inhabitants that 'all is lost that is not saved by active effort', and that 'by direct active struggle in the streets, houses, etc., of Warsaw the moment of final liberation will be hastened and lives of our brethren saved . . . . . . ' "

"The news [of the uprising] reached London next day, and we anxiously waited for more. The Soviet Radio was silent and Russian air activity ceased. On August 4 the Germans started to attack from strongpoints which they held throughout the city and suburbs. The Polish Government in London told us of the agonizing urgency of sending in supplies by air. The insurgents were now opposed by five hastily concentrated German divisions. The Herman Goering Division had also been brought from Italy, and two more SS divisions arrived soon afterwards. I accordingly telegraphed to Stalin.

Prime Minister to Marshal Stalin 4 August 1944

"At urgent request of Polish Underground Army we are dropping, subject to weather, about sixty tons of equipment and ammunition into the south-west quarter of Warsaw, where it is said a Polish revolt against the Germans is in fierce struggle. They also said that they appeal for Russian aid, which seems to be very near. They are being attacked by one and a half German divisions. This may be of help to your operation."

The reply was prompt and grim.

Marshal Stalin to Prime Minister 5 August 1944

I have received your message about Warsaw. I think that the information which has been communicated to you by the Poles is greatly exaggerated and does not inspire confidence."

One could reach that conclusion even from the fact that the Polish emigrants have already claimed for themselves that they all but captured Vilna with a few stray units of the Home Army, and even announced that on the radio. But that of course does not in any way correspond with the facts. The Home Army of the Poles consists of a few detachments which they incorrectly call divisions. They have neither artillery nor aircraft nor tanks. I cannot imagine how such detachments can capture Warsaw, for the defence of which the Germans have produced four tank divisions, among them the Hermann Goering Division."

*

On the 12th of August Churchill again asked Stalin to help Warsaw, and eventually:

*

"On the night of August 16 Vyshinsky asked the United States Ambassador in Moscow to call, and, explaining that he wished to avoid the possibility of misunderstanding, read out the following astonishing statement.

The Soviet Government cannot of course object to English or American aircraft dropping arms in the region of Warsaw, since this is an American and British affair.

But they decidedly object to American or British aircraft, after dropping arms in the regions of Warsaw, landing on Soviet territory, since the Soviet Government do not wish to be associated themselves either directly or indirectly with the adventure in Warsaw.

On the same day I received the following message couched in softer terms from Stalin.

After the conversation with M. Mikolajczyk I gave orders that the command of the Red Army should drop arms intensively in the Warsaw sector. A parachutist liaison officer was also dropped, who, according to the report of the command, did not reach his objective as he was killed by the Germans."

*

"According to Mikolajczyk's account the first paragraph of this telegram is quite untrue. Two officers arrived safely in Warsaw and were received by the Polish command. A Soviet colonel had also been there for some days, and sent messages to Moscow via London urging support for the insurgents."

*

"The struggle in Warsaw had lasted more than sixty days. Of the 40,000 men and women of the Polish Underground Army about 15,000 fell. Out of a population of a million nearly 200,000 had been stricken.

The suppression of the revolt cost the German Army 10,000 killed, 7,000 missing, and 9,000 wounded. The proportions attest the hand-to-hand character of the fighting.

When the Russians entered the city three months later they found little but shattered streets and the unburied dead. Such was their liberation of Poland, where they now rule. But this cannot be the end of the story."

CHAPTER 16

THE FIGHT FOR THE OLD CITY

THE CHILDREN DREAMT OF POLAND
AWAITED FOR MANY LONG YEARS.
FOR WHICH OUR FATHERS HAD FOUGHT,
BROTHERS DIED, AND MOTHERS SHED TEARS.
SO THE BOYS WENT TO THE DUGOUTS
TO FALL AT POLAND'S FEET WAS THEIR LOT,
THEY'LL FIGHT FOR THE CAUSE WITHOUT ANY DOUBTS,
SO HELP THEM, PLEASE, DEAR GOD.

Doroslaw Kobielski (approximate translation).

*

In the chaotic fighting Warsaw was split into tiny sections, each one conducting its own war and finding it difficult to communicate with each other. A concrete building more than ten storeys high towered over the area close to where Tadek and Bolek were fighting. It was held by the Germans. From its great height they were able to cover a substantial area with constant machine-gun fire. An assault company was created to take it, but the attackers had to cross an open square in order to approach it. Because of this the casualty rate was so high that volunteers were sought to replenish the ranks and Sergeant Bolek tried to gather people to go from his section when, after two days of attack, the Germans were still holding out.

In the end only he went, taking Egon and Stach with him, because the rest of the scout group had enlisted in the postal delivery service. By the time the three of them joined the assault, the Home Army had been able to cut off electricity, water and gas to the building. Up to then the Germans lit up the square below, so that they could continue shooting at their attackers in the hours of darkness. Mercifully, when Sergeant Bolek and the two boys found themselves in the open space below the looming mass of the block, all was in darkness, although the Germans still maintained continuous machine-gun fire so that now and again a dark figure trying to cross would fall. It was luck helped by good training, which enabled them to reach the building. But luck was with them that night. As they approached, the German soldiers began throwing grenades. One grenade came hurling towards the little group, but if fell at their feet and did not explode. It was purely a reflex action, too swift to require thought or consideration, which made Egon scoop up the familiar rounded object and hurl it back. The ensuing explosion knocked them back and they were scratched by splinters, but it enabled them to get into the ground floor through the aperture it made. The fighting continued floor by floor, and it took the insurgents another two days to occupy the building.

From now on the boys no longer knew when one day ended and another started. They ate when there was food and slept, when they could no longer go on.

When they re-joined Tadek, he told them proudly that he was a second lieutenant in the A.K. – the Home Army, and that they were under his command. The chief commander of the uprising was General Bor Komorowski. The boys thought Tadek looked very handsome in his German uniform decorated with the red and white armband and a genuine Polish military four-cornered hat, which Mrs. Ostrowska had kept for him. He explained that they had "liberated" a whole store-room full of ordinary and combat uniforms, but these were too big for young boys.

"To tell you the truth," he continued, seeing the disappointment in their faces, "they're too big for most of us grown men as well. Those bastards have had plenty to eat and are much fatter than we are. In any case, you'll not be so hot in your own clothes, and Aunt Ostrowska has been keeping a couple of real scout hats, which you can pick up later. Before you do anything else I want you to report to Lieutenant Sas. I have important papers which have to be delivered to him. It is more important for me to stay here, and I know I can trust you two. I will also give you a note for him, and you can have something to eat in the field kitchen down the road. Now dismiss."

"Yes, sir," the boys saluted smartly.

"I wish to report," Egon said suddenly. "I have a map of the sewers from Witek. He was teaching me how to go through them and said the map may be useful. Can I give it to you?"

"No. Keep it for the moment. I'm told that a number of people who have been working for the Sewage Company have reported for duty. There's nothing I can do with it. When the time comes you'll make a better use of it than anybody." It was evident that Tadek did not really see himself having to use the sewers.

"But, Tadek," Stach suddenly forgot the military language. "Couldn't we have some guns?"

"There's a shortage of weapons and a shortage of ammunition. We're bound to have some dropped by parachute to us by the Allies, or supplied by the Russians. You can have some then. I know you two are exceptionally good shots, but I can't give guns to boys, when some of the men have none. Dismiss!"

A plane flew over them, and everybody ran into the cellars, but all that fell were leaflets. Stach picked one up and gave it to Tadek, who laughed.

"These must have been written by the same author who did the placards. The man signs himself General Bor, and tells us to surrender, but I am sure the General's Polish is better than that. They say that everybody will be protected, and the population of Warsaw will be looked after. As if we could believe anything they say after living under their occupation for five years!"

This time they dismissed, and went first of all to the field kitchen Tadek had recommended. To Egon's delight it was supervised by none other than *Pani* Zofja Golabek. She was helped by a number of pretty girls eager to become a part of the uprising. Among them was Marylka. The girl's dark hair was severely tied back and her enormous brown eyes were set under straight sweeping eyebrows. Her ankles were slim and her legs long, shapely and strong. She was the very image of a ballet dancer. Stach sauntered towards her, not aware of the fact that he was blushing.

"How wonderful to see you here," he said very bravely. She smiled at him.

"It's nice to be doing something real at last. Even this," she pointed towards the kitchen. "But now we have it all organised, I am going to do some assistant nursing. I am to report to Kilinski Street as soon as I finish the last food distribution. Perhaps I'll see you there."

Stach would have preferred to stay and worship, but of course it was out of the question, and they took their leave after eating the generous helpings of food issued by Mrs. Golabek, who was too busy to indulge in her usual gossip.

"It's wonderful," she said only. "People are all helping each other."

It really was marvellous, in spite of the constant sound of shooting from other parts of the city.

They now went in the direction of Senatorska, where they had been told to report. Their elation grew as the enthusiasm of the people around them communicated itself to them. They noticed groups busily tearing down German street names.

An elderly woman stood in front of her house with a basket of rolls:

"Have one each, darlings," she said, as they passed, "I've been baking them all night to give to the likes of you."

They thanked her and crunched the delicious fresh bread, as they went along. Having been hungry for so long, they were prepared to eat at any time, and thought that they would never have enough.

Further on, a young girl was selling or giving out newspapers. They could not see either her or the papers very clearly, because a crowd surrounded her, literally tearing them out of her hands.

"Romek!" a familiar voice sounded behind them. It was Dr. Alina Korouski, looking exhausted but happy, walking on the other side of the street.

"Good to see you," she said, catching up with them. "I'm just off home for a few minutes to see if Susanna is alright. She has broken her ankle, poor thing."

"We know," Stach butted in before Egon could gather his thoughts. "She very kindly fed us and let us rest in your flat."

"How're things at the hospital?" Egon hurriedly changed the subject, afraid that Dr. Alina would notice something in him which might give him away.

"Amazing. People bring sheets, and food, wash bandages, in fact do anything they are allowed to do. At the moment we have more helpers than wounded in our section, but I'm afraid it's rapidly changing. We hear a new vocabulary of the various types of weapons and methods the Germans use. There are 'the pigeon shooters,' who sit on roofs and shoot at anything that moves, the big guns, which people call 'the pirates,' and mine throwers known as 'cows' or 'cupboards.' On our side we also have original weapons, though I'm afraid not so effective: homemade grenades called 'Filipinki' and baskets of grenades called 'Sidolki'. You see, I get to know everything in the hospital. I am even improving my German. We have a few German wounded. Jerzy doesn't leave at all. We do not have enough doctors, although I have learnt that some Jewish doctors have been freed in Gesia. They have arrived bringing not only their skills – but also some bags of potatoes. I'm glad you're well. I must run."

She didn't look much older than Susanna, Egon thought, as he looked at her slim figure disappearing round the corner.

Second Lieutenant Sas, to whom they were told to report, was very busy. The Headquarters' office, where he occupied a desk on the ground floor of a large house, was full of people. A secretary was typing something at the next desk, and briefly looked at them.

The young officer hurriedly read through the papers and the note Tadek sent, and said: "Glad you made it. Take these letters and documents to Panska. There is a Community Centre there with which I want to establish contact."

"Yes, Sir!" The boys stood to attention, collected the papers and would have been on their way, when Sas stopped them:

"Wait a minute, you two. You'll need passes to move around Warsaw. You'll find that you will be stopped otherwise. Miss Palinska will give you identity cards and today's password." He turned to the secretary:

"Please give them passes and make them valid for the whole city. It'll avoid having to give them new ones every time."

He then looked at the boys sternly and said, "Don't ever lose these. Very few people have them."

They were very impressed by the honour, and both kept their passes till they died.

Stach's circle of acquaintance within the A.K. youth was considerable, because many of them had at one time or another stayed with or visited *Pani* Ostrowska.

Now a voice called him.

"Stach, you don't by any chance know anyone who can speak German? I have a prisoner."

The speaker was a boy scout a little older than they carrying a machine gun, which was much too heavy for him, and a revolver, with which he did not quite know what to do. He was accompanied by a hefty young man in his late teens, who wore a German uniform, and held a white handkerchief in his hand.

"He came up to me," the boy scout said, pointing at his prisoner of war, "and gave me his weapons. He keeps saying that he is with us, but that's about all he can say. I'm taking him to my commander, but it would be useful to know whether he's not a spy."

"Who are you?" Egon asked in German.

The man's relief to be able to communicate was almost painful, and the words came out in a rash."

"My name is Karl Müller. I'm a Bavarian student. The last thing I wanted to do was to fight for Hitler. Some of my friends have been shot for trying to resist, so I kept quiet, but now they have put me in the army, and I don't want to be any part of the murderous gang, which has been brought over here. Most of them are not even German. Many are some kind of Mongols they brought from Russia, some White Russians, Ukrainians and German criminals. I want to be on your side."

"That's all very well, but it's your people who're in charge," Egon said coldly. "You don't blame the dog that bites you because his master had set him on you." He paused, as other thoughts came into his mind, and asked quietly. "Are there other Germans who think like you?"

"I think that nearly anyone with any sense must by now have realised what goes on, but of course that's why people are afraid. Like I was." Karl Muller answered, ignoring Egon's first outburst.

"I don't know if I can believe you," Egon said quietly, and then translated what he had heard. They had no time to dally then, and he never found out what happened to the young Bavarian, whom he could not help liking, in spite of the fact that he had decided that he hated all the Germans.

No sooner had they started moving once more when German planes appeared in the sky again, but this time it was not leaflets but bombs that fell from them.

"It's on the Elektoralna, I think," whispered Egon, as they crouched in a cellar surrounded by strangers, who seemed to be living there permanently.

"So much for their promises of safety for the population," said Stach. "Pigs!"

It was terribly hot. The sun shone brilliantly adding to the awful heat produced by the burning houses.

Although the shooting and bombing continued without stopping, groups of local people were trying to stop the fires, but when the boys reached Plac Mirowski it was lying in ruins in spite of everybody's efforts. Crosses appeared in the streets with the names of the killed.

Different sort of placards, thought Egon, but did not dare to say it to Stach.

They found the Community Centre quite easily. It was in an office,

where desks had been replaced by long tables and benches, and a group of ladies welcomed all comers. One of the first to greet them was *Pani* Ostrowska, looking as elegant as ever, her blue eyes shining with excitement:

"I was expecting the Uprising, and we've been organising this place for a long time," she told them. "All the ladies in the neighbouring houses have agreed to cook in turn and everybody shares what they have." She was interrupted by the entrance of a large group of "our lads", as all insurgents were affectionately called. A wonderful meal of pea soup followed by macaroni was being served to everybody, but Egon and Stach had to leave in order to deliver the papers to the officer stationed at the centre. Fortunately he told them to join the others while he prepared dispatches to go back. The boys were only too willing to have another meal, and obeyed promptly.

This was the official opening of the Centre and speeches were made, followed by singing accompanied by a guitar. All present sang as loudly as they could, compensating for the five years during which such singing was forbidden. All the old Polish soldier songs, the sad and the happy ones sounded and resounded through the hall – the people were drunk with freedom. Egon too was totally carried away by the music and by the poetry of the words.

The strong voices and the melodies they sang escaped through the open windows, provoking the Germans in the neighbouring house to increase the volume of their fire. The bullets whistled outside, but the singing went on with a relentless joy – nobody took any notice whatsoever of the deadly din beyond the walls. It was not done to show fear, the singing was the most important thing at the time.

Pani Ostrowska crept up to Egon and Stach and gravely handed them two scout caps which she had decorated with the red and white colours of Poland. They were singing the solemn and patriotic "*Rota*" as they received them. It was all most appropriate.

The way back was more difficult. They were supposed to return to Lieutenant Sas, but, because of the constant shooting and bombing they frequently had to break their journey and dive into the cellars, where all the population of Warsaw appeared to be living.

It was just as well they had their permits and knew the password, because they were stopped on every corner. Their training and quick reactions helped them to remain alive. They had been taught to stop and shelter in doorways at regular intervals, and they observed this routine all the time. On one occasion they took cover faster than usually, reacting to an unexpected sound. They heard the deafening explosion at the very moment they stopped inside.

"That must have been what *Pani* Alina called a 'cow,' Egon said.

Very cautiously they crept out of the doorway. There was no damage in the immediate vicinity, but then they saw a man lying dead in the street.

"He was killed by a splinter," said the woman, who was bending over him.

The missile had landed in the next street. They did not even notice the destruction to buildings. It was the massacred bodies, without arms and legs, strewn all over the pavement, which held their attention. Silently they plodded through the area, carefully avoiding the dead and the wounded, already being cared for by young nurses, called over by those of the passers-by, who had managed to survive.

The streets now began filling with streams of stunned-looking people, carrying bundles. They were refugees from Warsaw suburbs. Some of them took refuge in the cellar into which the boys jumped when they saw another approaching plane.

Apart from the noise of explosions outside and quiet whimpering all that could be heard in the semi-darkness was the voice of a woman who sat on a heap of rubble under the window.

She was motionless and rigid like a carved figure. The only moving part of was her mouth. It articulated the words precisely, and dispassionately, as if she was making a prepared speech, or a report. Her face looked ashen under her dishevelled dark hair lit by the shaft of light coming from outside.

"We lived on the Wola," she recited. "The Germans came and told us all to come out of our houses. They said we would be allowed back later. But for the last five years everything they had told was lies, so many mothers with small children tried to stay behind. My neighbour said I could hide out with my two children in a locked room he had at the back of his flat, so we went. My son Tom is six years old, and my daughter Marysia is six. We were sitting there with other women and children, and I was telling them a story to keep them from hearing the shooting outside, when the door burst open and in came a group of Mongols and a few drunken White Russians.

"First of all they took away all our rings, watches, and anything else of value, and then they repeatedly raped us. Also the bigger girls. I was thanking God that Marysia is only four, but then they all got annoyed because we were trying to defend ourselves.

"They thought what they were doing was perfectly normal and this increased our horror. In their fury they started to shoot, trying to kill everybody. When my children fell, I fainted. I thought I was dead, but I woke up in front of the house with those who had left at once. They told me that a big Russian threw me out of the door. There were other groups like ours standing in the street, and on the ground lay the bodies of the men they had shot. That was the shooting we had heard. Then all of them, the Germans, the Mongols and the White Russians systematically burned all our homes and everything and everybody who was still in them. The flames rose high, and into them they threw the bodies of those they had killed, without giving them a Christian blessing and burial so that at least their souls could have rested in peace. The Germans then separated the remaining men from the women, but the other mob went on to pillage the next house, and we escaped through burning streets, which were full of dead and burned bodies. May God punish them, for they do know what they are doing."

Again there was a silence in the cellar, interrupted only by sobs, and the air was filled with pity and fear, as they listened to the woman's precise speech and the explosions outside. She stopped for breath and started speaking again, repeating exactly what she had said before.

"She keeps saying all this over and over again," a man said to nobody in particular, as the boys started towards the door. Egon looked back at the woman, and the grief on her frozen face was so tangible that it seemed to be a separate presence. He made himself turn away and followed Stach out of the cellar.

Lieutenant Sas and his office were no longer where they had been before. There was a heap of rubble, where it had been, and the area was occupied by the Germans. They turned back, and showed their passes to a young officer who was passing with a group of soldiers. He told them that Lieutenant Sas was in the Old City.

"But," the young officer added, "carrying papers does not require two of you. One's enough. The other can be doing another job. No doubt they'll tell you when you report."

"We'll stick together as long as we can, no matter what he says," Stach said as they struggled off again.

"That's right. We will," answered Egon, hating the very idea of being on his own again.

When they finally arrived at the Old City, there were many people in the streets. Soldiers' uniforms could be seen everywhere. News reports were being broadcast from a loudspeaker in the market place and services held in churches.

They managed to reach their lieutenant, but found it difficult to recognise him, because a big bandage hid a part of his face.

"It's not as bad as it looks," he said, noticing how studiously they avoided looking at him. "Miss Palinska will assign you to the postal service. The boy scouts have been doing a superb job delivering letters for people. It is marvellous for the morale. At least people know what is happening to their families, however bad it may sometimes be. Report to Kilinski Street. Your scout group is located there, and you can get some food and rest before you start on your next assignment."

They did not know how long the Uprising had lasted. Was it days or weeks? Time did not exist, but suddenly they were aware of utter weariness, and were glad to be directed somewhere where they could rest. Stach also felt happy because Marylka had said that she too was going to Kilinski Street.

Kilinski Street was humming with life. There were AK soldiers, sanitary personnel and boy and girl scouts, moving purposefully around. On the ground floor of the house to which they were directed was a kitchen, where hot "coffee" was prepared for the those who manned the barricades. Stach and Egon were delighted to see all of their "cellar" crowd, but too tired to talk. A couple of mattresses on the floor in a neighbouring house were assigned to them, and they went to sleep.

In the morning little Bronek woke them because he had collected their food issue and brought some warm coffee from the kitchen downstairs to go with it.

"Where are the others?" asked Stach, when he completely woke up.

"Piotr is in charge of our unit, and very pleased to have you two with us. He's gone to get our instructions for the day. All the others are still on duty but will be coming back soon, except Jasiek Augustyn. He was one of the first to go," answered Jurek, trying to appear unaffected and matter of fact. "He had delivered his letters, and was coming back, when a shot got him. He managed to get back, and we found him in hospital. He said that he knew he was going to die, but he was glad that the priest had come and he could confess. Not like his mother, who had been shot when smuggling meat from Karczew, and like his brothers and sisters, whom the Germans burned in their house while Jasiek was delivering meat to Warsaw, doing his mother's job. Poor souls! They had no priest to give them peace."

They were quiet for a time, and Egon remembered what *Pani* Golabek had said about big Maria Augustyn. Jasiek must have been her son, but now it did not make any difference. He would never be able to talk to him about his mother's deliveries, which had made life better for them. He wished they had all said a little more about themselves to each other, but, of course, at the time, it had been better not to do so. If he survived, he thought, he would try to get people to tell him who they were and what they did.

And then Stach said in his solemn way, "Let's face it. Some of us are bound to die, but the important thing is that those of us who live should be happy. It's no use always living in mourning. Tadek and I started off like that, but it was no good and we thought that our parents would not have wanted it. So we always try to remember them, but also try to go on living and laughing."

"Yes," said Egon, voicing the thoughts of the others. "I suppose we've all been doing this, but it's always hard at the beginning."

The days in the postal service were a blur for Egon and Stach, because the constant danger made them concentrate entirely on surviving their

rounds. They would collect the letters from the boxes assigned to them and try to deliver them, after they had been checked to ensure that unsuitable information did not fall into enemy hands. The notes had to be short, unsealed and referring only to the whereabouts and health of families. Usually they simply consisted of basic information such as: "we are alright," followed by names of the family members, "and are at" giving the address." Finally there was nearly always the question: "Who else of the family is known to be alright?"

Although Stach and Egon were given separate bundles of letters, they would re-sort them, and, by moving as fast as possible, distribute them together within the same time taken by those who operated singly.

The first time they saw Russian planes flying above Warsaw, made them feel quite sure that the Uprising would be victorious within days, especially when they were told that some food and arms had been dropped, but they were so tired that even hope was not clear. All their journeys consisted of constant diving through holes in the walls of cellars and fences, where chalked signs indicated the neighbouring streets accessible from a given point.

There was only one place where you could cross one of the main arteries of Warsaw – Aleja Jerozolimskie. It was secured with bags of earth, and, if you were very lucky and kept very low, you had a good chance of getting through without injury. The scouts arranged a string with a pulley on which they could move their letters from one side to another without actually going across.

It was while waiting with a group of other people, for the bundles to be pulled through that they talked to a young woman liaison officer, who had recently been to the river area.

"A Russian major came over with some of his men to make contact with us," she said "He was still there when I left and was disgusted that his people were delaying taking Warsaw. They're just standing there in the suburbs and doing nothing."

"They're waiting till we're all killed," butted in an older man, who was listening to their conversation. "Then they can take over without any opposition. There will be no fighters left, and they can have their own kind of government."

"And the Allies," said another woman, "are no better. They've liberated the French, who have never done anything to fight the Germans, and seem to be having a holiday instead of coming over quickly."

"There've been some British air drops of food and weapons," the man said, "but most of it seems to be falling in the wrong places and going to the Germans."

The first wave of enthusiasm was beginning to wear thin, as water supplies to the city were cut off, and food began to be scarce. But, still people seemed to manage. Wells were dug throughout the town, and the boys saw long queues waiting for water.

The Germans saw them too, and, whenever possible directed their fire at them, so that getting water was becoming extremely dangerous. Furthermore, quarrels arose, because the army had priority, and people grumbled. They also grumbled about being dragged out of the cellars to help rebuild the damaged barricades. It was no longer always beneficial to be wearing the army insignia.

However, the scout postal service was both popular and efficient, each "postman" doing his or her utmost to bring some kind of an answer to their customers. Often the answers were indirect, given by neighbours. Sometimes hopeful. "They have left Warsaw. She said they were going to Aunt Wikta in the country." At other times they could not be traced however hard the boys tried to question all around. Sometimes the reply would be that there had been a direct hit on the house, because in some districts the Germans were now bombing regularly and methodically house by house with a truly Teutonic thoroughness and deliberation.

So much so, that when, while returning from their delivery round they found themselves by the house from which they had watched the Germans executing hostages, Egon calculated that it would be at least fifteen minutes before it was hit, because two buildings separated it from the last targets. Both boys looked up. The cage was still in the window and something bright yellow fluttered in it. An irrational desire to save the canary overcame Egon.

"Wait for me here," he said to Stach.

The two boys stood by what used to be a basement window of a house still a reasonably safe distance away on the other side of the street which had already been bombed. They had rested there for a while, but moved on because of the stench of dead bodies coming from the ruins. Egon asked Stach to wait in a tone he used rarely, but Stach knew him well enough by now, not to argue with him when he spoke in this way. There was no point. He would not even appear to hear. As fast as he could, Egon raced to the house and up the stairs. The door to the flat was hanging open, there was no glass in the windows; all the rooms were completely empty, except for some dirty papers on the parquet floor. He did not stop to think why the canary was still there, but simply grabbed the cage and started running back.

He had been sure that he had at least another ten minutes to go, but suddenly there was an enormous crash.

When he regained consciousness he was lying flat on his back still holding the cage which was resting on his chest. He looked up and noticed that the canary in it was dead, and then, raising his eyes further, he saw Stach's dirty, tear stained face above his.

"It's alright," Egon said. "I'm O.K."

"But you can't be," Stach said incredulously. "It was a direct hit. The bastard came back too early. Must be in a hurry to get off duty," he added, trying to sound nonchalant. "Besides, there's blood under your head."

Egon became aware of a pain at the back of his head, and an unpleasant stickiness around his neck. He put the cage beside him and using both hands to support himself managed to sit up.

"There can't be all that much wrong with me," he said, remembering his First Aid training, "if I can do that, as well as talk and think properly, though I do feel a bit dizzy and bruised. I must have been thrown out through the window by the force of the explosion. Perhaps I'm not meant to die just yet," he tried to smile, but the muscles of his face did not quite make it, because of the pain. They always carried field dressings, and Stach expertly stemmed the blood.

The cut in the back of the head was not big but looked ugly. A sudden noise above them made them look up, and Egon thought he was hallucinating. It was broad daylight – an enormous American Superfortress moved through the sky dropping large boxes on parachutes.

"Now we must win!" Stach said happily, "but in the meantime I'm taking you to see Dr. Korouski at the hospital."

"I hope that this time the stuff will not fall into the German hands, but we'll get it." Egon's pain made him pessimistic.

Stach managed to get him to the hospital as well as obtain Dr. Korouski's personal attention, although normally only the most serious cases were referred to him.

"Hm" said the Doctor, "you've been bloody lucky. There's a small splinter in there, but the wound is clean and will remain so if I stitch it up. After the war you can have an operation to get it out, though it shouldn't do you much harm where it is. I am not going to try removing it, because I would only enlarge the wound, and possibly cause infection under present conditions. You seem to be bruised all over, but if any of your bones had been broken you'd undoubtedly have noticed it during your walk here. I'll put a dressing on your head in a minute and you'll be as good as new."

He proved to be right. The splinter did not give Egon any trouble, though he never had it removed but he often wondered whether the feeling of unreality, which stayed with him for weeks from the moment he looked at the dead canary was a direct result of his injury.

There was no anaesthetic, and the pain of the stitching was excruciating, but mercifully short, because of Dr. Korouski's skill.

"You'd better both have some rest. There's a bit of room in that corner over there," said the doctor looking at the space longingly. He would have liked to lie down there himself.

"I still think that it's only by the grace of the Holy Mary and Jesus Christ that you are alive," Stach said as they settled to sleep. "They must be looking after you."

It was late afternoon when they went to report back to Kilinski Street, but it was difficult to recognise it.

Instead of being full of the energetic, cheerful crowd of happy young people it was grotesquely covered with small bits of human bodies. Odd arms and legs, as well as half-burned corpses lay scattered amongst the ruins. A group of people had just finished digging a communal grave, while others collected the pieces, wrapped them in white sheets and started putting them into the freshly dug hole.

Stunned they rushed into "their" house, which was still standing. It was empty. In their room an arm lay next to a rucksack, but there was no body attached to it. Piotr sat on the floor. His face was twisted with hatred.

"I wasn't here when it happened. I have just returned from collecting the letters. The others were resting and waiting for me."

"Do you know what happened."

"Yes. Our soldiers captured a tank on Podwale. The boys managed to get it down to here, and then stopped, because a funeral cortege was passing by. Lots of people came out to look at the tank, all the girl guides rushed out, as well as the girls from the kitchen. It was a booby trap! I don't know how much explosive the bastards put in it, but even the people who stayed inside their houses have been killed. We're the only ones of our lot left."

"And Marylka? She was supposed to come here. Is she alive? D'you know?" Stach whispered through clenched teeth.

"I saw her. She is one of the few who survived, because she had not run out to take a ride on the tank with the other girls from her room. She was buried in the rubble, but they've got her out. Only," he paused and took a deep breath, "her legs are missing."

Stach did not say anything for a while, but his face turned white, and then he was violently sick.

"I must go to her. I must go to the hospital," he whispered, when the sickness passed.

"Don't," Piotr said. "You can go tomorrow, when you've taken control of yourself. Now you're under orders to stay. And she's stronger than you. You know what she said? She said, 'I wouldn't have been a very good ballerina anyway. I'll study something important after the war.' "

And then the three of them forgot that they were grown men, brave soldiers of the Home Army, and cried, like the children they really were. They cried because they did not know that Marylka would do exactly what she had said.

"We would have been here too," Egon said eventually, "if it wasn't for a small yellow canary."

Somebody told them that Lieutenant Tadek was on the barricade very close by. Piotr did not bring any instructions with him, so they decided that it would be good for Stach to see his brother.

They all felt that they had to be where the fighting was in order to hit back. Just as they reached the barricade, keeping low, as they had been taught in the forest, and then climbing to the top to meet Tadek, they saw a large German tank. It was still some way down the road, but was relentlessly coming towards them.

They knew from experience that it was possible to deal with tanks by throwing petrol bottles at them, but the Germans knew it too. The tank moved slowly, and all around it walked a dense crowd of Polish women. They were herded at gun point. Behind them walked German soldiers holding their guns at the ready to shoot any of the women who swerved, or anyone who would impede the tank in its progress towards the barricade.

"Please, Tadek, give Stach and me guns," Egon shouted, and Tadek nodded. "You're now acting sergeants and entitled to weapons. Lend the boys your guns," he ordered.

Egon had noticed the perfect spot that could be reached direct from the barricade through a hole, which had been a window on the first floor of an adjoining house. He climbed up to it followed by Stach. Moving to the other side of the house, they found themselves behind the tank, directly above the soldiers.

Now, exactly as Sergeant Bolek had shown them, they took aim. They had been used to sports guns, similar to those which they now held in their hands, and one by one they started to shoot down the soldiers who guarded

the women. It was almost like an exercise, Egon thought, and heard shouts
from the barricade telling the women to run. The women were not slow
to do so. Some of the soldiers shot at the women, the others tried to see
from which direction the shots came and then turned back and took cover,
before the tank was first immobilised by expert petrol bottle throwers, and
eventually blown up. Stach jumped up in excitement, the plank on which
he stood broke and he fell into the German held street beyond the barricade.
It was not too high, and he did not seem to be too badly hurt, but before
he could move, a hand grabbed him and drew him into a doorway.

Egon braced himself to shoot, but the German soldier stayed in the
doorway. He soaked the stunned boy with petrol, leisurely took out his
lighter, and lit him like a cigarette. During all that time Egon was climbing
down from his aerie, and Tadek, who saw it all from the barricade went
berserk. He grabbed a machine gun and went running into the German
soldiers, shooting as he went. Others followed him, pushing the Germans
back, but Tadek was killed minutes before Egon managed to reach Stach,
who was now no longer covered with flames. The German had either been
in a hurry, or did not have much petrol. Stach was light and Egon managed
to pull him out of the danger zone. It was all too late, because Stach was
so badly burned that he could not survive, despite the efforts of the
ambulance staff, who were on duty at the barricade.

"I'm glad I'm dying," he mumbled to Egon, "because I hurt too much,
but remember what we talked about . . live . . happy."

He lost consciousness and mercifully did not regain it until he died some
long minutes later. During that time, too, Egon was not aware of very
much. Stach's head, with burned-off hair and unrecognizeable face, lay in
his lap. There was a ghastly smell of fried meat coming from him, and
Egon felt sick like Stach had been when he heard about Marylka. But he
did not want to move, and kept swallowing hard, fighting the sickness and
trying not to think at all.

CHAPTER 17

THE LAST FIGHT

WE NEEDED TO GO A LONG WAY INTO HATRED.
WHEN THE FIGHTING STOPS,
MY SKELETON WILL HAVE IN ITS HAND
MY FATHERLAND'S FLAG,
COVERED IN BLOOD AND STINKING OF DEAD BODIES.
ONE GOES THAT WAY IN ORDER TO BECOME A MAN.

Krzysztof Kamil Baczynski.

*

"I'll see to it that you get a medal for that," a voice said behind Egon. "It was bravery above the line of duty."

Perplexed, Egon looked up to see none other than Lieutenant Sas, who was now, judging by his insignia, a captain, but he could not answer him. He knew he would cry if he tried to speak, and his eyes closed, as if any effort to communicate was too much for him.

"Let the boy rest," somebody said, and he felt himself being lifted and put on one side, like a piece of luggage, which happened to be in the way.

Suddenly he wanted to laugh. Orders, he thought. Who needs orders when they lose a friend. And what about poor Tadek. What a waste! What a typical bloody, unthinking, wonderfully brave Pole. And why am I still alive? What is it that saves me every time? My parents' prayers? Basia's little Madonna? and he made sure it was still on the string around his neck, Fate? Or simply luck.

Suddenly bits of Ecclesiastes he had memorised while learning Hebrew with his father came into his mind. The Hebrew had all gone, but the words had been like a magic incantation and remained with him. His father had told him their meaning in Polish.

"There is a time to be born and a time to die;

A time to plant and a time to uproot;

A time to kill and a time heal;"

There was a lot more of that, but he could not remember it. Perhaps there will be a time to heal, but now it was time to kill. He picked himself up and walked up to the barricade, where there appeared to be a lull in the firing. Probably, as had been the case wherever he and Stach had been, the Polish fighters were running out of ammunition. Captain Sas was still there. He was not as young as he had seemed when Egon first saw him. He probably came from the real army, so Egon reported in proper military fashion.

"Acting Sergeant Zbigniew Baranski, pseudonym Zbyszek, reporting for duty."

The captain looked puzzled. He knew that all his NCOs were very young, but this was a child. Before he could say anything one of the soldiers butted in.

"That's correct, sir. Lieutenant Tadek made them both Acting Sergeants before he let them have our guns." He was obviously pleased to have his weapon back.

"Tadek reported that his brother's friend had a map of the sewers. Are you the one who's supposed to have it?" asked Sas.

"Yes, sir. I think I still have it." Egon looked through his pockets. The map was still there.

"Lieutenant Tadek mentioned it again, when we discussed a possible retreat to the City Centre. The sewers appear to be the only way through. Go to the field kitchen. Perhaps they still have some food. Eat something and report back to me."

"We've pulled the riding boots off the Germans you shot, and there are also some hip guns and ammunition. Here's a pair of boots for you and a gun, if you want it."

Of course Egon wanted both. His feet were big, and the boots were only a bit too large, and very comfortable. And who could possibly refuse a gun? He was also sure that if that particular field kitchen still had any food, some of it would be given to him.

Pani Zofja Golabek continued to be in charge, but she no longer looked happy.

"Are you alright, Romek?" she said when she saw the dressing protruding from under his cap. "Go and sit in the corner over there, and I'll bring you some soup," she continued without waiting for an answer.

She brought him a bowl of gruel, which he started to eat greedily, suddenly realising how hungry he was. In spite of his hunger, he had to keep stopping to spit out the husks of which the soup was full.

"That's right," Pani Zofja said, "the boys call it 'spit soup'. There's no other way of eating it. Take your time. I've tried to give you the thick."

Slowly now he continued to eat, the pain within him dulled by the general discomfort. He was dirty and sweaty, he could not get used to the the stench of dead bodies, and his head hurt. *Pani* Zofja's words came to him as if they had been spoken in the next room, but he listened attentively out of habit; he had always liked hearing her stories.

"The Germans are calling the population to give up, but who can trust them? They've burned the hospital in Wola together with all the wounded; they kill everybody they take prisoner too, though sometimes they mutilate them first. And then they burn the bodies without even giving them a Christian burial. Our soldiers are forbidden to kill prisoners, but they shoot the SS and the Gestapo. You can't stop people doing that; the others are made to carry water, and are often killed by their own snipers, but otherwise they're treated as prisoners of war. But the city . . . Our beautiful Warsaw is being deliberately destroyed. Palace after palace, monument after monument and church after church, not to mention house after house, and all the museums have been looted a long time ago. If there is any justice, I hope and pray to Jesus and Holy Mary, that before this war is over each and every one of the German cities will also be destroyed, though I doubt if anyone will be as thorough as these bastards."

She was silent for a while, and then went on more quietly.

"One has to hand it to them. They plan all they do, and everyone obeys orders. Not like us Poles. We're capable of enormous self-sacrifice, and our bravery has no match, but when it comes to organising or obeying we're no good. That's why our greatest king brought in the Jews, but now they've all been killed, so even if we have anything left to be organised, there'll be nobody left to do it. Now look at this uprising. Nobody made sure that it will all work. Everybody wanted to help, but nobody really knew what they were doing, and now the fight in the Old City is all but over, and I hear that the army is getting out to the City Centre, but the civilian population is being left behind. There's still food for the fighters, but a lot of ordinary people are dying of hunger, and lack of water, not to mention every kind of illness, so there's a lot of resentment. Anyway, now that you've finished eating I'll stop talking and you must tell me all your news."

Mrs. Golabek listened with all her soul and all her attention, as with great difficulty he told her all, except for the night with Susanna.

He might have even told her that, although in his mind it would have been a kind of betrayal, because *Pani* Zofja possessed the ability to listen with such complete sympathy, that one felt like pouring out all the pain and all the happiness one had accumulated.

Then something made him look up and he saw Dr. Alina Koronski standing a few steps away from him. She was swaying with exhaustion, so he ran up to her, and brought her to the place where he had been sitting.

Wordlessly, *Pani* Zofja brought in another plate of soup, and handed it to her. Alina ate in the absentminded way of a sleepwalker. She did not even spit out the husks of barley, but choked from time to time, and *Pani* Zofja produced a glass of the precious water, which the other woman drank greedily. Then she whispered;

"It was a direct hit on the house. Jerzy had gone to a look at Susanna's leg and close his eyes for an hour. He was completely exhausted. He'll never open them again. They're both dead. I wanted to go too, but there was work to do, and I thought he needed the rest, and now the hospital is gone. They burned it with all the patients. I don't know how I came here."

Egon put his arms round her, and was not ashamed to cry with her.

First Stach and now Susanna, he thought.

All his friends were being killed around him. He tried not to think of Susanna lit up by the pink glow of fires. His brain was numb anyway, but the picture persisted, bringing with it a further pain of a kind he had not yet experienced.

Eventually he said. "I have to report to my superior officer, but I'll be back."

"Don't worry," *Pani* Zofja said. "I'll look after her."

There was not much left of the barricade, or its defenders by the time Egon returned. Captain Sas now had his arm in a sling, but was calmly arranging the retreat. Egon noticed that Piotr was also there.

Why is he alive, a thought came to him unasked, if Stach and Tadek are dead?

"I hope you're better now," said the captain. "We're going to retreat to the City Center. There are guides seeing people through the sewers, but it'll be useful to have you as well."

"I'm fine, thank you, sir. There are two women there, whom I've promised to lead through if I go. One is a doctor, the other is in charge of the field kitchen in which there's no longer any food. We'll need people like this. They can hardly be counted as civilians."

"Very well," the older man agreed. The boy had an astonishing air of authority, but he was not cheeky. His voice was most respectful and his request would have been sensible if it had come from a fellow officer.

They were not the only ones leaving. It was not dark during that night, because the entire city was burning. The whole of Dluga Street was full of soldiers. The wounded were carried on stretchers; those who could still walk were supported by their comrades. Rockets fell, putting even more light on the scene, giving it a further similarity to hell, as described to Egon by Father Michal.

*

Egon walks mechanically, when they are able to move forward, or sits, or stands, leaning on any available piece of ruin, when the column comes to a standstill. It takes many hours till their turn to enter the sewers comes. The heat is unbearable, and there is no water unless you can afford to buy it at 600 zlotys a glass. Egon does not have 600 zlotys, but the amount stays in his mind, because he wishes he had it.

Somebody says that the way down is through Plac Krasinski, so he looks on his map, and tries to memorise the whole area of the sewers leading to the City Centre. The rockets give the extra light he needs. Why don't they bomb them all? Perhaps the Germans are also confused.

An officer instructs the soldiers to preserve silence and refrain from using lights while walking through the sewers, because the Germans have established posts at various sewer exits. There is also danger from grenades, which they have hung on strings from the ceilings and which detonate on touch. Some passages have reportedly been blocked by bags of cement, and parts of the sewers have been filled with poison gas. It all doesn't really matter, because Egon knows now that survival is merely a matter of accident. An officer at the entrance tells people to throw away any luggage they carry, and Egon finds himself walking on various bags, blankets and bedding. He walks in front of their little group, and is grateful for his familiarity with the awful descent into the blackness and stench below. This time there is no ladder but metal hooks offering unsteady support for feet and hands.

The memory of his first time in the sewers is still clearly in his mind, and he feels terribly sorry for the others. They have no light and no Witek with them; so he goes down first only to find that he is up to his knees in water. He shouts a warning, and holds out his hands to help. There is nothing to guide him, but he glimpses a flicker far ahead, so that must be the right direction, except that he has to fight a strong current to go that way.

After a while there does not seem to be anybody in front or behind their group. Are they lost? Judging by the continuous stream of people going into the sewers there should be a similar crowd down below. The walk seems to last for an eternity. This time Egon is weaker than when he was walking from the ghetto, but he does not have to semi-carry a child. He holds the small hand of Dr. Alina, and tries to visualise the picture of the sewer map he had just memorised.

It is really pretty simple, except that in the dark, time and distance lose all proportion and the absence of others is worrying. Where have they all disappeared?

Only much later Egon found out that those who were escaping through the sewers were supposed to be following a string stretched along the walls for their guidance. So many people had held onto the string, trusting it to lead them through, that nobody realised that it had broken, because it was held up by the hands which clung to it. They had lost their way and many died. Egon did not know about the existence of the string, and that saved his group. Even so it took them more than three hours to reach the City Centre. They were among the last. The later groups perished when the Germans built further dams across the sewers, and continued filling them with burning petrol and gas.

It was daylight when they emerged, and the sun blinded them all. They blinked and looked around. The whole thing was difficult to believe.

Here too there were barricades, but they were perfectly constructed and everything around them was calm, because the German attack had not yet reached the area, they were concentrating their efforts on one district at a time. There were leaves on the trees, which still stood around as if they had a right to grow, and as for the people . . . They were clean, and seemed unbelievably elegant. Many of the men wore ties. Quite a few of the houses in the street were still intact. A lot of them even had windows. Captain Sas took charge.

"We're to report to section Bogumil at the Plac of Three Crosses, but anyone who can find somewhere to clean themselves up and have a rest first can do so."

"I have relatives who have lived here near Marszalkowska," said *Pani* Golabek quietly to Egon. "I don't know if they are still there, but I could take Dr. Alina and you with me."

The only relative, who was still in residence was *Pani* Renata Filipek, who proved to be a very practical woman, just like her cousin, *Pani* Zofja. She was plump and energetic. Having taken one look at the filthy and malodorous little group, she directed them into the courtyard, and showed them where there were buckets and a well.

Queues for water had already formed, but it was still available, which was not the case a day or two later, when the situation generally worsened. It was very difficult to get clean, although *Pani* Renata gave them some soap, old rags, two clean towels and a few clothes for the women. Their shoes had soaked up the sewage, but Egon's good German boots seemed to be pretty resistant to everything; probably through constant polishing by their previous owner.

In addition, *Pani* Renata gave him some of her absent husband's old socks.

"Last time I saw my husband," she said, "he was heading for the forest. That was a year ago, and I haven't heard from him since. I don't think he will start counting his socks when he comes back."

There was the smell of freshly baked bread in the flat when they finally considered themselves fit to go there. *Pani* Renata was already giving shelter to others, and they had all together ground some corn and made bread. A wonderful feeling of well-being came to Egon in the comparative quiet and orderliness of the flat.

A neighbour came in with news that a number of armed young people from Pyry near Warsaw were on their way to give help, and this encouraged them to hope, but the fragile moment of contentment was shattered when a piece of shrapnel flew in through a window in the adjoining room.

It damaged one of the walls, covered all surfaces with fragments of broken window glass, and splintered a chair, but no one was hurt. They simply moved the remaining furniture to the dining room and tried to settle down again, but it was no longer possible. It became the same as it had been in the Old City. Having systematically "cleared" one area, the Germans moved to the next. The "cows" exploded around, and somebody came in calling all men to build a new barricade, but the men in the house did not move.

"Our enthusiasm to help," said *Pani* Renata in a flat matter-of-fact voice, "has now evaporated."

That was the last thing Egon heard before he fell asleep on the comfortable settee where he had been chewing his piece of bread. When he woke up, *Pani* Renata was still or again talking, this time about the marvellous service she had attended in the cinema in Pius Street.

"The priest preached beautifully. We were all so moved that nobody took any notice of the planes and bombs, which could be heard outside," she was saying with great feeling.

"Thank you very much for your hospitality," Egon said in the lull that followed. "I must now report to my commanding officer."

Dr. Alina embraced and kissed him and *Pani* Zofja followed him out.

"While you were asleep," she said, "people from the Home Army came in. They had to order all men under forty-five to help with the barricades. People here are tired of fighting, and are talking of surrender. Not the fighters, of course, but the soldiers can't fight without the support of the people. They will surrender. It's only a matter of time. See how things go. You don't have to go with all the others. Try to get back to your uncle on the German side, and get out. The others don't have an option, but you have. You're very young and have a right to live."

He found that Captain Sas had also only just reached the Plac of Three Crosses. Except, of course, that it was difficult to recognise the place, because the Church of Holy Aleksander, which had dominated it had been burned, and all the other buildings were heavily damaged.

They were told that Lieutenant Colonel Bogumil was in charge, though at the moment he was busy at another section, but there were three SS men, who had to be executed, and they could do that as their next job.

Egon saw the distaste in the face of Sas, and a certain excitement in Piotr. He had always thought, that given half a chance he would like to kill them all, SS and Gestapo alike, not to mention any other Germans he had seen in action. Now he stood in front of the elite.

They were tall, blonde and blue eyed – everything that Hitler was not, and they fell on their knees and cried for mercy. Tears ran down their large faces, making inroads into the dirt that covered them. There was a sharp contrast between the well-fed giants and the two half-starved boys and one man. Egon did not want to shoot them. It was one thing to fight, to shoot at anonymous shapes, who were trying to kill you. It was quite another thing to shoot an unarmed man, however much you hated him. He felt a tremendous disgust, and wanted to leave them there with their own thoughts, that is if they were capable of thinking. Personally he wished to be as far away from them as possible because their presence revolted him. Captain Sas's distaste communicated itself to him, but then one of the SS men spoke.

"I have some diamonds here," he said stretching out his hand on which a number of bright stones glittered. "We got them from the Jews. We've always been friendly with the Poles. We can get you some more if you'll help us."

It was then that Egon fired the first shot and others followed suit. They shared out the diamonds. Egon thought that the two he was given were but a small part of the jewels that had been his mother's. His conscience did not trouble him.

From now on life consisted only of being under fire, shooting back and trying to escape the bombs. A few Russian planes appeared in the sky from time to time. They were a welcome sight, but were often dangerous, because their bombing was indiscriminate. More often they were German planes against which they could do nothing. Sometimes there were friendly planes, which dropped supplies. Unfortunately these seemed mostly to fall into German hands. It was too difficult to see from the air who was where. All around people were dying, or being horribly wounded. Soldiers and civilians, women and children. When he managed to slip off to the cellar, where his friends now lived, Dr. Alina was no longer there. She was working in another cellar, which was converted into a hospital. Her place was taken by an old lady, whom the others had adopted and were trying to nurse. She had lost one eye, but lay quietly, in spite of her pain, which she bore with remarkable fortitude.

It was difficult to know when days and nights passed, because they flowed into one long nightmare of noise and blood and dirt. Egon was not sure whether he was asleep or awake. He was in a delirium produced by constant hunger, tiredness and thirst.

They periodically snatched sleep in cellars, and then went to get water. Civilians grumbled when the soldiers went in front of the long queues, but the fighters argued that they had no time to wait.

There were quarrels and even fights. It was a far cry from the initial rapturous happiness of the uprising, which was supposed to last for a few days, and was now lasting for nearly two months.

*

Towards the end of September Egon was standing guard, when he overheard a discussion between two officers.

"It's just a question of time. General Bor is negotiating surrender."

"He can do all the negotiating he wants, but we know that the Germans do not honour any agreements," answered the other.

And Egon remembered what *Pani* Zofja had said. He had done his best. He had fought. It would not help anybody if he also should die, but what could he do?

The decision was taken out of his hands, because on that day General Bor sent a message to his government in London saying.

"1. We have established that the rations of food will suffice for only three days. We do not see any chance of the Russians taking Warsaw within that time, nor of their ensuring the city sufficient cover from bombing attacks or providing supplies of food, which would enable the town to last out until its liberation.

2. I have informed Marshal Rokossowski about the situation and asked him for help. However, if I do not immediately receive it in great quantity, I will be forced to surrender on the German guarantee of granting combatant status.

3. Due to the fact that after the fall of Mokotow the Germans took the initiative in talks on removing the civilian population from the town and the possibility of ending the fighting, which they consider to be senseless, I agreed to the talks.

The evacuation of the civilian population is expected to take place from the morning of 1st October and will last, I should think, three days . . ."

On Sunday the 1st of October the guns went silent. People trudged through the ruins, searching for any of their friends and family who had survived. They were afraid to go to the Germans, because they had heard what was happening to those who fell into their hands, but by the 3rd of October, the civilian population was instructed to leave Warsaw, and the army, or what was left of it, was going to march out in full formation to be treated as prisoners of war.

"I'm going to try to escape," Egon confided to his chief officer, when he saw him.

"You should try to join the civilians instead, or come with us, so you can be looked after," Sas told him. He had become fond of the lad. "You'll never manage alone. They'll catch you and kill you."

Egon did not contradict him, but he had heard different advice from Uncle Otto.

"Never follow a crowd, unless you know exactly where the crowd is going, and you really want to go there yourself," Otto had said on many occasions. "A mob does not think. It can be easily intimidated, whipped up into a frenzy, or given a sense of power, which can be used by a skilled manipulator. Always try to stop and think for yourself."

And that is what Egon did now. With great regret he left his gun, his battle trophy, for which he now had no ammunition, but not his faithful penknife.

"You would've had to give them it anyway, either as a civilian or as a soldier," he cheered himself up.

He then went to find *Pani* Zofja. She and all other residents of the cellar were sitting down and eating up their supplies:

"We'll be robbed anyway," explained *Pani* Renata, "so we might as well give ourselves some strength. There's enough here. Come and join us."

There were all kinds of tinned foods, which people were saving till the end, and this was the end. Egon did not need to be asked twice, and his morale improved with eating.

Pani Zofja was completely ready to go, but she and *Pani* Renata had been vainly trying to convince the one-eyed old lady, that there was no other way, but to surrender.

"Cowards!" the old lady was saying in an indignant high-pitched voice. "If I had been younger, and a man, I wouldn't have let them stop fighting. Once we let the Russians in, we'll never get rid of them. They'll trick the people. The Germans murder everybody, but the Russians only those who stand in their way. Why doesn't anybody understand?" Her voice now sounded querulous, and there were tears in the one eye.

She had not cried when she was in pain, or when she knew that her eye was irrevocably lost, but now she was pitiful in her distress.

"She's been going on like this for the last couple of days," whispered *Pani* Zofja to Egon.

"Madam," Egon bowed in his best Fraulein Hedwige manner, "you must go now. People with your understanding must survive so that they can explain things to others."

The old lady measured him with her remaining eye, which she wiped with her sleeve, and said firmly:

"I think you're right, young man. People need to be told." She then stood up and professed herself ready to go.

"Could you possibly wait for just a little while," Egon said, "because I need some help from *Pani* Zofja."

And *Pani* Zofja helped him to clean himself up, and take off the bandage from his head. The wound had healed sufficiently to be covered only by the thick fair hair, which *Pani* Zofja trimmed with a pair of scissors from the old lady's manicure set. She also used them to detach the now dirty red and white band from his scouts cap, which he wanted to keep.

"I can always say that I found it, if I meet any Germans. They'll believe me, because I'll be unable to speak any Polish."

"I wouldn't risk it," said *Pani* Zofja, after having taken the give-away band, "but I can understand. I've done all you wanted, but do this for me. Leave it behind. It's never worth giving a life for any possession, however much you may value it."

Egon looked into her wise eyes, in which there still lurked the ever-present trace of mocking laughter, and nodded in agreement. She gently put the cap down with the things she was taking with her.

"Perhaps, one day, I'll give it back to you. We never know where we all land up," she said cheerfully.

Then she kissed him on the forehead, gathered her friends, and they set off into the rain, slithering in the mud, towards the Western Railway Station, where the civilians had been ordered to assemble for deportation.

Egon was left alone, feeling almost as desolate as when he had set off for the Station at Gorsk. He looked after the women as they disappeared between the ruins, and *Pani* Zofja turned and waved to him. She wore the same coat she wore the first time he saw her. He remembered her saying then, and many times after that.

"These loden coats are very practical. They protect you from the cold, and they protect you from the rain."

Now it was raining. It was the last time he saw her. He later found out that she was killed by a Ukrainian guard, when she proved unwilling to accept his advances.

Then he watched his comrades gather and follow a captain in Polish uniform, holding a German sabre. They walked straight, holding their heads high with great effort to show their defiance. Seeing them like that, he felt that perhaps he should have gone with them – they looked so proud even in their defeat – but it would not have made sense.

Once in prison, assuming that they would be allowed to live at all, there would be nothing more he could do, and he had learned to fear inaction.

Now the silence became awful. There were still far off explosions, but nothing moved in his immediate vicinity, and he became afraid. The only cure for that was to do something.

Very carefully, as he had been trained to do, Egon started moving through the cellars and subterranean passages he had used when carrying letters and despatches. Except, of course, in the past all the "safe" underground trails had been full of people and signs helping to find the way but now they echoed with silence and emptiness. Had everybody left? Perhaps not, because he suddenly heard explosions in a cellar on his right. Very quickly he moved in the opposite direction and froze in a half-broken cornerstone of a house.

A German patrol was making its way through what used to be a street. Whenever they came to a cellar, where they thought anyone could still hide, they released a stream of machine gun fire into it, before checking it out. He had known he had to be careful, but now he realised the extent of the danger. Finally, after a long time, he reached what he thought was his destination, except ... Of course he should have expected it, but he did not.

The house where the shop had been, where he had always been sure of a refuge, that house was no longer there. Had he made a mistake? After all it was almost impossible to recognise anything, except that it was easier for him, because he had watched the destruction, and could tell one ruin from another. He was pretty sure that he was in the right place.

After trekking through the cellars he had hoped that now there would be a welcome, a release from responsibility, almost a homecoming. Instead, a heavy hand fell on his shoulder:

"And what have we here?" a voice asked in German, and he looked up, not yet afraid, but at that moment more annoyed by his own silly carelessness caused by the shock of not seeing the house where it should have been. There were two men, fortunately in the less threatening Wehrmacht uniform; not the Gestapo or the SS.

"I'd shoot him, just in case," said one of the soldiers, who was squat, and dark. "There were lots of kids just like him in the fighting," and he took the safety catch off his gun.

He was not going to be caught so stupidly after all he had been through. Egon was still so cross with himself that when he spoke there was no fear in his voice.

"Please, can you help me," he said in his clear unaccented German. "My uncle had a shop somewhere here, and his stock was kept in the NSDAP Headquarters in the Aleja Roz, where I left him. I am not sure if he is there now, because he told me we would soon be leaving. He sent me to collect some papers, but the house is no longer here. I've been wondering around for hours, because I can't recognise anything. Uncle had not realised it was all like this, otherwise he would not have sent me. He thought it was quite safe now that the uprising had been put down."

"D'you have any documents to prove all this?" the second soldier asked suspiciously.

"Of course not," Egon replied. "Uncle thought I'd be back quickly, and he kept all my documents to get them properly stamped in case we had to be evacuated."

"Well," said the first soldier. "All our people are being evacuated from the Hauptbanhoff, and we're going there ourselves. You can come with us, but God help you if you don't come up with the papers. It is our duty to deliver you to the Gestapo."

"Search him first," said the squat dark soldier. "We don't want any surprises."

They found the penknife, but the taller soldier said that it was not unusual for boys to have them.

"Possibly," the dark one was not convinced, "but just in case, let me take it."

Parting with his father's last present was like loosing a friend, but he had by now lost so many real ones that losing a possession should not matter, as *Pani* Zofja had said. It was just as well that he had listened to her and not kept the scout cap.

Moving with the Germans was a lot quicker, although they were not taking any chances, and took it in turn to keep a good grip on him.

They did not have to dive into cellars at the slightest noise, but simply walked through the spaces, which were clear of rubble. Egon was now trying to think what he could possibly do when they reached the Station.

It did not take them very long to get there. All the area was full of Germans with or without uniform, and there was a train standing at the platform, but there was not one familiar face to be seen by Egon. He tried to prolong the time before the soldiers felt they had to do their duty, hoping that somehow he could slip away in the crowd.

"If everybody is leaving, uncle just has to be here somewhere," he said, trying to sound sensible and matter-of-fact. "You can see that I can't possibly know where he is exactly."

Vainly he looked around, but he could not even find any of the Nazi troopers from the Aleja Roz. For a while the two soldiers patiently walked with him up and down the platform, but eventually, when they were near the Gestapo officers on duty, the older soldier said.

"That's enough of this game," and walked up to them. "Heil Hitler," all arms flew up at once. "We've caught this boy in the ruins and . . . "

"Why wasn't he shot at once?"

"Because he speaks only German, and a proper Hochdeutch without any accent it is at that. He also says his uncle had a stockroom in the NSDAP headquarters in the Aleja Roz, and is somewhere here with his documents."

"Quatsch! If you pull his trousers down, you'll probably find out he's not just a Pole, but also a Jew, but don't do it at the station. Take him outside. You have enough time."

Just as his arms were being grabbed Egon looked up at the train, and, with total disbelief recognised Otto standing in the door of a goods carriage.

"There he is!" he shouted as loudly as he could. "Uncle! It is me, Egon!"

Within moments the large bulk that was Otto towered over the Germans, who were still holding Egon. Both their thinking processes and their reactions were very much slower than Otto's, and they were still surprised and hesitant, when he reached them.

"Heil Hitler!" he said, unbalancing them sufficiently to grab the boy out of their hands. "Why was the child not brought to me immediately? I've been looking for him everywhere!"

The two soldiers were only too glad to be out of it, and the Gestapo had their hands full anyway.

"Next time don't let him run around without documents," said one of them. "He's jolly lucky he didn't get shot by the Poles, but I still want to see his documents."

Without a further word Otto presented them.

CHAPTER 18

PICKING UP THE PIECES

The freight truck was filled with the furniture and goods from Otto's shop and office as well as a great number of the familiar brown hardboard boxes. Egon was further reassured by the sight of Filomena who was sitting in one of the office chairs. She rose to her feet and hugged him.

"We didn't know where to look for you," she said. "We simply hoped you were alright." Then they were silent, afraid to speak in case anyone overheard them. The questions did not pour out, but remained poised on their lips, anxious to be released. Otto returned to his vantage point at the door, which he did not close until the train moved off.

"It was better to be standing there defying questioning, than having them open the doors and having to explain," he said, settling his big hulk on a wooden box. A cardboard one would not have supported him.

"But how did you manage it? How is it that we are not being herded off with the rest of the population of Warsaw?" Egon still could not believe that he was sitting in the comparative comfort of a private freight truck, and leaving all immediate danger behind.

"It was not too difficult." In spite of this denial, Otto was obviously very pleased with himself.

"I told Dr. Stein that all the important medical goods I had in the shop and those which were being stored at the Aleja Roz should not be wasted, but brought to the capital of the province. I don't know if you've realised, but the province is Poland and its capital is Cracow, which is, according to the Nazis, a city of old German culture. By the same token,

I'm a Japanese. It's to Cracow that we're going. He was most co-operative. Filomena has typed out a long and complicated permit, the wording of which I've composed myself. Apart from having it stamped by Stein, I went to everyone in the Nazi headquarters, whom I knew to be in the possession of a good rubber stamp, and had them affix it to the document. It has cost me the rest of the vodka which I have been storing with the boxes, but I think it was worth it. Everyone at the station was properly impressed, and this carriage was placed at my disposal. In one of the boxes are also the official receipts for all the goods confiscated from our original business. I'll see to it that after the war the swine will pay every penny of it. But now it's your turn. Tell us what's been happening to you."

They listened to him, almost without interruption, except when he told them of the death of Dr. Koronski and Susanna. The others they did not know, and dying had become commonplace.

"Oh, poor Alina," sighed Filomena.

"I hope that Andrzej lives," Otto had also sighed heavily on hearing the news, "at least Alina still has a son."

Egon did not know Cracow, the ancient capital of Poland, the home of its Kings. He had only been there in the ghetto, and that gave him no impression of the city itself. Even if it had been just an ordinary town, and not an enchanting, royal city evoking past splendour, it would have seemed beautiful to him, simply because it had not been bombed. There were trees in the streets and in the Planty (the park which circled the city in place of the original city walls) and there was glass in the windows of the house in the outskirts, where they managed to get accommodation. Egon helped to unload the precious boxes and all their other possessions, but when that was done he felt, as was usual with him, the need for some action. The Germans were still to be seen, but they were moving out. The landlady told them that an order had been issued by the Nazis to withdraw so that "the ancient German city" would not be damaged by fighting.

"I'll just go outside for a while to have a look around," Egon said to Filomena after they had cleared up the improvised meal they had put together.

"Please be careful. It'd be so silly to get yourself killed now, when the end looks near."

Filomena was not given to fussing, and realised that she could not longer issue orders to Egon, but she found it impossible to refrain from warning him.

"I'll be careful," he promised.

Egon walked down the lane, which led directly into the field at the end of which stood a few tall trees. He decided that one of them could easily be climbed to give a view of the surrounding countryside, and started moving briskly towards it. Suddenly, as he passed the last outbuildings, he found himself surrounded by a gang of boys about his own age.

"And where d'you think you're going?" the biggest of them asked belligerently, stepping in front of him. He wore his trousers tucked into his enormous boots, which now stood wide apart, covering most of his legs and supporting his sturdy body. The cheeky expression on his freckled face reminded Egon of Stach.

"Over to those trees," Egon answered, standing his ground.

"And I say you can't pass." The bulky figure of the boy barred the way, his feet still spread out and his hands on his hips. His companions arranged themselves behind him hoping for entertainment, which came quickly and suddenly. Their leader never knew what happened to him. Quite unexpectedly he flew backwards and hit the ground. It took him quite a while to pick himself up, even with the help of the others.

Egon had only hit him once, putting his foot behind his adversay as taught to him by Felek in the forest. Now he waited without moving until the brawny lad was again standing facing him.

"What's your name?" Egon asked amicably.

"Marek," answered the big boy rubbing his chin and the back of his head.

"Zbyszek," said Egon and put out his hand, having decided to continue being called by his last pseudonym. Marek shook the hand which had been offered to him.

"Where did you learn to fight like this?" he asked, shaking the dust from his knees.

"I'll tell you about it when we get to know each other better, but I can see that you've a good bunch of boys here. Any others around?"

"Yeah. There are other gangs. We know some of them. Why?"

"I think we need to form a scout group. Learn to march. Sing songs, help others. I'll teach you some First Aid if you like, but in the meantime I'd like to look over the terrain. Can we climb up those trees?"

The boys were very keen to show him which trees were the best to climb. From their high vantage point they could see a little valley below, in the middle of which was a small knoll.

Just after Egon had settled on the last sturdy branch of the tallest tree, and the rest disposed themselves around, they noticed a multitude of dark shapes moving quickly towards the hill from a road leading through a meadow. As the shapes came nearer the boys recognised them as human figures wearing padded jackets. A few minutes later they glimpsed red stars in their hats and saw that they were Russian soldiers, running bent forward, holding their rifles at the ready. They ran in waves. One wave would run, fall flat on the ground, and allow another wave to overtake them. When they neared the mound the first wave was completely cut down by machine gun fire directed at them from the top of the hill. This did not stop the second wave running forward, and they, likewise were shot down by the firing from the summit. In horror the boys watched the bodies piling up, until at last the firing stopped, and a final wave, running over their comrades, reached the top, which had been held by two Germans with machine guns. The Germans had run out of ammunition, and were now casually shot by the advancing soldiers.

"What a stupid way to fight," whispered Marek contemptuously from the branch next to Egon's. "There'll be none of the Russians left by the time they finish."

"These poor bastards must've been ordered to do that," answered Egon also whispering.

They stayed in the trees until the Russian waves passed them, having buried their dead with an efficiency which showed much previous experience, and carrying their wounded.

They moved on presumably to wipe out any remaining German positions.

*

People were, of course, happy on the day the end of the war was officially announced, but they could not give themselves totally to proper celebrations. It was as if they were slowly coming out of the anaesthethic after a serious operation. Some part of them was missing, never to be replaced again, and the pain of healing was just beginning. Furthermore, news was beginning to come through that many of the AK (Home Army) officers had been shot or imprisoned by the advancing Russians. It was difficult to believe that this was the reward for all the heroism. It took the savour out of peace.

*

Egon spent his time training his new friends and a few extra boys who wanted to join them. There were now twelve members of his scout group. He made them march up and down the lane, which they did quite creditably after a short time, keeping in step and wheeling around like real soldiers.

One day when they were parading up and down the field, through which the unfortunate Russians had advanced, they noticed a tall man standing by the copse of trees and watching them. Egon marched his troop towards him and made them stop in front of the man, who detached himself from the tree on which he had been leaning and said.

"You're doing a good job. I have been told that somebody was trying to do some scout training, and I just had to come and have a look. I was a scout leader before the war. My name is Stanislaw Prochowski."

"My name is Zbigniew Baranski, and this is Marek Kobylka. I'll introduce you to the others in a minute, but it would be wonderful if you could help with the training. All I have learned was during the occupation in Warsaw and with the partisans. Now we need quite different things."

"Yes. There's going to be a celebration in the town, and we could do a march past. If you would really like it, I could help you to make some Red Indian head gear for the boys to make it more interesting, and perhaps a couple of shields and spears."

Stanislaw's suggestion met with universal approval and everybody wanted to help. Some unfortunate cockerels must have suffered because feathers were found for the head gear, and somebody gave Egon a real Polish mountaineers hat, which he could wear as leader.

Stanislaw insisted on marching at the end of their group.

"It will be much more exciting if people see that you boys have trained of your own initiative," he said firmly.

And on a wonderful sunny spring day in 1945 the first scout troop marched through the ancient streets of Cracow, past the red and white flags, which fluttered in the wind and had not been allowed to be seen for such a long time. They were not a very impressive group. Their leader wore a mountaineer's hat with a feather, and (although nobody could possibly know it) thought with tremendous longing and regret about a scout cap he had left in Warsaw. The others wore feathered Indian head dresses, two carried painted shields and spears, and one a small axe. They all wore short trousers, jackets and white shirts, except for the two Pietrzynski brothers, who wore long trousers and belted shirts, which they considered to be closer to Indian clothing. The tall figure of Stanislaw Prochowski in full scout uniform, which somebody had kept for him, completed the troop, and the people loved the whole thing.

"Look at our children," they said. "They're the first to know that we are free."

Women with wrinkled faces and scarves on their heads stood quietly with tears running down their cheeks, thinking perhaps of their own sons, who were either dead or somewhere far away.

The scouts marched, singing all the marching songs they knew, gathering people behind them. Everybody joined in the singing. Windows opened, hands waived and finally a realisation of the end of the war was felt by all and filled them with elation.

*

Stanislaw Prochowski had spent the war with the partisans, and was now a part of an organisation employed in checking if any weapons or explosives had been left in the houses previously occupied by the Germans. He was always glad to have Egon come on his rounds with him.

Usually they inspected office buildings, but on one particular day they were asked to look at a house, which had first been occupied by an SS General and his staff and then by the Gestapo. It was close to the town centre, and stood in its own gardens surrounded by a tall brick and wire fence, covered inside by a hedge. With some difficulty they managed to open the rusty metal door, placed in one corner of the wall, and stepped into a garden, which still retained signs of previous care.

As the gate closed behind them with a loud protesting squeak they seemed to have stepped out of the ugliness and pain of the war into a remnant of a better world. This strange sensation may well have been caused by the overpowering scent of lilac, which filled the garden. It came from unbelievably thick clusters of mauve and white lilac flowers, which almost completely covered the many lilac bushes scattered around the tall fences.

In the middle of the front lawn stood a slender cherry tree, its branches proudly and tremulously displaying pure white blossom.

"It looks like a beautiful young bride," Stanislaw Prochowski whispered, and Egon lifted his head to see it better. All at once he became aware of the fact that he had largely stopped perceiving the world around him properly since Brzesko. Since that awful day he had only concentrated on finding a modicum of safety. He had looked at people's faces mostly to evaluate their future actions. Were they likely to be reliable? Were they going to pry? Were they pro-German, and were they in the business of betraying Jews. He had looked at his surroundings primarily to find some-where warm in the winter and somewhere cool in the summer – above all to find food and drink. He registered all the kaleidoscope of horror and destruction around him, but he did not allow either his eyes or his thoughts to dwell too long on it.

It was an instinct of self-preservation – a desire to remain sane, which made him act in this way. And now, for the first time in many years, in that magic garden, he truly saw again.

Soft breeze touched the white petals on the cherry tree and he felt as if a switch had been turned within him and colour had returned to the world around him.

"Yes," he confirmed quietly. "That tree really does look like a beautiful young bride." He said it with complete conviction, but suddenly realised that he had never seen a bride dressed in white.

Stanislaw unlocked the front door with the key he had been given and they walked up the comfortable shallow stairs, leading to the three large apartments into which the house had been divided. The rooms inside it were completely empty. The parquet floors on the ground floor still looked good, the golden timber showing through the dust. In one of the rooms of the first floor the rays of the sun came in through cut glass windows which broke them into a multitude of small rainbows illuminating the dirty walls with magic colour. There were no weapons anywhere within the expanse of the echoing empty rooms. Silently they walked to the back of the house, and found a large yard with a garage block, beyond which there was a small orchard. Incongruously, in the middle of a group of apple trees, stood a bunker. The door to the bunker hung open.

They were startled by somebody clearing his throat behind them, and turned round to see a skinny man in his late thirties, whose shifty pale blue eyes darted around them, without meeting theirs.

"I'm the caretaker here," he said. "My name is Piotr Ropek. Can I be of service?"

"I have a weapon search warrant, if you want to see it." Stanislaw answered. "And we have already satisfied ourselves that there are no weapons of any kind in the house or garden. But since you are here, perhaps you could tell us something about this place."

"Nothing much to tell, really. This house, like many others, belonged to some Jews before the war. They went away before the Germans got here. Don't know if they caught them or not. A German general arrived and took most of the things. He had special vans, into which they loaded the furniture, and the way in which they packed the pictures, crystal and china was something to see. Didn't let us take much, the son of a bitch, but we still managed to save a bit for ourselves before he got here. Of course the furniture was too large for us, so we didn't begrudge him that. The whole place was full of books. They didn't take those, but burned most of them. Many of them were very old and no good to anybody anyhow; probably written by Jews too, so it's good riddance. Later on the Gestapo moved in. It was they who built this bunker. D'you know who'll have the place now?"

Egon felt such loathing for the man that he had to restrain himself from hitting him, but Stanislaw merely said that he had no idea. His job was merely searching for weapons.

"Well, you've searched and found nothing, so you might just as well get off the premises," Mr. Ropek decided to assert his authority.

"We haven't inspected the bunker yet," Stanislaw said mildly, and walked towards it across the soft young grass of the orchard, but the bunker was also empty. "Go ahead," said Piotr Ropek following them. "The general cleared the place out, but, as I said, the Gestapo were here after that. Don't know what they did in that bunker. They didn't do me any harm."

Egon no longer felt the need for violence. His feeling of revulsion was such that he could not have brought himself to touch the man.

Stanislaw recommended Egon for all kinds of scout courses that wonderful summer, and he was always away with various groups of boys and girls learning photography, rafting, and even gliding. They camped, played and sang, happy with their sudden freedom and the possibility to behave like young people normally do.

At the end of the summer Otto and Filomena moved back to Katowice, where Otto's original business had been, and, in compliance with Otto's promise, they were married at the local registry office.

With some of the proceeds of the sale of the contents of the brown boxes, they bought a little house, which they started to furnish.

"There are two businesses, which will always thrive," Otto said. "Food and medicines. People must eat and they can't help being ill. I've chosen medical supplies and they've always provided me with a living."

He established himself as a supplier to the returning doctors, and travelled to far away places on the German border, where he somehow managed to contact his previous suppliers in Solingen, who in turn . . . But Egon did not know and did not care much about all this.

Life was so full of excitement that he took the plentiful nourishment he now received for granted. He soon made contact with the scouts in Katowice and rushed around collecting certificates of achievement, in everything possible from photography and boxing to first aid, riding and gliding. They were all full of hope about the wonderful new Poland they were going to build.

Egon shared Otto's delight when Filomena gave birth to little Lila. The happy event was quite unexpected by the unitiated, because, as soon as food became available, both Otto and Filomena became exceedingly fat, and nobody suspected that a baby was concealed in the ample folds of Filomena's large body.

The rush of everyday life suppressed the constantly recurring thoughts of the past events, though Otto started enquiries through the Red Cross and placed advertisements in newspapers, trying to find out if any of the enormous Weiner clan had survived. As he had suspected it was all in vain.

No trace remained of the old people, of the fine musicians, the doctors and the lawyers, the teachers and businessmen, the cripples and ne'er-do-wells; the women, both old and young, plain and beautiful, clever and stupid. Not even of the laughing children so many of whom had showed much promise. Otto went to the various towns where they had lived, and came back more depressed every time. He never talked about it. There did not seem to be any point. However, when Egon asked about his brother and his parents, Otto told him the truth:

"Nobody knows for sure, but it appears that they were taken back to the Cracow ghetto and from there to Auschwitz. They did not survive, otherwise they would have tried to get in touch."

They did not cry any more. They pushed the awful knowledge deep into the recesses of their subconscious, and tried not to allow it to poison their minds, but it was not an easy task.

"It is important to live for today and for tomorrow," Otto did not trust himself to put his arms round the boy, because he was worried about creating mutual self-pity, "and possibly for the day after. It's no use looking too far forward, or too far back. You can't bring back the past and you can't foresee the future."

"But shouldn't all the Germans be killed now?" Egon wanted to know.

"At the very least all those who are guilty, and surely it'll be better to kill them all, just in case. That's what my friends say anyway, and not many of them lost all their family like we did."

"Yes, of course. We can try to kill all of them, but some will survive and they in turn can try to kill all your friends, and any of us who survived, and we can go on like that for ever. The Good Lord and the Allies will do the vengeance job, though, I hope it will be justice rather than vengeance, but you and I have to concentrate on living. And in order to live properly you will have to start learning. That's your most important job now. You have to go to school."

CHAPTER 19

TIME TO LEAVE

That is what must be engraved on Polish memory – like on a
boulder.
Our common home was destroyed, and through spilled blood,
united is our fate.

Execution walls unite us, and Dachau and Auschwitz, and dying
shoulder to shoulder,

And every nameless grave and every prison grate.

Wladyslaw Broniewski: "To Polish Jews".

*

The idea of school did not appeal to Egon, simply because he had never
previously attended school, and the concept was alien to him. He had
learned to read and write and do some mathematics when Kurt and his
father were still alive, did some mental arithmetic with Otto, had a few
lessons with Basia and listened to one or two lectures with the scouts, but
that was the sum total of his education. Most of the Polish children had
had some tuition during the war. One way or another their parents managed
to send them to people who could regularly teach them something, but
Egon had had to hide.

His apprehension proved unjustified, however, because, when he eventually went to school it did not prove to be too bad. As always in the past,
he found that he enjoyed the company of boys of the same age. Of course

it was difficult to sit without moving for long periods, but many of the lessons were interesting, although, increasingly Egon found it disturbing that he did not have the basic knowledge possessed by his fellow students.

There had been no opportunity to get documents in his proper name, and he was still using his papers made out in the very Polish sounding name of Zbigniew Baranski, which proved to be fortunate, because he heard his friends say, with depressingly increasing frequency, that all Poland's troubles had been caused by the Jews. Walls and fences displayed lines written by some unknown "poetry lovers", proclaiming that:

> Katowice and Cracow
> Are cities for the Poles,
> And you, Jewish swine,
> Should go to Palestine.

He did not question his friends about this. To the best of his knowledge, he was the only Jew in the school and, as anti-Jewish remarks were being made within the hearing of teachers without exciting any criticism whatsoever, he knew that he would have no support from those in authority if he disagreed.

Father Boniface, who taught them religion, and was one of the teachers in whose presence these remarks were particularly freely made and well received, liked him very much, because Egon displayed an amazing knowledge of prayers, reciting great lengths of them from memory. As a mark of favour, the priest entrusted him with the honour of carrying incense round the church during the services, and Egon's only act of retaliation against his religious teacher's anti-semitism was an occasional introduction of grass into the container, so that it produced evil smelling smoke instead of pure fragrance. He pretended to be as puzzled as Father Boniface about this, and sagely nodding his head advanced the opinion that the quality of incense before the war must have been better.

Egon was also popular because he won the area lightweight boxing championship for the school, but his academic achievements left a lot to be desired, and his reports were not very good, although he tried hard. There was just too much catching up to do, and too many subjects he did not fully understand, having never learned the basics. As Otto's education had been in German, and Filomena was busy with the baby, neither of them could be of any significant assistance.

"Alina Koronski is in Katowice," Filomena said. "She has her mother's flat here. Her mother was a teacher, you know, and she may have kept some of the old school books which would be a great help. Alina could, perhaps, give Egon some lessons in the evenings after school and help him to catch up."

That evening, Otto and Egon went to the address Filomena had given them, where Alina Koronski lived on her own since the recent death of her mother. Until then young Andrzej was with them, being looked after by his granmother, but two weeks ago *Pani* Alina had decided to send him to his paternal grandparents in Cracow. She did not want him to be on his own when he returned from school and she was still at work. The flat was in one of the modern buildings built shortly before the war. It was small, modern and full of the polished walnut furniture with rounded corners, which had been so fashionable in the thirties. The rooms were low, but the large windows made them seem airy.

Alina was delighted to see her friends and happy to give Egon lessons. She was lonely in the evenings, and Egon's company would be welcome. With tacit agreement they did not speak of their dead; it was all still too fresh, and it hurt too much. Instead they concentrated on admiring the little flat, which had a small kitchen, a modern bathroom and a separate bedroom as well as the room in which they were sitting. It all seemed very luxurious at that time.

At first Alina did not want to accept any money for teaching Egon, but Otto convinced her that she should, explaining simply.

"At the moment I can make money, and this is the most important thing to spend it on. You can teach him for nothing when I can't pay."

She agreed a fee on being re-assured that she would really be told when funds were low, and then made them coffee. A parcel had arrived from some friends in America, and *Pani* Alina wanted to share her treasures. The pleasure of receiving friends made her talkative and she told them about her work at the hospital.

"It's nearly all women," she said. "Most of the men are either dead or abroad, but people still tell funny stories. My favourite is the one about the prostitute and a policeman who is trying to make her move on. 'And what did you do for Poland in the years of occupation?' she says to him beligerently. 'Not much, I'll bet. But I've infected at least twenty Krauts and I don't even remember how many revolvers I stole and took where necessary. I may die like I live somewhere in the streets, but my conscience is clear.' "

They left Alina's flat still chuckling, having agreed that Egon would come at seven o'clock the following evening.

He arrived punctually, and noticed that there was a lift in the building, but pressing the button proved futile. The lift did not work. It seemed that he would always have to climb the stairs in order to reach her. As he walked up to the fourth floor, he thought how different these clean modern stairs were from those in the Koronski's flat in Warsaw, and then felt the usual contraction in his throat when he thought of his night with Susanna. The memory of that night always lurked at the back of his mind, but he tried not to dwell on it, because the very thought of her fragile body being torn to pieces brought nausea.

Pani Alina opened the door almost immediately he rang the bell. Again a picture of Susanna standing by the open door of the Warsaw flat flickered in front of his eyes, but they soon focused on the woman in front of him. Her brown hair curled round her face, and her greenish, cat-like eyes were smiling. She wore a simple white shirt, which showed the cleavage between her round breasts. The smile in her eyes deepened when she noticed the direction in which he was looking, but she was very businesslike that evening, and helped him with all the homework he had to do, so that for the first time he was able to go to school fully understanding what he was doing. It was a good feeling, and on the following day he bought her a few flowers to show his gratitude.

"Thank you," she said, putting them in water. "It's lovely to be receiving flowers from a handsome young man again."

Egon found himself saving his pocket money to buy *Pani* Alina flowers. At first it was only in gratitude for teaching him so well but, as the days went by, he had to admit to himself that it was also to see her smile with pleasure when she received them. Instead of hating the thought of home-work he looked forward to going to *Pani* Alina's flat, and paid careful attention to everything she taught him. His school marks improved out of all recognition, his vocabulary grew, and he developed a passion for history, initially because of his wish to emulate Janusz. Later his desire to learn increased in proportion to his knowledge. He became fascinated by the motives leading to the terrible conflicts, which humanity inflicted upon itself through the ages.

"Primarily," he said to Otto, "it's economic necessities that motivate people. They seem to be the basic cause of wars. Of course, there is also greed, but that comes second. I really need to learn a lot more."

"You're right there," said Otto, pleased to see that the boy was thinking.

"But take care not to take other people's opinions as knowledge. Also, I don't think that you're a true academic, because you're far too practical. As a businessman I have always been able to buy expertise, but the experts need somebody to tell them what to do, how to exploit their skills, and how best to apply them. It's the people with a broader view who make the world go round.

"When I wanted to know what medical instruments were needed I asked the doctors and the surgeons. Then I went to the toolmakers, engineers and metallurgists and asked them how it should be made. Only when I knew all that, I went to the manufacturers and asked them how much it will cost to produce. Finally, I checked whether my clients will be willing to pay the price, which would include my expenses and profit. This is just an example, but you see what I mean. Most people need to be told what to do. There are not many people who can tell them. If you can do this, you are really achieving something useful. Anyway, whatever you do, try to think for yourself."

But it was only rarely that Egon could talk to Otto properly, because his uncle was either travelling or working. When he was at home Filomena and Lila were there, and serious conversation was impossible. At other times Otto was preoccupied with letter writing trying to find if anyone else was alive. For a long time they hoped against hope, but when the full enormity of the holocaust came to light and no answers came from anywhere, they had to face the terrible truth.

The same problem seemed to occupy people abroad, because, through the Red Cross, Otto received a letter from Frieda Weiner's brother, Paul Bernstein, who lived in New York, enquiring if anyone of the family was still alive. Of course, Otto wrote to him at once, and correspondence ensued, followed by parcels. Paul was particularly interested in Egon, the only Bernstein survivor in Europe, but to Egon it was all very remote, and not only in the geographical sense.

"I've fought for Poland," he said staunchly, "and here I'll stay to rebuild the country."

Otto did not say anything. He sighed and looked at Egon strangely, nodded, and went on with his letter writing.

One day in late October, the autumn suddenly gave way to winter. It became exceedingly cold. At seven o'clock, when Egon walked to his lesson, the sky was dark and threatening, the wind blew hard and the first drops of icy rain started to fall. He was glad to have reached his destination before it started in earnest.

When *Pani* Alina opened the door to him, a wave of stale cigarette smoke floated past her, bringing with it the smell of food and vodka.

She remained standing still for a moment, letting him take in the fact that she was not wearing her usual skirt and blouse, but a soft clinging dress of gentle coral, which clung to her body, accentuating the full breasts, small waist and softly rounded belly. He had to make a special effort not to reach out and touch the dress and the softness beneath it. Instead he silently and awkwardly handed her the flowers he had brought. She took them, smiling and expressing her thanks as usual. Then she turned and went back to finish clearing up in the small kitchen.

"Some friends from the hospital came in to celebrate my birthday," she explained. "Sit down for a moment, and have a cigarette, while I just clear these few things away, and put your flowers in some water."

"Thank you," he said, helping himself from a box on the table, and feeling very grown up. Of course, he had been smoking since his time in the forest, but his smoking was still unofficial, and this was the first time that an adult had offered him a cigarette.

He was also pleased that this was one of the times when he had bought flowers. They were only three beautiful gold tinted rich cream dahlias, but he thought that they were just like *Pani* Alina. Susanna had been like a delicate pink rosebud, not yet wholly unfolded, but the dahlias were like a ripe woman in her full glory. He followed *Pani* Alina to the kitchen, and saw her putting them into a vase.

"Can I help in any way?" he asked.

She looked up at him, and said, "No. Just stand there and talk to me. You look very sophisticated with that cigarette. These dahlias are really very beautiful, and it's so nice that you brought them even though you didn't know it was my birthday. You are very kind to your old teacher." Her eyes twinkled. She was obviously in a very good mood.

"My friends brought me a bottle of vodka. Would you like a drink? I have no wine," and her eyes laughed knowingly.

She poured out two generous glasses, and he suddenly knew that Susanna had told her of their love making. He gulped the vodka in one go, as he had been taught in the forest, and did not refuse the second glass.

"It shouldn't bother you that Susanna talked to me," *Pani* Alina said. "We talked about everything. Most of the psychiatric troubles people have are caused by lack of communication. They cannot talk to each other openly, and it is difficult to talk about some things, but talking, like everything else, becomes easier and better with practice, and alcohol can help. It relaxes the inhibitions. Of course, it can lead to indiscretion, and that's why it is important to drink only in the company of friends."

"Your very good health," Egon said, ponderously lifting the third glass. "I am grateful that you think of me as a friend."

Then, suddenly, he found the whole situation very funny, and managed to contain his desire to giggle by singing the traditional Polish birthday wishes.

> "Hundred years, hundred years,
> you should live with us.
> And once more, and once more,
> go on living with us."

He had a pleasant voice, and his even teeth sparkled in a broad smile, as his full lips opened to display them. Quite unexpectedly *Pani* Alina kissed his mouth. Not just lightly, but lingeringly. So lingeringly that her body became limp, and threatened to drop. He was very strong and found it easy to pick her up to prevent her from falling, and carry her to her bed on which he carefully put her down. When he tried to move away, she put her arms round him and pulled him to herself. Then, remembering his experiences during the nights spent camping with girl-guides, he started fumbling under her clothes, but she stopped him.

"Not like that," she said. "When I make love, I want to feel that I make love," and she took off the soft coral dress, the brassiere, which supported her breasts, and the knickers, which covered the abundance of hair between her shapely legs. He watched her silently, taking in the curves of the beautiful body, and then stripped with a speed of which he did not know he was capable, and slipped into bed beside her.

"You are beautiful," said Alina when they lay together after the first flush of lovemaking. "You're made like a V. Your shoulders are broad, and your bottom so small that I almost think I could take it into my hand, but I never thought that you were a Jew."

"What a way to discover it!" Egon was still finding everything amusing. "If the Germans had hit on this idea, they would have found all the Jewish men without any trouble."

"Jerzy must have known," reflected *Pani* Alina, "but he never told me. He was a wonderful man, but not terribly good in bed. Perhaps he was right not to tell me. I wouldn't have been sufficiently heroic to die for hiding Jews, though probably not sufficiently nasty to give you away. It would have been a dilemma. You know, my family are small landed gentry.

They never liked Jews, and some of it must have rubbed off on me, though I know it's quite illogical."

"It is," agreed Egon. "But all I want to do now is to look at you, because you are the most wonderful woman on earth." This was definitely not a time during which he wanted to have a discussion on anti-semitism.

"I am glad you think so, and it is a lovely thing to hear. I was saying that Jerzy was not much good in bed. You will be very good, but you need some tuition. You will have to have lessons in lovemaking as well as in everything else. And the first lesson is that the first time is for you, if it is all going to happen so quickly, and from the second time on it is for your lady. Come back to me."

He came back to her many times that evening, and each time he learned something new. At ten o'clock, when he would normally have gone home, she telephoned Filomena.

"It's absolutely pouring and extremely cold outside," she told her. "I'm going to let Egon spend the night on the sofa, otherwise he'll catch his death of cold. He has neither a raincoat nor an umbrella with him."

Filomena evidently agreed, because Alina turned to Egon with a mischievous smile.

"See. Even the weather conspires with us."

And it was true. Outside wind and sleet heralded the approach of winter. Inside it was cosy. The double glazing kept the warmth in, and it was very warm in bed.

"This is the most splendid thing that can happen to anybody," Egon said eventually. "I'd never had dared if you hadn't kissed me. Not that the thought hadn't crossed my mind, but I wouldn't've dared. I had no idea that anyone could be so kind. You are wonderfully beautiful, and I love you."

"Now that's where you must be careful. Never say 'I love you' until you've given the matter a lot of thought. You like me very much. You enjoy making love with me. You probably respect my education, but love is a lot more than that. One day you'll love, and then my lessons will come useful to you, because you'll know how to make a woman happy.

"On my side it's not kindness. As a psychiatrist I consider frustration one of the most unhealthy conditions. A young man like you certainly needs a woman regularly, and a mature woman like me needs a man. There are not many men about at the moment, and those that are, are either drunk, or sad, or nasty. I may have made you a little tipsy, but you're not a drunkard. You hide your sadness well and you're certainly not nasty. Let's go to sleep."

Every evening she taught him well. First the school lessons; and until he mastered them properly there was no chance of the tuition he really wanted. He summoned all his powers of concentration in order to get through his homework quickly, and his progress was amazing.

All that autumn, winter and spring they worked and loved together. He was her son, her pupil and her lover. The very knowledge that their kind of love had to be transient, added a special poignancy to every moment they shared.

When the summer came, and school holidays started he, very shyly brought her a sketch he had made of her face. She was so impressed by it, that she called on an artist friend of hers to give Egon lessons.

He, noticing Egon's highly developed sense of the ridiculous, asked his pupil to do a few caricatures as an exercise, and found them so good that he sent them to the best known satirical magazine in Poland, called *"Szpilki"* – ("Pins). It was a great triumph, when they accepted them, and Otto asked Filomena to organise a tea party to celebrate the event.

It was a lovely warm evening in the early July, 1946. By that time Otto and Filomena were very comfortable in their little house. There was a housekeeper, who looked after them, and the tea she served that afternoon was wonderful.

"Just like before the war," *Pani* Alina said happily, looking at the cakes and the open sandwiches displayed on long china trays carefully placed round the table covered with an embroidered white linen cloth. It was then that the telephone rang. Otto excused himself and went into the study. He was away a long time, and returned with his face white.

"What has happened?" demanded Filomena. She knew that it took a lot to upset Otto.

For once he was unfair, "Your countrymen have been at it again. I have just had some news from Kielce. They've butchered all of the Jewish Committee. You remember Dr. Seweryn Kahane – he was the chairman. The lucky man was shot. The others were either stoned to death, clubbed or killed with axes. But they didn't stop there. They also found some children, a few teenagers, who had stopped there on their way to Palestine, and a chap who had been at the Birkenau concentration camp. That's all they know about him, because he was so disfigured when they found him, that the only thing they could see was his concentration camp number on his arm. Your great patriots and practising Christians – I forgot to tell you that it was all done to protect Christian children from being made into matzos, though Pesach is long time over – have also murdered two Jewish officers who had served in the Polish army, not to mention others, whom I don't know. They managed to dispose of more than forty people."

The stoic Filomena burst into tears and rushed out of the room. *Pani* Alina and the artist left. The food on the table remained untouched, and the world lost colour again.

Eventually Otto raised his head.

"We have to leave, and you must leave first of all," he said to Egon heavily.

*

Extract from "*The Holocaust*" by Martin Gilbert.

On 1 February 1946 "*The Manchester Guardian*" published a full report of the situation of the Jews still in Poland. The four headlines to the report read:

JEWS STILL IN FLIGHT FROM POLAND
DRIVEN ABROAD BY FEAR
POLITICAL GANGS OUT TO TERRORIZE THEM
CAMPAIGN OF MURDER AND ROBBERY

Since the beginning of 1945, the newspaper reported, 353 Jews had been murdered by Polish thugs. "Unfortunately," it added, "anti-Semitism is still prevalent in spite of the Government efforts to counteract it." As a result of the war, this anti-Semitism, "always present in Polish society", had been "greatly aggravated by German propaganda". Since the end of the war, ritual murder accusations had been made against Jews in Cracow and Rzeszow. In Radom a hospital for Jewish orphans had been attacked. In Lublin two Jews already wounded by thugs while on a bus, had been tracked down to the local hospital and murdered there, in their hospital beds.

On 5th February 1946, four Jews were killed in Parczew, the forest of which had been the scene of so much Jewish suffering and heroism scarcely two years earlier. Six weeks later, on March 19 one of only two survivors of the death camp at Belzec, Chaim Hirszman, gave evidence in Lublin of what he had witnessed in the death camp. He was asked to return on the following day to complete his evidence. But on his way home he was murdered, because he was a Jew.

Five days before Hirszman's murder, the British Ambassador in Poland, Victor Cavendish Bentinck, reported from Warsaw that food supplies belonging to the Chief Rabbi's Emergency Council had been allowed to proceed in a car flying the Union Jack. Yet even with this protection, the car had been stopped "and four Polish Jews one of whom was a woman, travelling in it, were taken out and shot by the roadside for being Jews". The Ambassador added that anyone with a Jewish appearance was "in danger" and on March 28 the Foreign Office learned that a group of Jewish leaders travelling from Cracow to Lodz had been seized, tortured and murdered.

Martin Gilbert continues with a long list of similar occurrences until he comes to:

The climax of these post-war killings came on 4th July 1946. Three days earlier, an eight-year-old Polish boy from Kielce, Henryk Blaszczyk, disappeared from his home. Two days later he returned, claiming that he had been kept in a cellar by two Jews who had wanted to kill him, and that only a miracle had enabled him to escape. In fact, he had been to the home of a family friend in a nearby village. The friend had taught him what to say after his return.

On July 4 a crowd of Poles, aroused by rumours of Jews abducting Christian children for ritual purposes, attacked the building of the Jewish Committee in Kielce.

Almost all the Jews who were inside the building, including the Chairman of the Committee, Dr. Seweryn Kahane, were shot, stoned to death, or killed with axes and blunt instruments. Elsewhere in Kielce, Jews were murdered in their homes, or dragged into the streets and killed by the mob.

Forty-two Jews were killed in Kielce that day. Two, Duczka and Adas Fisz were children. Four, Bajla Gerntner, Rachel Zander, Fania Szumacher and Naftali Teitelbaum were teenagers on the way to Palestine. Three, Izak Prajs, Abraham Wajntraub and Captain Wajnreb, were officers in the Polish Army. Seven could not be named. One of those whose name was unknown was a survivor of Birkenau, a fact disclosed by the tattoo number on his arm, B 2969.

Following the Kielce "pogrom", one hundred thousand Polish Jews, more than half the survivors, fled from Poland, seeking new homes in Palestine, Western Europe, Britain and the United States, Latin America and Australia.

CHAPTER 20

PARTING

E xcerpt from *"Poland between the Hammer and the Anvil"* by Konrad Syrop.

As the Red Army pushed the Germans out of Poland and advanced on Berlin, it nominally handed over the administration of the country to the Provisional Government set up by Stalin with real or crypto-communists and some other left-wing elements. The country, ravaged by the war, was the scene of a veritable migration of people. Millions of Germans fleeing from Poland's new "Regained Territories" or expelled from them, millions of Poles drifting away from the eastern provinces incorporated into the Soviet Union, and in addition millions of refugees, deportees, prisoners of war and inmates of concentration camps returning home, often to find the home either destroyed or on the wrong side of the new frontier. Russian troops were everywhere, proclaiming to be friends, but behaving like an army of occupation.

*

The open windows of the house looked out into the sunny garden, where little Lila gurgled happily, watched by the housekeeper. Otto, Filomena and Egon sat on the small verandah, drinking coffee.

"It's obvious that there's not much future here for us," said Otto in his special matter-of-fact voice, which he kept for difficult family decisions. "But one should not allow oneself to panic. Filomena and I must stay for a while and consolidate the business we have started. It is still possible that

Poland might be able to manage itself in spite of the likelihood of Russian occupation. Then, when we've established it sufficiently to hand it over to others who could run it on our behalf, we can also leave. In this way we will all have a livelihood.

"But you, Egon, must leave at once. The sooner you learn another language and the way of life elsewhere the better your chances will be. You must consider yourself as the first of us starting abroad on all our behalf."

"That's all very well," Egon was not at all sure that he wanted to leave his present life, "but where am I going to go?"

"That is, of course, a very important question. Uncle Paul in America is very keen that you should come to him, but the Polish quotas for going to the States are full. They are only admitting a limited number of people per year, and it'll take a long time until your name comes up, because nearly all Jews are trying to leave Poland, and most of them want to go to America. The incident in Kielce was not just a local, isolated act of violence. There have been many similar ones on a smaller scale in other parts of the country, and everybody is afraid. Filomena and I are reasonably safe here, because the neighbours know us, and the anti-semitic violence is not supported by the government like it used to be. The police are also on our side. We don't go around too much, and when I go anywhere I go with one or two hefty Polish assistants.

"So far nobody at your school knows that you are a Jew, but, if they found out, there would be no way I could protect you. I don't want you to go back to school this autumn. You must leave the country as soon as it can be arranged, in any way in which it is possible."

"Surely you're not talking about sending him to Simon in England with that Rabbi," Filomena said, sipping her coffee, and obviously not happy with this possibility.

"And why not?" Otto asked tersely.

"Well, for one, things in England are pretty bleak from what one reads in the papers. Everything is rationed, and it's been bombed almost as badly as we were here. It would make much more sense for him to wait, and go to America, when his visa comes through. There's no reason why anybody at his school should find out that he is a Jew."

"So you think it's alright for him to live with a lie all his life?"

The conversation was becoming heated, and Egon decided to butt in.

"Please!" he said holding out his hand, as if he was in the classroom, and asking permission to speak "I know there was an Uncle Simon, but

how come he is alive and in England, and who's this rabbi you're talking about?"

"Simon Susskind married your mother's sister." Otto gave the information briefly and concisely, because he was anxious to get back to the point. "He was called up to the Polish Army during the mobilization before the war, and his division left Poland through Romania. He was eventually demobilized in England. His wife and two children were killed in Auschwitz. He is not very well-off. A week ago I had a letter from him that a Rabbi Schonfeld has received permission from the Polish Government to take out orphaned Jewish children to England. The British Government has given conditional permission for their entry. However, a guarantee has to be given that no child will become a burden to the State. Simon is prepared to give you such a guarantee."

"But he can't even remember me much. I certainly have no recollection of him at all."

"There are so few of us left. His elder son would've been your age. He is alone. He writes that it would be easier to live with his pain if at least he had somebody with him who could understand. He says that people in England are extremely kind. He has a friend whose wife is something called a Justice of the Peace, and she would help him to arrange things."

"But you yourself say that he's not very well off," Filomena obviously did not like the whole idea. "He'll not be able to buy food on the black market, and you know the amount that Egon can eat. How on earth will they manage?"

"He writes, that the amount of food you get on your ration books in England is adequate, and that the food you are allocated is cheap. Also, they believe that it is dishonest to buy on the black market."

"They've obviously not lived in Poland during the war," commented Egon dryly. He was for ever hungry. Though his food consumption was enormous, he was still as thin as a rake, and had to be given a plate of food before going out to a meal, so as not to appear greedy when at somebody else's table.

Conscious of these excessive demands on his part, he added somewhat defensively: "Besides, I wouldn't want to cause him hardship."

"You wouldn't. Those two diamonds you have collected from your SS friend will see you through for the initial period, and I have already written to ask Uncle Paul to start making enquiries about the money your mother left in Switzerland. It's not a large sum, but together with the proceeds from the sale of the diamonds it should last you until you finish your studies. After that you'll be able to earn a living."

"You're talking as if it's all been decided," Filomena was not giving up.

"Nothing has been decided. We all have to think about it, but it seems to be the only way out."

They were quiet then; each lost in thought. Filomena felt that she would be losing a son. She had come to love the lad, and was very doubtful about sending him off with a rabbi of all people. Under no circumstances would she have voiced her misgivings. Nobody could accuse her of being anti-semitic, but sending a boy off with a rabbi was a bit much.

He probably had a black beard and side locks, was dressed in some medieval costume and smelled bad. One never knew what sort of super-stitions he might teach the lad, who, after all was not much of a Jew. He knew the Catholic religion a lot better than his own. If he met the right sort of girl he might even become a Catholic and be a credit to his country.

Otto also regarded Egon as his son and thought that he would be sending the boy into the unknown, but he hoped to follow him there. It was as if he was sending an emissary, he told himself. At least he will be safe, and he will be able to be himself. He knew, that, in the final analysis, a little discomfort and a little hunger did not do much harm, provided you stayed alive and healthy. The greatest luxury is to be allowed to be what you are, and that did not appear to be possible in Poland.

He also could not express his views, because he had a good idea what Filomena was thinking, and he did not wish to hurt the mother of his child. She was a Polish patriot and a good Catholic.

Egon too did not want to leave. He loved his substitute parents, who had helped him during the worst period of his life and represented his only security. Furthermore the possibility of parting from *Pani* Alina seemed almost impossible to bear. At the same time, a sneaking thought of the great adventure of going abroad was beginning to thrill him.

He was glad that the decision had been shelved, because at that moment he had something else to consider. The Jewish sports organisation Maccabi was playing in a football match against a Polish side in Katowice. The problem, which exercised his mind was how to go to see the match without being seen by anyone from school, who might then suspect him of being Jewish, and if anyone should see him, how to justify being there. Should he go at all?

In the end he decided to go. He approached the football ground carefully, looking around and prepared either to turn back, or walk on casually if he saw anyone he knew. There were crowds of people, because any kind of entertainment was scarce and therefore welcome, but he was pleased that there were no familiar faces to be seen around him.

Egon found himself a good seat and settled down to watch. The game started, and he was just beginning to relax and enjoy the fact that Maccabi appeared to be winning, when he became aware of somebody looking at him. He turned and saw another boy from his school.

He was not in his class, but he had seen him and might tell the others. Egon did not even know his name, but he was sure that the recognition was mutual. As soon as he turned round the other boy appeared to have eyes for the game only, and took no further notice of him. Egon decided to do the same. After all, the other boy would also have to justify watching the match if he wanted to tell tales. Was he also a Jew?

Egon did not enjoy the rest of the game quite so much.

*

Things had a habit of happening quickly once Otto started thinking about them. Although he had said that nothing had been decided, he proceeded to make all the necessary enquiries, and about a month later had all the answers. Full of his news he walked into the living room and saw Egon playing with Lila, who was a smiling, dark haired, energetic little thing with the big dark eyes so typical of the Weiners.

She liked nothing better than crawling around the floor with her big Uncle Egon, who obviously also enjoyed this occupation, because he gave it quite a lot of his time. Filomena watched them with a smile on her face, her corpulent body spread comfortably on the sofa, her hands busy filing her nails.

He seems so grown-up, thought Otto, but rolling on the floor with the baby, he becomes what he really is – just a young child.

He cleared his throat to draw their attention to him, hating to interrupt the pleasure of the moment, but impatient to tell them his news.

Filomena slowly raised her head. A frown of concentration replaced the smile on her face. She knew at once that he had something important to tell them. Egon looked up, and Lila crawled full speed ahead straight into her father's legs. Otto picked her up, and sat down on the sofa next to Filomena. Egon stayed on the floor, looking up at the two kindly mountains of flesh with the little baby girl wedged in between them.

"Now we have to decide what's to be done," said Otto heavily. "I have established that, if that's what we want, you could leave Poland on the ship, which sails from Gdynia for England in November. All you would have to do, is go to the Jewish Committee and prove who you are. I have all the necessary documents, which confirm your original identity, and naturally I can be a witness to it. You need two witnesses, but there will be no problem in finding another one among my acquaintances. The committee will issue you with a stateless passport. Uncle Simon wrote that he has provisionally put your name on the list at the other end. All you will have to do is to join the others in Gdynia."

Filomena's eyes filled with tears, and Egon instinctively stood up and put his arms round her neck. He knew from experience that it was no use trying to embrace her properly. His arms were simply not long enough.

Then he looked across at Otto, and said doubtfully.

"If you think that this is right, and there is no other way . . " His voice trailed off, because there really was nothing else to say.

That evening Egon went to see *Pani* Alina. He stopped at the stall on the corner of her street, where he usually bought her flowers and chose a bunch of golden chrysanthemums.

As soon as she saw him *Pani* Alina noticed the sadness and hesitation in his eyes and knew that the beginning of the end had come. Moving unhurriedly with her usual grace she closed the door behind him, and took the flowers. Then she turned her back on him to give herself time to regain her composure. Without saying anything she carefully arranged the chrysanthemums in a crystal vase, which she had taken from the top of a cupboard and washed till it sparkled.

"There," she said at last, putting the flowers on the table. "Just like in the song, only I haven't got a piano."

He could not help smiling and they sang the lovely melancholy song, which was as popular now, as it had been during the war.

> Golden chrysanthemums
> in a crystal vase,
> Stand on the piano
> Awakening sadness and regret.

She stopped abruptly and said. "Except, of course, we will have no regrets. We have always known, that it was only a borrowed time, a borrowed fun and . . . " she whispered, "a borrowed love."

He did not answer, but took her in his arms, and they made love like they did that very first time, so many days ago.

"I shall always remember, and I shall always love you," he said.

"Don't say that about our love. It never was the kind which could last for ever. I'll also always remember, but we both know that life will go on for us. We're the sort of people who will always have fun while we're alive, and your life is just starting."

"I'm going to England."

"How exciting. I'm going away too, but not quite so far. My father wrote that there's a vacancy for a psychiatrist in a Cracow hospital. Naturally I applied, because I cannot go on indefinitely being parted from Andrzej, and they have accepted me. One day you too will have children and will realise that they have the first priority. In addition, the new job is better than the one I have here, and I love Cracow. It will be wonderful to live there. So you see, you are not leaving me and I am not leaving you. It's life that is parting us. All partings are a little sad, but life is always full of the unexpected and that's what makes it worth going on living. When are you going and how?"

Egon told her all he knew and found out that she was leaving at the end of October. Letting the flat should not be difficult, and her new job required her to live at the hospital.

They were both very busy during that last month, during which Poland tried to show Egon how beautiful it was in the autumn. Or was it *Pani* Alina, who made him see it like this during the odd moments they managed to snatch together? She made him look at and admire the golden trees, and picked the shiny conkers with him, taking them out of their prickly green shells. They looked out of her bed at the brilliant blue sky and the clouds, which sometimes chased each other in gentle play and sometimes in anger.

It rained on their last evening together, just as it did on their first, and Egon thought that it was as if their tears, which neither of them had allowed themselves to shed, were flowing across the windows.

Pani Alina cradled his head on her round shoulder, so that his face was buried in the softness of her breast and said.

"We will most probably never see each other again after today, and it's just as well. I want you to remember me as I am now. In about ten years you will still be a very young man, and to you I would then appear to be a wizened old woman. I don't want us to keep in touch – otherwise you might be tempted to see me again out of sheer curiosity, and I want to avoid this."

Egon tried to protest, but she pressed his face tighter to herself and continued,

"No, don't contradict me. I've given this a lot of thought. Let's both be grateful for what we've given each other."

"You've given me so much; you've taught me so much, but I have given you nothing."

"Little do you know, my young friend. You gave me laughter and flowers and song, which are all most wonderful things for the spirit, but on the purely physical level you gave me the sort of pleasure an older man could never manage."

"With madam's excellent tuition – all is possible," said Egon, trying to execute a formal bow in bed, which proved to be exceedingly difficult and sent them both into gales of laughter. And that is how they always remembered each other.

Otto, Filomena and Lila went with Egon to catch the train which went to Gdynia from Katowice. They came to the station in good time to get him a window seat, so that he could wave to them as long as possible. Little Lila sat on Otto's shoulders and waved with great enthusiasm, but burst into tears when Egon could no longer be seen and she noticed that her mother was crying.

The train was delayed and Egon was late in Gdynia in spite of having taken a taxi from the station. Otto had been generous with zlotys for the trip. Egon thought that it was just as well to spend them before leaving: they would be of little value in England. When he finally reached the assembly hall in Gdynia, it was full of young people of varying ages. There were small children, teenagers and some youths who must have been in their twenties. A few adults milled among the crowd as well. They had come to see their charges off into the world.

A tall man in a British officer's uniform had just finished making a speech. He was handsome and looked impressive, but his red beard was unusual for an army man and his announcement seemed to have left the assembled children disgruntled. Egon decided to approach two young men, who stood on the edge of the crowd, to find out what had happened.

"Excuse me," he said having elbowed his way to them without dropping the two heavy suitcases he carried, "My name is Egon Weiner. My train was late and I haven't heard what the man said." This time he was careful to use his real name in case it was going to be checked against an official list.

"Hello, nice to meet you," said the stocky, broad faced young man facing him. "I'm Lolek Bierman, and he's Joseph Pelz. The man who has just finished speaking is Rabbi Dr. Schonfeld. We've just been treated to some words of wisdom, which I shall not bother to repeat, but the bad news is that, like your train, our ship has also been delayed, and will not reach Gdynia till tomorrow. It will then have to be cleaned etc., which will take another day or two, and that would mean that we would have to travel on Saturday, which is the Shabbat."

He grinned broadly as he continued. Obviously he was not a believer.

"Now that, according to the laws of our forefathers, would be the ultimate calamity, and God and Rabbi Schonfeld, forbid us to sin in this awful way. The good news is that we don't need to wait here, but can stay at The Grand Hotel in Sopot till Sunday. There will be lorries along to take us, but Joseph and I thought of taking a taxi. I see that you too have a bit of luggage. Perhaps you would like to share one."

"I'd love to."

The driver piled up their cases on the roof and in the trailer of his shaky vehicle, and they came to the beach resort of Sopot ahead of the rest; the concierge at the reception desk had been given a list of names and they were expected. The hotel was almost empty in November, and the management were glad of the business. The three early arrivals were allocated a double room into which an extra bed had been brought. They had their own bathroom and a view of the sea, both of which impressed them almost equally: the first by its luxury and the second by its expanse. Not one of them had seen the sea before and their first sight of it was disappointing because that day it was grey and flat, merging on the horizon with an equally flat and grey sky.

In spite of this, they decided to go out on the pier and have a closer look outside, after they unpacked the few things they would need. By then a strong wind had sprung up bringing with it strong smell of sea-weed, which their nostrils registered for the first time. Great foam topped waves noisily hit the pier supports making the three friends realise the enormous power which lay tamed under their feet. It was very cold and trying to rain. Somewhat subdued they returned to the hotel in time for supper.

When they came back all the members of Dr. Schonfeld's group were already seated in the vast dining room, where dinner was about to be served.

Joseph, the tallest of the three, spotted some free chairs between a boy called Stefan Fischer, whose name seemed to ring a bell with Egon, and a small, monstrously fat boy, who could not speak, but only grunted, though he managed to tell them his name, which was Adam Weiss. Then his round blue eyes focused on Egon and an expression of disbelief, fear and finally a sort of triumph came to his face, as he turned it away to look down the white table cloths on the long table. He looked at Egon again, closed his eyes for a moment, stared at the table and Egon again and something like a smile flickered on his podgy face, but he said nothing.

Egon disregarded Adam's strange behaviour, and was just going to sit down next to him when a few chairs away he saw a familiar face. Delighted he ran towards his school fellow whom he had noticed at the Maccabi match. The recognition was mutual. The boy immediately stood up and stepped back so that they could talk out of hearing of the others. The habit of being careful remained with both of them.

"I never imagined you were Jewish, and was worried that you'd tell the others about seeing me at the match," the boy said smiling.

"Same here," Egon answered, "until I comforted myself with the thought that you would then have to explain why you were there yourself."

"Me too. We obviously think alike. My name is Victor Feldman. What's yours?"

"Zbyszek. Zbyszek Weiner." Out of habit Egon stuck to his assumed first name when speaking to a school fellow. Anyway, he did not like to use his German sounding name and preferred the pseudonym, which had helped him to survive.

They did not continue their conversation because the waiters started serving the meal, and the two boys returned to their places, having promised each other to keep in touch.

The food was plentiful, tasty and quickly served. It was much appreciated by the children, who had vivid memories of being hungry, and consumed every dish with the greatest possible zest. When the meal was over, and most of the others started leaving, Egon smiled at the waiter who had been serving him The man smiled back and asked;

"Did you enjoy your dinner, sir?"

"That's just it," Egon said. "I enjoyed it so much, that I could manage to eat the whole thing again."

"I don't believe you could," the waiter said incredulously, "but I'll ask in the kitchen."

The astonished kitchen staff peeped from behind the doors, as the waiter once more brought first the hors d'oeuvre, then the generous plate of thick soup, the large omelette with potatoes and vegetables and a huge piece of chocolate cake to finish.

The Jewish authorities had requested a vegetarian meal.

Egon consumed his second dinner with relish and without difficulty.

"I don't know where you put it all," said the waiter, forgetting polite phraseology in his amazement. "You're nothing but skin and bone."

"I manage," Egon answered modestly.

That evening there was a dance at the hotel. The three boys still had some money, so they decided to go down, see people dance and buy themselves a drink.

They sat in the dimly lit room, listening to the music, and watching the whirling couples, when Egon noticed three people making their way to a table at the far corner. There was a tall man, slightly balding, but straight and handsome, the boy called Stefan Fisher who had sat next to him at dinner, and a girl.

There was something almost familiar about her, though he was sure he had never seen her before. She passed under a lamp, and for a moment the light reflected from the honey blond of her hair, which she wore plaited and arranged in a crown round her head.

It appeared to him for some reason that he saw her eyes laugh, although she was talking to the tall man and he could not actually see them. The three newcomers sat down at a table a short distance away, and the man lit a cigarette.

Egon could not stop himself from looking at the girl, and his new friends were quick to notice.

"Stop staring, but I admit she's bit of alright," Lolek said with conviction.

"Yep. Goes in and out in all the right places," agreed Joseph.

"Don't be so common," Egon admonished before he had time to stop himself.

"The child is struck," Lolek said kindly.

"I can't do ballroom dancing, but I'll buy you two a beer each if you ask her to dance," said Egon so seriously, that they accepted his offer.

He sat watching them, and tried to think why it seemed to him that the girl was someone he knew. Indeed, he felt that he knew her well. Suddenly, and for no reason, the picture of the blossoming cherry tree came to his mind. He dismissed it as irrelevant: a vision produced by excess of food and drink.

"Well," said Joseph, sipping the beer he had earned by having a dance with the girl. "I've found out that her name is Nina, that she effectively refuses to dance close to strangers by putting her hand firmly on her partner's shoulder, and pushing him away if he comes too near. Also, that she doesn't really like dancing with people, who trip over her feet."

"Yes," agreed Lolek. "I also overheard the older man, who's her father, telling her that it's rude to refuse to dance if somebody had plucked up courage to ask her."

This information did nothing to explain Egon's odd feeling about the girl, but he did not have time to continue thinking about her, because at that moment a laughing throng of girls from their group entered the room. Joseph gallantly stood up and invited the young ladies to join their table, and Lolek proceeded to confide in them, with great sadness in his voice, that Egon could not dance.

"And it would not look right, if you see what I mean, if my friend and I try showing him how to do it," he added looking appealingly at the girls.

Tuition was, of course, promptly offered and Egon was plied with drink by his new friends to overcome his shyness. At the scouts he had learned all the Polish dances – the Polkas, Mazurkas, Krakowiaks the Polonaise and a fast waltz. With his innate sense of rhythm and love of music, coupled with the intensive instruction offered by his laughing partners, he soon mastered the simple steps of the quickstep, which could be adapted to all the other dances, and by the end of the evening began to enjoy himself on the dance floor. He glanced at the table in the far corner of the room, but the girl called Nina and her two companions were no longer there.

The music, the dimmed lights, and the whole atmosphere of a nightclub gave the youngsters self-assurance. After all, they had to be real, almost grown-up people to be in a sophisticated place like this.

The following day fish was served at lunch and Egon, still hungry as usual, decided to supplement it with a meal in a nearby restaurant, where he ordered a whole chicken. He was just beginning to tackle it, when he thought he felt somebody looking at him. There was just a glimpse of a grey coat in the window, but for some reason he was sure that it was the girl with the laughing eyes. He hoped that somehow one day he would meet her in some very special circumstances, but he could not simply walk up to her like he had done to the others. Fate had played such a large part in his life that he had faith in it, and was prepared to leave to it all things that really mattered. It decided on death; it probably also decided on life.

On the other hand, there were immediate decisions which one had to take oneself.

The one Egon took now was to spend the rest of his zlotys on a telephone call home. Otto answered almost at once:

"Is that you Egon?" he asked. "I thought the transport had already sailed."

"We have been delayed and are staying at a super hotel in Sopot. I'm having a lovely time," Egon told him. "There are lots of people here who can become my friends, because we seem to have a lot in common. Don't worry. It'll not be too long before we're together again. I'll find a way. You can be sure that I'll do my best." The telephone crackled and the line went dead.

Egon walked slowly back to his room. They were going to sail in the morning. One of his lives was ending and another one was just going to begin.

Bibliography

Bartelski, L. *Powstanie Warszawskie (Warsaw Uprising)*, Iskry, Warszawa.

Bartelski, L. *Warszawa Jako Ośrodek Ruchu Oporu w Kulturze (Warsaw as a Centre of Cultural Resistance)*, Iskry, Warszawa.

Bartoszewski, W. *Prawda Młodych (The Truth of the Young)*, Monthly Underground Publication.

Bartoszewski, W. *Organizacja Małego Sabotażu (Organisation of Minor Sabotage)*, Zachodnia Agencja Prasowa, Warszawa.

Churchill, W. S. *The Second World War Volume VI Triumph and Tragedy*, Cassell & Co. Ltd.

Czarnecki, R. *Lata Niezakończonej Walki (The Years of The Unfinished Fight)*.

Czarski, A. *Najmłodsi Żołnierze Walczącej Warszawy (The Youngest Soldiers of Fighting Warsaw)*, Pax, Warsaw.

Filipowicz, J. *Miałem Wtedy 14 Lat (I was then 14)*, Pax, Warsaw.

Gilbert, M. *The Holocaust. The Jewish Tragedy.* William Collins.

Hanson, J. K. N. *The Civilian Population and The Warsaw Uprising of 1944*, Cambridge University Press.

Hillebrandt, B. *Młodzież Warszawy w Walce z Hitlerowskim Okupantem (Polish Youth in the Struggle Against Hitlerite Occupation)*, Wiedza Powszechna Warsaw.

Hitler, A. *My Struggle*, The Paternoster Library, Hurst & Blackett Ltd, First published in England in October 1933.

Krakowski, S. *The War of the Doomed*, Holmes and Meier New York.

Krawczyńska, J. *Zapiski Dziennikarki Warszawskiej*, Państwowy Instytut Wydawniczy Warsaw, (Notes of a Warsaw Journalist).

Landau, L. *Wybór Pism, Kronika Lat Wojny. (Selected Works. Chronicle of the War Years)*, Państwowe Wydawnictwo Naukowe Warsaw.

Lemke, A. *Wandel Einer Stadt*, Das Generalgovernment 1940.

Lewin, A. *A Cup of Tears*, Basil Blackwell Limited.

Orpen, N. *Airlift to Warsaw*, University of Oklahoma.

Serwanski, E. *Życie w Powstańczej Warszawie (Life in Warsaw during the Uprising)*, Pax Warsaw.

Smolski, W. *Za To Groziła Śmierć (For that Death threatened.)* Pax, Warsaw.

Szarota, T. *Okupowanej Warszawy Dzień Powszedni. (Everyday Life in The Occupied Warsaw)*, Czytelnik Warsaw.

Syrop, K. *Poland Between The Hammer and The Anvil*, Robert Hale Ltd.

Tazbir, S. *W Obronie Dzieci i Młodzieży w Warszawie. (In Defence of Children and Young People in Warsaw)*, Państwowy Instytut Wydawniczy.

Tomaszewski, J. *Epizody Powstania Warszawskiego (Episodes of the Warsaw Uprising)* Krajowa Agencja Wydawnicza Warsaw.

Tushnet, M. *To Die With Honour*, Princeton Press.

Wistrich, R. *Wer War Wer in Dritten Reich Who's Who in Nazi Germany*, Harnack Verlag. Weidenfeld & Nicholson.

Zbyszewski, K. *Warsaw was a Beautiful City*, Superior Printers The Library of Fighting Poland.

Other publications

Biuletyn Żydowski – several issues. (Jewish Bulletin).

Studia Warszawskie – Warszawa z Lat Wojny i Okupacji. (Warsaw Studies – Warsaw in the Years of War and Occupation).

The Holocaust – issued by Yad Vashem, Jerusalem.

Biuletyn Informacyjny – informative buletin – several numbers.

Życie w Pówstańczej Warszawie – relacja Świadków Zainwentaryzowane w Archiwum Pracowni Badania Dziejów Okupacji Hitlerowskiej. Instytutu Zachodniego w Poznaniu.

(Life in Warsaw during the Uprising – eyewitness reports registered in the archives of the workshop for the examination of the events of the Hitlerite occupation at the Western Institute in Poznan).

Kronika Historyczna Armii Krajowej – (*The Historical Chronicle of the Home Army*) printed by Pollkann, Chicago.

Warszawa – Różne Zeszyty. (Warsaw – Various magazines).

The New Standard Jewish Encyclopedia – edited by Cecil Roth and Geoffrey Wigoder – publishers W. H. Allen, a division of Howard & Wyndham Ltd.

The Haggadah – published by the Soncino Press Ltd.